Translators Writing, Writing Translators

TRANSLATION STUDIES
BRIAN J. BAER, EDITOR
Albrecht Neubert, Gert Jäger, and Gregory M. Shreve, Founding Editors

Translators Writing, Writing Translators

Edited by

Françoise Massardier-Kenney,

Brian James Baer,

and

Maria Tymoczko

The Kent State University Press   KENT, OHIO

© 2016 by The Kent State University Press, Kent, Ohio 44242
All rights reserved
Library of Congress Catalog Card Number 2015012331
ISBN 978-1-60635-232-8
Manufactured in the United States of America

Library of Congress Cataloging-in-Publication Data
Translators writing, writing translators / edited by Françoise Massardier-Kenney, Brian James Baer, and Maria Tymoczko.
    pages cm. — (Translation studies ; 9)
  Includes bibliographical references and index.
  ISBN 978-1-60635-232-8 (hardcover : alk. paper) ∞
1. Translating and interpreting—Study and teaching (Higher). 2. Academic writing—Study and teaching (Higher). 3. Translating and interpreting—Vocational guidance. I. Massardier-Kenney, Françoise, editor. II. Baer, Brian James, editor. III. Tymoczko, Maria, editor. IV. Maier, Carol, 1943– honouree.
  P306.5.T723 2016
  418'.02—dc23   2015012331

20 19 18 17 16   5 4 3 2 1

For *Theorôs* Carol Maier,
Mentor, Collaborator, and Friend

Carol Maier is professor emerita of Spanish and translation studies at Kent State University. The inspiration for this book, she is a prizewinning translator of the works of Octavio Armand, Severo Sarduy, Rosa Chacel, and María Zambrano and a leading scholar in translation studies who has published widely on topics ranging from the poetry of Ramón del Valle-Inclán to issues of gender, ethics, and the pedagogy of translation. She was instrumental in giving voice to translators in the United States through a number of interviews and many collaborative works. She has had and continues to have a profound influence on many students, scholars, writers, and translators, several of them contributors to this volume in her honor. Her work displays a rare combination of extreme precision, erudition, daring, and generosity. She is currently the book review editor for *Translation and Interpreting Studies* and a member of the advisory board of *The Translator, TTR,* and the book series Literatures, Cultures, Translation (Bloomsbury). She is also translating work by Octavio Armand and Rosa Chacel and editing a volume in honor of another formidable translator, the late Helen Lane.

How the Brain Works

Like a peony. Full white blossoms,
so heavy. Heavy and damp with the scurrying
of a hundred ants over each petal.
From this comes language:
Morning sun. Afternoon shower. This, that.
I think can do to say.
Gathers to fit in open palms, heart shape
that wants to carry one flower as far
as it has to, as fast as it's able, to the dark
oak table, the red cut-glass bowl.
Black ants will drop and crawl to the windowsill.
Soft petals will brown and slime,
fall down to re-enter the earth.
And the brain says *Over to do.*
The brain says *Happy, happy.*

—Maggie Anderson

Contents

Acknowledgments

We have many people to thank for making this volume possible. First and foremost, we must thank Carol Maier for inspiring so many leading scholars in the field of translation studies to contribute. We also wish to thank Kent State's Institute for Applied Linguistics and the Office of Research and Sponsored Programs for supporting the copyediting and indexing of the volume. Copyright fees to reproduce the visual images in Moira Inghilleri's chapter were covered by a Publication Subvention Award from the Office of Research Development at the University of Massachusetts Amherst. Thanks are also due to Marilyn Kiss for donating the photograph featured on the cover, to Kelly Washbourne for his wonderful translation of Octavio Armand's "Un brindis por Carol Maier," to Valerie Ahwee for her meticulous copyediting, and to Christopher Mellinger for his help in preparing the manuscript for submission.

Introduction

*Maria Tymoczko, Brian James Baer, and
Françoise Massardier-Kenney*

Translation studies is one of those rare fields in which it is common for a person to be both a practitioner and a theorist. This combination sets translation studies apart from most other disciplines, particularly in the humanities. Professors of English literature, for example, are sometimes producers of literary works but not usually, and historians rarely make history. But translation scholars routinely produce translations, a fact that makes the separation of theory and practice untenable. In this regard, Carol Maier is exemplary, having achieved an especially productive balance between theory and practice. Her suspicion of totalizing theoretical approaches and her advocacy for unflinching self-reflection ensure that neither term assumes primacy over the other but that both exist in a relationship of mutual interrogation. When Maier theorizes, she keeps the real-world implications of that theorizing in view, including the implications of theory for translator training, for teaching literature in translation, and for rethinking professional codes of ethics and the translator's positionality. This complex orientation is what has lent her work relevance over the course of her professional life as a scholar, a teacher, and a translator, and it is something that her work shares with that of other scholars whom she admires outside translation studies proper—bell hooks and William Boyd Smith, for example—and inside the field.

When Maier published "The Translator as an Intervenient Being" in 2007, she articulated the need for more "raw material" about translators, including investigation of translators' memoirs, diaries, autobiographical material, correspondence, drafts, and notes, as well as fictionalized accounts and empirical data about translators, including data about the cognitive activity of working translators. The result in translation studies has been a closer scrutiny and deeper exploration of translators themselves and their position with respect to their work, questions that she observed were still relatively little explored at the beginning of the twenty-first century. This book is a contribution to the emerging body of research on those topics. Many of the authors have responded directly to her call for more "raw material," and the material presented and explored here ranges from Rosemary Arrojo's exploration of a fictional translator to direct accounts by translators and the historical research of Noël Valis, who contributes a biographical study of two nineteenth-century sisters-in-law related through poetry, politics, and translation. The autobiographical pieces include strikingly honest portrayals of their own lives in translation by Lawrence Venuti, Susan Jill Levine, and Christi Merrill. Other essays—including those by Peter Bush, Moira Inghilleri, Roberta Johnson, and Maria Tymoczko—explore specific aspects of the processes of translators translating.

Like Carol Maier, to whom this volume is dedicated, many of the contributors to this volume are known for sustained self-reflexive engagement with translation. In some cases contemporary theorizing of translation and cross-cultural communication are inseparably linked to their work as practicing translators. The primary purpose of this volume is therefore not merely to pay tribute to the work of one of the founding figures of contemporary translation studies. It is not a backward-looking volume. Instead the authors extend some of the lines of thinking that Maier has initiated, and they attempt to deploy and elaborate on the insights she has offered. Indeed, the rapid globalization of the world's economy and the militarization of diplomacy that have occurred alongside the "discovery" of translation by promoters of world literature have made Maier's explorations of the position of translators more relevant than ever. Specific aspects of Maier's work—including her focus on the translator's body, the processes of translation, and the positionality of translators—have taken on new immediacy in a world that is moving to the use of global English as an international link language and in a world where the threat to translators and interpreters in war zones has become widely known through the mass media.

This focus on the body is something that Maier shares with Severo Sarduy, the Cuban-born novelist, poet, playwright, book editor, and critic, whose works Maier translated periodically beginning in the late 1980s. Such a felicitous pairing of translator and writer is, of course, the stuff of chance, but in hindsight their collaboration seems inevitable. Never a neutral conduit, Maier reveals in her thoughtful introductions to her translations of Sarduy, particularly his collection of essays *Written on a Body* (1989), how profoundly she engaged with his writing, how it pushed her to deepen her thinking about the fundamentals of translation once it is freed from the burden of textual mimesis, as expressed in the opening paragraph of her essay, which serves as both translator's preface and scholarly introduction.

> The suggestion that simulation is an essential, biological force promises an exhilarating freedom for a translator, that most mimetic of readers who is ever aware of how much her work will inevitably be something of a disappointment, a mere attempt at likeness, a flawed reproduction. By apparently legitimizing, even welcoming transgression, Severo Sarduy's definition seems to contend that the original is the copy, that the simulacrum throbs with life. (Maier 1989b:i)

Such a rethinking of the translator's role presents the translator as a co-constructor of meaning, a collaborator, whose body is thoroughly engaged in the process of translation.

We should note that Maier's work as a whole is characterized by an ethos of collaboration, of which her work with Sarduy is merely one example. She promotes and practices collaboration not only between translator and author but collaboration with creative people across academic disciplines and across the arts. It is, therefore, fitting that this volume opens with a poem by Carol's friend and colleague Maggie Anderson, and includes a reproduction of a photograph by her long-term colleague and friend Marilyn Kiss. The theme of collaboration is a leitmotif of her essays on the role of the translator, and many of the people involved with this volume have collaborated closely with Maier on various translation projects. Several of us have had the distinct pleasure of teaching with her or of observing her teach. In his essay in this volume, Kelly Washbourne contemplates the nature of author-translator collaborations.

Translation and Gender

Throughout her long and productive career as a translation scholar, teacher, and practitioner, and through her translations and reflections on translation as a process, Carol Maier has documented the ways that translators view and perform their work. In light of her definition of translation as an "activity in which a literary work is rewritten in a different language," it is not surprising that her description of this process of rewriting has led her to interrogate the "understanding of originality, gender, and nationality" (in Palatella 1997:19). Gender is a marked aspect of the body in most human cultures, and thus Maier's focus on the embodied nature of translational work leads naturally to an exploration of gender and translation. In the cultural context in which she first began to translate—second wave feminism and the rise of feminist criticism in the 1970s—the intersection of gender and self-reflection on the body in relation to translation became one of Maier's central concerns as a translator and as a translation scholar. In this regard her writing has been at the forefront of translation studies; not surprisingly this aspect of her work is another facet extended here in contributions with a similar focus from some of her many collaborators and colleagues, including Christi Merrill, Noël Valis, and Roberta Johnson.

In her critical writing on translation, the trajectory of Maier's thinking follows an arc starting from a gender-based identity to questioning of the very notion of gender and its implications for writing and translating—from a "woman-identified" to a "woman-interrogated" positioning. Her reflections on her own activity as a translator over the last 40 years, as well as her translations themselves, bear witness to a dynamic and evolving view of what constitutes "woman" and gender in translation. After establishing herself as a scholar of modern Spanish literature through her work on Ramón del Valle-Inclán, Maier began her career in translation by translating the works of Cuban poet Octavio Armand (1976, 1977, 1979, 1980) and Chicano poet Ana Castillo (1978). She accompanied these translations with reflection on her own writing—in the words of Isabel Garayta, "taking the pulse of her own development" (1998:74)—and using her own work as an object of study. Far from being a solipsistic inner turning, this sustained analysis of the principles that guide her practice has allowed her to bear witness to the largely unacknowledged and untheorized *labor* of translation, providing a rare glimpse into the complex process by which a text becomes a literary work. Maier's insistence that a translator be aware of the factors that affect her practice led her to acknowledge the ways in which her social (if not biological) identity as a woman has influenced her translation process. As Garayta makes clear, although the resulting translation, the "product," may not reveal the workings of Maier's position as a woman translator, her critical essays and notes bring to light the importance of these considerations.

In this sense, Maier's discourse about translation takes Borges's statement below one step further.

> No problem is as consubstantial to literature and its modest mystery as the one posed by translation. The forgetfulness induced by vanity, the fear of confessing mental processes that may be divined as dangerously commonplace, the endeavor to maintain, central and intact, an incalculable reserve of obscurity: all watch over the various forms of direct writing. Translation, in contrast, seems destined to illustrate aesthetic debate. . . . Translations are a partial and precious documentation of the changes the text undergoes. (Borges 2000:69)

Maier's body of writing in and about translation documents the way these changes occur. We see many aspects of her thinking in her statements about translating the works of Armand. For instance, in "A Woman in Translation, Reflecting" (1985), she describes how Armand's erasure of the mother's voice in his poetry leads her to feel anger and discomfort. Her drive to translate Armand and her admiration for his work are complicated and inflected by her identification as a woman. She writes, "Armand's texts in English were written by me and because of that they convey my femaleness and my antagonism as well as my affection" (1985:7).

Interestingly, this unease does not lead Maier to adopt the interventionist tactics of feminist translators, such as those of Canadian author-translator Suzanne de Lotbinière-Harwood. Maier does not rewrite or censor the masculine/patriarchal text; she does not bring back the voice of the erased mother. Instead, she uses a paratext to establish a dialogue with the poem outside the translation itself, questioning the author's erasure of the mother. This approach allows her to provide a broader context for Armand's work and to speak about the difficulties of her position as a woman translator without adopting aggressive translation strategies. She returns to this technique again and again in her work.

Maier discusses her early identification with women and its problematic nature directly in "Notes after Words" (1989a). Elsewhere she describes how being a woman translator, which she hoped would lead to an "egalitarian working mode" with the author Ana Castillo (Garayta 1998:128), turned out to matter less than her status as an Anglo academic with stylistic preferences at odds with those of the author she was translating. At this early stage of her career, Maier's working assumptions still involved gender as a category that placed the female/translator below the male/author, but her "feminist" positioning led her to seek a less authoritarian relationship. With Castillo, as with Armand, Maier the translator decides to respect the integrity of the author and to recognize the limitations of her gender identification while at the same time bearing witness to the process of "setting aside one's terms and attempting to perceive something in a new way" (Maier 1996:59). What is significant in this statement is not so much her final choices or decisions about translation (to change or not to change the character of the text based on the translator's preferences), but her focus on the thinking/translating process. Rather than leaving unthought the complex workings of gender, Maier is one of the rare translators who provides a window onto the mind of the translator, exposing the work of translation as the writing of a tension, that is, the writing in the translator's own words of two experiences sometimes sufficiently different as to be antagonistic.

Maier's interest in and interrogation of gender as part of her position as a translator is also visible in her choice of writers to translate: all lived part of their lives in exile, and issues of gender are central to their writing. Sarduy lived in exile in France and investigated gender and transvestism in his work. Spanish writer Rosa Chacel was an advocate for women as early as 1915; she lived in exile for many years (in Brazil and the United States) and presented her novel *Memoirs of Leticia Valle* (1994) through the mind of a young girl narrator. Similarly philosopher/essayist María Zambrano left Spain for Cuba, Italy, and France. As part of her "life-long resistance to the historical idealization of women she found so crippling," Zambrano "continually questioned the sense of 'woman' in history and society" (Maier 1998:106, 108).

Living in exile and writing from exile inevitably led these writers to question what it meant to be Cuban, or Spanish, or American, and to interrogate the notion of a stable identity, be it national or gendered. For Maier (and consequently for her readers), translation becomes the site where certainties about our identities are held in suspension and ultimately dissolved. Her call for viewing translation as a rewriting that "is best realized and discussed interrogatively" (Maier 1998:108) should therefore be read not as a tentative gesture but as a radical positioning.

Reading Literature in/as Translation

Although for most of her career Maier has trained translators, she has seen that raising awareness of translation and the role of translators outside the translation classroom is a pressing concern. Maier began arguing in the early 1990s that translated texts were being read in schools and universities as if they were written originally in English, thus erasing the very differences that make such texts valuable for instilling global awareness and sensitivity. Therefore, Maier has called for a special pedagogical approach to the teaching of texts in translation, aimed at instructors and students who do not know the language of the original. Such a pedagogy is a way to make difference visible and in doing so to resist the powerful homogenizing tendencies that accompany globalization.

As a result, many of Maier's writings are directed less to her colleagues in the field of translation studies than to colleagues in Spanish and Latin American studies, literary studies, and feminist studies. For many years Maier's was one of the few voices to pose what David Damrosch refers to as "the problematics of translation" (2009:8) outside the field of translation studies proper, as evidenced by the fact that Maier authored the entry on translation in the 1997 *Encyclopedia of Feminist Literary Theory*, edited by Elizabeth Kowalski-Wallace; the entry on translators in the 1995 *Oxford Companion to Women's Writing in the United States*, edited by Cathy N. Davidson and Linda Wagner-Marin; the essay "Teaching Monolingual Students to Read in Translation (as Translators)" in the roundtable discussion on teaching texts and translations, published in the *ADFL Bulletin* (Maier 2001); and the chapter on translation, entitled "Teaching the Literature of the Spanish Civil War in Spanish-to-English Translation," in the 2007 MLA volume *Teaching Representations of the Spanish Civil War*, edited by Noël Valis.

Maier consistently opposes the focus on origins and originals that continues to organize the study of (national) literary traditions in many parts of the world today by calling upon instructors to make translators and translations visible. She writes, "Instructors must also ensure a discussion not only about the author of the work and the historical, political, and literary climate at the time the work was written but also about the climate in which the translation was made, the translator, and the response to the translated work" (2007a:248). We must not forget, out of expediency, to ask why any specific work was published at a specific time and by a specific translator. We must, so to speak, *see* the other, a metaphor that brings us back to the importance of the body in literary studies, including the body of the translator whose work has produced the text being read. Maier also advocates giving monolingual students the opportunity to experience—through work and the involvement of mind and body—the complex decision-making involved in the translation of literary texts by having them compare multiple translations of a single work and then create their own translations from those texts, explaining why they made the choices they did. In addition, Maier has advocated strongly for the position that students who read texts in translation must be introduced, "however briefly, to important principles of literary translation and the challenges that translation involves" (2007a:248). By involving students in the process of translation, Maier sensitizes students to their own positionality.

Carol Maier's concern that the monolingualism of many American students prevents them from understanding the complexities of cross-cultural communication in general, and those of literary translation in particular, leads her to advocate not only for explicitly addressing translation theory in the literature curriculum but also for reading literary texts featuring translators and interpreters as a way to encourage discussion of the translator's role. Among Maier's favorite works featuring fictional translators are Lydia Davis's *The End of the Story* (1995), Barbara Wilson's *Gaudí Afternoon* (1990), and Banana Yoshimoto's *N.P.* (1994), translated by Ann Sherif. These "intimate portraits of translators," Maier argues, "prompt a reader to ponder the effect translation can have on one's understanding of originality, gender, and nationality" (in Palatella 1997:19). In this way her emphasis on self-reflection extends not only to the writers of translations but to the readers as well.

Maier has turned regularly to the theme of fictional translators as a way to think about translation and identity as, for example, in "The Translator as an Intervenient Being," which appeared in the volume *Translation as Intervention* (2007), edited by Jeremy Munday. Fictional portrayals of the translator, Maier asserts, "provide insights into the translator's work with language, originality and creativity. This work, in my opinion, contributes to some of the most profound discomfort occasioned by intervenience" (2007b:7). It is in this article that Maier calls for more autobiographical writings by translators and interpreters to provide the data necessary for an understanding of the complexities of the translator's task.

Many of Maier's views on teaching literature in translation have been consolidated in the two collected volumes that she has edited on the subject: *Between Languages and Cultures: Translation and Cross-Cultural Texts* (1995), which she coedited with Anuradha Dingwaney, and *Literature in Translation: Teaching Issues and Reading Practices* (2010), which she coedited with Françoise Massardier-Kenney. *Between Languages and Cultures* was daring, ahead of its time in a number of ways, perhaps most obviously in its interdisciplinarity, with almost all the contributors coming from fields outside translation studies proper but united in their concern over the ethical representation of otherness. In that volume Maier and her coeditor provide one of the most succinct and nuanced statements of the issues that must be addressed when teaching literature in translation. Advocating for a practice of reading literature in translation that is based on a "subtly dialectical interplay of identity (identification) and difference," one that neither sacrifices nor appropriates difference, Maier and Dingwaney caution:

> The dangers of mobilizing solely one or the other category are many. An uncritical assumption of identity is, as we have shown through Rigoberta Menchú, a mode of appropriation. Similarly, identification is a function of recuperating the unfamiliar "other" in terms of the familiar; reading this way relies on the stereotypes one culture utilized to understand, and domesticate, (an)other. An uncritical assumption of difference, which presumes that (an)other is never accessible, allows readers to abandon, indeed exonerates them from, the task of ever reading cross-cultural texts. Deployed solely, each category produces an impasse. (1995:312)

The act of reading translated texts, they advise, should be organized around this "complex tension," which can serve as a site from which to question and destabilize linguistic and cultural identities.

Their emphasis on the dialectical relationship between identification and difference is especially important today in view of the popularity of Lawrence Venuti's (1995) concepts of foreignization and domestication, which are often treated as a simplistic binary opposition. To the extent that the assimilation of new knowledge always involves some degree of scaffolding or identification, that is, making connections with our previous knowledge and experiences, any encounter with the foreign must to some extent be domesticating for it to make sense at all. The only truly foreign work, then, is the work that is not translated. At the same time the promise of new knowledge—the experience of the foreign—is precisely what motivates most readers to read translated literature and most teachers to use such texts. Thus, domestication and foreignization cannot be understood as a binary choice; they are inseparably linked and their relationship constantly negotiated in any act of translation and in any teaching using translations. This productive tension, for which there is no easy resolution, no quick fix, is at the heart of Maier's theorizing on translation and of her translation practice.

In the volume *Literature in Translation: Teaching Issues and Reading Practices* (2010), Maier again addresses the need—made more urgent by the increasing popularization of world literature—to develop a pedagogy for teaching translated literature. Recognizing translation to be a mediation of a mediation, the book outlines a pedagogical approach that attempts the difficult but ethically sound task of reading translated texts in such a way as to neither erase the difference of the source text nor reify it. The organization of the book operationalizes the two-pronged approach Maier has advocated since the mid-1990s.

Maier opens section one with an article advising instructors on how to choose a translation for a course. Maier's concern with the application of theory is most evident when she discusses, in her typically undogmatic fashion, what instructors should consider in selecting a translation or translations and why explicit discussion of that choice should be a part of the presentation of the work. Maier recommends that instructors and students alike critically reflect on their expectations of a translation as a necessary first step in opening themselves up to the experience of the foreign, in allowing themselves to be surprised by the language of translation. "After all," Maier writes, "readers guided solely by their expectations and preferences jeopardize their chances of experiencing the risky readings that can put one unexpectedly in touch with language used in unanticipated ways" (2010:21). That risk, as Maier acknowledges elsewhere in her work, carries with it certain ethical considerations.

Toward an Ethics of Translation

In discussing Carol Maier's views related to the pedagogy of translated texts, we have already drawn attention to the ethical concerns that permeate her discourses on translation. Inevitably, self-reflective translators and those who explore the position of translators grapple with questions about ethics, including the ethical responsibilities of translators; the relationship between ethics and specific strategies of translation; choices at both the macro and micro levels of translation; obligations toward the authors they translate; the role the translated text will play in the receiving culture; and the translator's responsibility to the writers and readers of both the source and target texts. These are persistent themes in the essays in this book and many of the authors have been inspired by the work of Carol Maier in formulating their own answers to these questions. Maier has been a strong voice in exploring the ethics of translation, and where she has led, others followed.

By setting Carol Maier's ethical explorations and discourses in a broad intellectual context and by showing their connections with her feminism and her approach to pedagogy, we can better understand the breadth, depth, and importance of her thinking about the ethics of translation and the ethical position of translators. The orientation to ethics in Maier's writings is not the classic ethics of the Greeks nor is it prescriptive and absolute. The sources she appeals to in her statements about ethics are both implicitly and explicitly diverse. They include, for example, Buddhist traditions, pragmatism, and existentialism, though not necessarily identified as such. Her ethical explorations converge on the position of writers, translators, and readers in an approach reminiscent of situation ethics. Proponents of situation ethics insist that there is no simple universal or absolute ethical position in any given circumstance but rather that a person—a translator or interpreter, for example—must adjudicate the complexity presented by each particular situation and act accordingly. Such an approach to the ethical questions faced by translators and scholars in translation studies illustrates the usefulness of complexity theory in the field of translation studies (cf. Marais 2013), which points to the necessity of considering the minute particulars of a translator's position even while taking into account larger ideological and global factors.

An important publication in relation to Carol Maier's ethics of translation that invokes situation ethics is Carol Gilligan's seminal study *In a Different Voice* (1982). Gilligan links the ethical choices of women to their assessments of situational criteria for ethical decisions rather than to their reliance on universal abstract principles, thus linking situation ethics and feminist issues. Carol Maier read this key book of second wave feminism with attention in connection with her early work in women's studies. It is not surprising, therefore, that Maier's orientation to ethics involves an interweaving of situation ethics and feminism.

The essays in this book here return persistently to the specificity of situations, particular nuances of specific texts, the production of translations in specific contexts, and so forth. Rather than attempt to make sweeping generalizations about ethics, Maier has taken the lead in showing the importance of the particular and the local in discussions of the ethics of translating, the situational dilemmas of specific translators and translation tasks, and the necessity for reading texts and translations with an informed consideration of context. Thus, specific political contexts are relevant to diverse times and places, demanding a nuanced ethical response from both a translator and a reader of translations. For a self-reflexive translator, the politics of a situation will be concrete: the events of the time of the text's writing and the translation's reception, the status of the nations involved in the translator's work, the specifics of gender politics, the identities of the writer and the translator, and so on. Political discourses will also be factors, whether they are discourses about postcolonialism, neocolonialism, violence, religious questions, or the many other discourses of any particular era. She advocates undertaking research and adopting practices reflecting such issues.

Maier's emphasis in "Translating as a Body" (2006) also has an ethical dimension, indicating that translators must approach their task not as a person with an abstract textual puzzle to solve but as a whole person in dialogue with another whole person, particularly when working with living authors. Here her ethical position reveals an existentialist orientation that can be compared, for example, to Martin Buber's *I and Thou* (*Ich und du,* 1923). Buber stresses that relationship is the essence of I-Thou modalities in contrast to the experiential qualities of I-it modalities in relation to the world of objects. Thus, Maier's ethics of presence and the importance of being attuned to the body in translating have implications connecting her views to both popular and theological existentialist positions in ethics.

A strength of seeing translation as a dialogue between a translator and an author as whole persons is that it enables the translator to retain her identity and her own ethical stance, allowing her to assume a face-to-face position in which she can "speak back" to the author; even while acting as translator, she can engage in critical, ethical, and social dialogue with the author. As we have already indicated, this is a practice Maier has embraced, again facilitating both her ethical and feminist position as a translator. A number of the essays in this book extend her exploration of the role of the body in the work of a translator, including those by Lawrence Venuti, Moira Inghilleri, Maria Tymoczko, and Noël Valis.

In "The Translator as an Intervenient Being" (2007b), Maier aptly points out that translation studies has neglected research about translators themselves, and she identifies various resources available for such research, many of which involve the ethos of particular translational situations. Ethical issues are central to this essay, which initiated an outpouring of research about translators at work, much of which has also addressed ethical questions. Maier initiated a new phase of descriptive translation studies, which has focused on translators rather than translated texts (as was the case in twentieth-century descriptive studies), and many of the essays in this book continue this wave of research.

Early on Carol Maier identified the necessity of incorporating the exploration of ethical dilemmas into teaching strategies for both translation students and students reading translations. Her desire to facilitate surrogate experiences of a translator's ethical dilemmas among students and readers of translations is akin to John Dewey's pragmatist philosophy of art outlined in

Art as Experience (1934). He argues that knowledge of art and understanding artistic creation are possible only if artistic production can be experienced bodily. In a sense, by having students rethink the decisions of translators, Maier, like Dewey, encourages them to assess translations experientially with their minds and bodies using ethical, esthetic, cultural, and linguistic frameworks, and to move beyond treating texts and their translations as sacrosanct, finalized, and static cultural artifacts. The experiential involvement of readers of translations—particularly student readers—in the ethical assessment of translation processes and the ethical dilemmas of translators who produced the texts being examined is an important technique for heightening ethical awareness of cross-linguistic and cross-cultural communication that has both local and global consequence.

Much of the force of Carol Maier's work on the ethics of translation is distilled in the powerful metaphors that she has created for conceptualizing the positionality of translators. Maier is eloquent about the power of metaphors, writing "one metaphor becomes another because the words of that metaphor sink in" (2006a:147). To be able to create new metaphors is a great intellectual gift and a notable contribution to any discipline. Metaphor is one of the most important means by which human thought expands in every sphere of activity and every field of knowledge, including translation studies (cf. De Man 1978, Hauser 2009, and St. André 2010). In turn, thus, the creation of important metaphors is a form of creating essential cognitive tools, because metaphors are used recursively as frameworks for the articulation of questions and problems and for exploration that leads to further knowledge, points that Maier articulates in her quote just cited. Not surprisingly, such recursivity is another of the fundamental characteristics that distinguish human and animal thought, according to Marc Hauser (2009), which together with human combinatorial facility results in the capacity for generativity of language, thought, and culture.

One of Maier's most productive metaphors related to the ethics of translation, found in her article "The Translator as Theorôs" (2006b), is her view of translators as a type of pilgrim. There she gives an extended explanation of the metaphor, indicating that in Greek thought the *theorôs* was originally "one who travels, observes, and contemplates, glimpses possibilities and learns about other people and their customs, but also risks becoming estranged, rejected, ridiculed" (2006b:163). Moreover, the theorôs was a type of "ambassador, witness, or reporter but not a pontificator of universals, norms, rules, or arguments" (163), who did not "mandate a particular practice" but in Greek thought was "associated with contemplation and wonder" as a precondition of practice (163). This metaphor offers a powerful reconceptualization of the situational and ethical positioning of a self-reflective translator/theorist. Implicit in Maier's metaphor is the proposition that translators are open and vulnerable and that their translations have the same quality: translations are essays in the etymological sense of the word as "attempts." Hence they are provisional reports of what translators have learned from their travels with source authors, from observation and contemplation of other people and customs in the texts they have translated, and from their role as ambassadors or witnesses of that learning for receiving audiences. The metaphor brings with it an appreciation of wonder, an open acknowledgment that translators do not fully master or possess what has been witnessed.

This metaphorical conception of the task of the translator seizes the imagination because it differs from popular views of the role of translators and their credentialed expertise. In many translation programs, efforts focus on instilling certainty into student translators, teaching them unquestionable knowledge, and preparing them to present themselves to employers as fully competent in two languages and the transpositions required in moving across those languages. The ethical problem with the conventional view—as Maier's metaphor indicates—is that a translator is thus figured as one who has certainty about meaning, valuation, and judgment. Maier's metaphor forestalls the tendency among translators to base their practice on the "largely unexamined certainty that their work [holds], or [makes] possible for others," namely, "experiences identical to experiences occasioned by work first written in a different language," as well as the "tendency to project oneself into the text of another and to assume that the projection [gives] rise to accurate, authentic, and truly shared feelings that [erase] or [transcend] mediation" (Maier 2006a:137). Such a reconceptualization of the task of the translator is inherently an ethical formulation. Moreover, adopting such a perspective radically reorients pedagogical practices in translation studies. The metaphor is a reminder of how thin the knife edge is in training competent translators who must remain open to their own ignorance, their own need to wonder and learn, and who nonetheless must learn to deploy the tool kit of translation studies in a competent manner.

In Maier's own methods of translating and writing, the roles of translator and translation scholar as theorôs are manifest. She is known for her extensive research on texts, authors, and contexts in both roles. Her wondering and wandering in ideas as she investigates the possibilities raised by her projects are models for a scholar in any field. In this way, she embodies the principal aspects of her most well-known metaphor.

The metaphor of the translator as theorôs can be seen as framing a second powerful metaphor that Maier has contributed to translation studies, namely the view of a translator's practice as *intervenience*. Here Maier chooses for her metaphor of the translator's position the term *an intervenient being* and for the translator's work, the term *intervenience*. These terms are conceptually related to *intervention* and *interference* but they are words that are less well known and that have been more commonly used to refer to the agency and activity of those who come between (often in legal contexts) rather than to the action itself. The notion of intervenience is also commonly used to describe the role of someone operating within a single or unified context where mediation may be required across different positions being held or contested within that context. One value of this metaphor is that the words are defamiliarized. Their metaphorical force helps to move translation studies beyond worn-out conceptual entrapments, ways of thinking that have lost their vitality, and trite associations associated with such words as *translation* itself, *transference,* and *between,* all of which entail significant conceptual difficulties that have been widely discussed in translation studies.

Again Maier's own practice embodies her metaphors. Her deep learning and impeccable and indefatigable research (involving wondering and wandering not just through the realm of books but also in mutual inquiry with her many collaborative colleagues), and her lucid verbal precision have often made her the ideal scholar to address and adjudicate quandaries and controversies both intellectual and ethical in the field of translation studies. She does these things with intervenience that never feels aggressive, interfering, or interventionist. She has invariably enriched the field and been a positive force for clear thinking in her intervenient roles.

The contributors to this book repeatedly deploy the metaphors and precision-crafted language that Carol Maier has developed to explore and reflect on the nature of translation, the work of translators, the positionality of translators, and the roles that translations and translators play in culture. The use of her metaphors and her language in the essays gathered here, as in a great deal of the current work in translation studies, is much more than a simple tribute to her that one expects in an honorary volume. Ipso facto by using her metaphors productively, the writers in this volume build on her project of self-reflexive investigation of translation. They attempt to explore, deepen, extend, and advance thinking about the very issues that Maier's work has highlighted in translation studies and the valuable frameworks that she has worked so hard to construct.

As a collection this book indicates the seminal importance of the work of Carol Maier in developing and shaping the field of translation studies. The explorations collected here both apply and re-enliven her insights, illustrating the key roles she has played in enlarging the domain of translation studies through her own work, her collaborations, and her influence on other scholars. Like herself, many of the authors are translators writing self-reflexively about their own work, processes, and lives. They take her practices and many of her views as points of departure for writing about the processes of translation and the position of translators in relation to pedagogy, ethics, and life. The book illustrates the ways in which Carol Maier has enriched the quality of thought in the field of translation studies about the agency of translators, the position of translators at work, and the social functions of translation in bringing individuals and cultures together in an ethical manner.

Works Cited

Armand, Octavio. 1976. "Indifference as Therapy." Translated by Carol Maier. *Review* 10(19): 73–74.

Armand, Octavio. 1977. "The Anthology as Systematic Ruin." Translated by Carol Maier. *Review* 11(21–22): 9–11.

Armand, Octavio. 1979. "Writing as Erasure, the Poetry of Mark Strand." Translated by Carol Maier. In *Strand: A Profile,* by Mark Strand, Octavio Armand, and David Brooks, 49–63. Iowa City, Iowa: Grilled Flowers Press.

Armand, Octavio. 1980. "A Mini-Course for Erasing the Cuban Writer from Exile." Translated by Carol Maier. *PEN Freedom to Write Report 2* (December): 6–9.

Borges, Jose Luis. 2000. "The Homeric Versions." In *Selected Non Fictions,* edited and translated by Eliot Weinberger, 67–72. New York and London: Penguin Books.

Castillo, Ana. 1978. Three poems by Ana Castillo. Translated by Carol Maier. In *The Invitation,* 14, 17, 27–28. Chicago: Self-published.

Chacel, Rosa. 1994. *Memoirs of Leticia Valle.* Translated by Carol Maier. Lincoln: University of Nebraska Press.

Damrosch, David. 2009. "All the Time in the World." Introduction. In *Teaching World Literature,* edited by David Damrosch, 1–11. New York: MLA.

Davidson, Cathy N., and Linda Wagner-Martin, eds. 1995. *The Oxford Companion to Women's Writing in the United States.* New York and Oxford: Oxford University Press.

Davis, Lydia. 1995. *The End of the Story.* New York: Farrar.

De Man, Paul. 1978. "The Epistemology of Metaphor." In *On Metaphor,* edited by Sheldon Sacks. 11–28. Chicago: University of Chicago Press.

Dewey, John. (1934) 2005. *Art as Experience.* New York: Perigee Books.

Dingwaney, Anuradha, and Carol Maier. 1995. "Translation as a Method for Cross-cultural Teaching." In *Between Languages and Cultures: Translation and Cross-Cultural Texts,* edited by Anuradha Dingwaney and Carol Maier, 303–19. Pittsburgh, Penn.: University of Pittsburgh Press.

Garayta, Isabel. 1998. "'Womanhandling' the Text: Feminism, Rewriting, and Translation." PhD dissertation, University of Texas at Austin.

Hauser, Marc. 2009. "The Mind." *Scientific American* (September): 44–51.

Kowalski-Wallace, Elizabeth, ed. 1997. *Encyclopedia of Feminist Literary Theory.* New York: Garland.

Maier, Carol. 1985. "A Woman in Translation, Reflecting." *Translation Review* 17 (1985): 4–8.

Maier, Carol. 1989a. "Notes After Words: Looking Forward Retrospectively at Translation and (Hispanic and Luso-Brazilian) Feminist Criticism." In *Cultural and Historical Grounding for Hispanic and Luso-Brazilian Feminist Literary Criticism,* edited by Hernán Vidal, 625–53. Minneapolis, Minn.: Institute for the Study of Ideologies and Literature.

Maier, Carol. 1989b. "Translator's Introduction." In Severo Sarduy, *Written on a Body,* translated by Carol Maier, i–iv. Washington, D.C.: Lumen Books.

Maier, Carol. 1995. "Translators." In *Oxford Companion to Women's Writing in the United States,* edited by Cathy N. Davidson and Linda Wagner-Martin, 883–85. New York: Oxford University Press.

Maier, Carol. 1996. "Carol Maier." An interview by Ronald Christ. *On Translation: The Translators,* edited by Ronald Christ, 56–67. Atlanta, Ga.: Atlantic College of Art Gallery.

Maier, Carol. 1997. "Translation." In *Encyclopedia of Feminist Literary Theory,* edited by Elizabeth Kowaleski-Wallace, 401–2. New York and London: Garland Publishing.

Maier, Carol. 1998. "Issues in the Practice of Translating Women's Fiction." *Bulletin of Hispanic Studies* 75(1): 95–108.

Maier, Carol. 2001. "Teaching Monolingual Students to Read in Translation (as Translators)." *Bulletin of the Association of Departments of Foreign Languages* 33(1): 44–46.

Maier, Carol. 2006a. "Translating as a Body: Meditations on Mediation (Excerpts 1994–2004)." In *The Translator and Cross-cultural Texts,* edited by Susan Bassnett and Peter Bush, 137–48. London: Continuum.

Maier, Carol. 2006b. "The Translator as Theorôs. Thoughts on Cogitation, Figuration, and Current Creative Writing." In *Translating Others,* edited by Theo Hermans, 163–80. Manchester: St. Jerome.

Maier, Carol. 2007a. "Teaching the Literature of the Spanish Civil War in Spanish-to-English Translation." In *Teaching Representations of the Spanish Civil War,* edited by Noël Valis, 248–57. New York: MLA.

Maier, Carol. 2007b. "The Translator as an Intervenient Being." In *Translation as Intervention,* edited by Jeremy Munday, 1–16. London: Continuum.

Maier, Carol. 2010. "Choosing and Introducing a Translation." In *Literature in Translation: Teaching Issues and Reading Practices,* edited by Carol Maier and Françoise Massardier-Kenney, 11–21. Kent, Ohio: Kent State University Press.

Maier, Carol, and Françoise Massardier-Kenney, eds. 2010. *Literature in Translation: Teaching Issues and Reading Practices.* Kent, Ohio: Kent State University Press.

Marais, Kobus. 2013. *Translation Theory and Development Studies: A Complexity Theory Approach.* New York: Routledge.

Palatella, John. 1997. "Breakthrough Books." *Lingua Franca* 7(February): 18–19.

Sarduy, Severo. 1989. *Written on a Body.* Translated by Carol Maier. New York: Lumen Books.

St. André, James, ed. 2010. *Thinking through Translation with Metaphors.* Manchester: St. Jerome.

Venuti, Lawrence. 1995. *The Translator's Invisibility.* London and New York: Routledge.

Wilson, Barbara. 1990. *Gaudí Afternoon.* Washington, D.C.: Seal Press.

Yoshimoto, Banana. 1994. *N.P.* Translated by Ann Sherif. New York: Grove.

Un brindis por Carol Maier/
A Toast for Carol Maier

Octavio Armand
Translation by Kelly Washbourne

Un brindis por Carol Maier, a quien conocí a finales de la década de los sesenta en un aula de la Universidad de Rutgers. Si no recuerdo mal esa clase se daba una vez a la semana de 5 a 7 de la tarde en un sótano de Livingston Hall, un dormitorio en cuyo quinto piso, y unos años antes, como estudiante de college, yo había sobrevivido. Creo que nos presentó una gran amiga mutua, Marilyn Kiss, de apellido inolvidable, pues en sus cuatro candentes puntos cardinales corresponde letra a letra al cariño y la lealtad que a gusto se deben los amigos.

Carol era una estudiante excelente. Y mujer de temperamento intenso, como de cuerdas tensadas—afinadas—para hacer buena música. Cuerdas para locos como yo, que

A toast for Carol Maier, whom I met at the end of the 1960s in a Rutgers University classroom. If memory serves, the class was held once a week from 5 to 7 P.M. in a basement of Livingston Hall, a dorm on the fifth floor of which I had survived some years earlier as a college student. I think a close mutual friend of ours had introduced us: Marilyn Kiss, with her unforgettable last name, for its four burning cardinal points correspond letter for letter with the affection and loyalty that friends so gladly owe each other.

Carol was an excellent student. And a woman with an intense temperament, like taut—finely tuned—strings for playing good music. Sane strings for madmen like me, who has had the good fortune to enjoy her

he tenido la suerte de gozar de su amistad desde hace más de cuarenta años—la suerte de gozar de su amistad y ojalá también de merecerla.

Lo cierto es que desde siempre Carol ha estado presente en mi poesía. De alguna manera yo soy un poema suyo y ella uno mío. Así de estrecha ha sido la amistad y la colaboración.

Cuando apareció mi primera publicación, casi de más erratas que poemas, Marilyn Kiss organizó una lectura en su apartamento. Aquello fue un beso de lenguas, pues lo mismo se habló en inglés que en español, aunque evitando siempre, en lo posible, el ingléspañol, ese híbrido.

Mi memoria elefantina, paquidérmica, proboscídea, no olvida aquella tarde. Y yo también, aunque algo esquizoide, la recuerdo agradecido. Estaban presentes varios profesores: Luis Mario Schneider, Frank Dauster, Conrado Guardiola, y un puñado de estudiantes. Entre ellos, por supuesto, Carol Maier, a quien desde hace añales llamo Carolus Maximus o Carolus Maierkovsky.

Pronto conocí a Fred, su esposo, y a sus dos hijos, Quentin y Eugene. A este último lo llamaba "Curly Wind" por sus rizos rubios y los

friendship for more than 40 years—the good fortune to enjoy her friendship and, I hope, to have earned it as well.

Truly, Carol has always been present in my poetry. In some ways I am a poem of hers, and she, one of mine. That's how close the friendship and the collaboration have been.

When my first publication was released—practically a collection of errata more than of poems—Marilyn Kiss organized a reading at her apartment. That was a kiss of languages, for both English and Spanish were spoken, though we took care, as far as we could, to avoid the "Spanglish" hybrid.

My elephantine, pachydermic, proboscidean memory never forgets that long-ago afternoon. And I, too, remember it gratefully if somewhat schizoidally. Several professors were in attendance: Luis Mario Schneider, Frank Dauster, Conrado Guardiola, and a handful of students. Of course, Carol Maier, whom for many years I have called Carolus Maximus or Carolus Maierkovsky, was among them.

Soon I met Fred, her husband, and her two children, Quentin and Eugene. The latter I would call "Curly Wind" because of his blond curls

portazos que daba cuando se ponía bravo. Ojalá que el buen vino que ahora cultiva y bebe le haya permitido olvidar ese apodo, que no creo le gustara. Y Carol también conoció a mi gente, a mis padres y mis hermanos.

Considero familia a Carol y los suyos y sé que ella también ha sabido ver—y sentir—en mí a un hermano. Un dato curioso que corrobora nuestro vínculo: su padre y el mío cumplían años el mismo día, el 6 de abril.

Como siempre he disfrutado muchísimo colaborar en las traducciones, no hablaré de nuestro trabajo sino de nuestro festín bilingüe, pentecostal, babélico. Si bien nunca hemos aspirado a hablar en lenguas de fuego, sí hemos tratado de acercar nuestras lenguas al fuego de la traducción. Hemos sido, en este sentido, como las mariposas que se acercan al calor de las luces hasta arder. Solo que tratamos de sacar alas a las cenizas, como si repitiendo—*vide supra* 'alas a las'—de un idioma a otro lográramos repicar en ecos el bronce de las campanas.

Aunque la traducción necesariamente obliga a ceñirse al punto de partida, que es un texto ajeno—y ajeno en dos sentidos: de otro autor y otra lengua—, todas las decisiones

and the way he would slam the door when he would get mad. I hope the fine wine he makes and drinks now has let him forget that nickname, which I don't think he liked. And Carol in turn met my family, my parents and siblings.

I consider Carol and kin to be family, and I know that she, too, has learned to see—and sense—a brother in me. An odd fact cements our connection: her father and mine have the same birthday: 6 April.

As I have always greatly enjoyed collaborating with her on the translations, I won't speak of our work but rather of our bilingual, Pentecostal, Babelian feast. Though we never aspired to speaking in languages of fire, we have sought to draw our languages together into the fire of translation. We have been, in that sense, like moths that are drawn into the heat of the lights until catching fire. Except we tried to set the ashes to flight, as if by repeating from one language to the other, we were succeeding—repeating, succeeding!—in making the pealing echoes of brass bells ring out.

Although translation means one must perforce hew close to the point of departure, a foreign text—foreign in two senses: from another author,

siones últimas han sido de Carol.
He querido que tenga tanta libertad
como yo, que sienta suyos mis poemas para que pueda hacerlos míos
en inglés.

Soy consultado, reviso, opino, sug-
iero, enrollo la cabuya en el trompo,
pero es ella quien hace la trampa y
lo suelta, obligándolo a girar hasta
que baila como un derviche el bolero de Ravel.

Carol Maier merece el homenaje
que ustedes sus colegas le hacen,
y al cual yo, que además de tradu-
cido me llamo amigo, hermano, me
sumo en español y hasta en árabe y
en chino:

تهنئة   祝賀

Caracas, 14 de septiembre 2014

and from another language—all the
final decisions were Carol's. I have
wanted her to have as much freedom
as I did, and for her to feel my poems
as her own, so that she might make
them mine in English.

I'm consulted, I read over the work,
weigh in, suggest, I wind the string
on the spinning top, but she is the
one who plays the game and sets the
toy free, making it whirl until Ravel's
Bolero dances like a dervish.

Carol Maier is deserving of the
homage you, her colleagues, pay
her. In addition to being her translated author, I also call myself friend
and brother, and now join the tribute in Spanish, via English, and
even in Arabic and Chinese:

تهنئة   祝賀

Caracas, 14 September 2014

The In-Between

Scenes from a Life in Translation

Lawrence Venuti

I am waiting for a train at the Stazione Termini in Rome and suddenly I spot it: a spanking new vending machine blazoned with the words "Self Bar."[1] It contains the usual drinks and snacks, many of which would not have been available a few decades ago when I first began traveling to Europe, and certainly not in that way, mechanically. What grabs my attention, however, is not the chance to shop but the language, the peculiar use of English, so strange to a native speaker.

The shorthand tag *self* for *self-service* shows how deeply English has seeped into current Italian usage, even though transformed in the process. It has joined a growing pool of Italianized English words, such as *bar,* always more suggestive of coffee than alcohol in Italy, or *OK,* sometimes pronounced to rhyme with *mai* (the Italian word for "never," *mai* sounds like "my"), or *golf,* usually applied to the sweater that anglophones call a "cardigan." For most Italians, these words are not merely comprehensible, but naturalized, perceived as Italian, their English origins imperceptible or forgotten.

Self Bar. Testimony to the worldwide domination of English, but also to the hybridity of being Italian today. Step right up and get a new self. The machine makes change in the most literal of senses. The brave new world of globalized capital creates niche consumers that are invariably anglicized, to some extent.

Yet what does that sign do to me, the American abroad? It moves me to translate with an automatism worthy of the very machine it names. To make sense of the words I am compelled to recast them in a familiar form. And in that split-second operation I confirm my own identity as an anglophone, although unmoored, set adrift in a sea of languages where English has been fragmented and the fragments recombined, demanding translation to be recognizable.

Seeing those words gives me a pleasure that is not unlike what I hope my translations will give. The pursuit of an uncanny foreignness has become ingrained in my thinking, very much part of my work as a translator. I see it as tempting readers with a calculated deviation, whether from the most commonly used language or from the most widely valued literature. Whatever enjoyment a translation might offer seems to rest on a betrayal or test of received wisdom—but only in favor of some higher fidelity. I prefer instead to be true to the foreign work, or a newly conceived idea thereof, even to innovation itself, the unique beauty and power that a translation can introduce into the whorl of simulacra in which we live.

But is this aim strictly professional? To what degree is it a matter of personal taste, plain willfulness, mad obsession? Do I simply want my translations to produce an effect that I experience on a day-to-day basis, an experience that has become second nature to me? To be precise, it isn't so much my nature as my culture, a trait or tic of sensibility acquired over many years, so that any distinction between first and second and subsequent has long ago been obliterated.

My train arrives punctually, and I am glad to be leaving Rome, filled with nostalgia for a city where I recently lived for several years. My destination is Trento, far to the north, an area of Italy where I have never been. It is Sunday. When I arrive many hours later, night has fallen, and the narrow, winding streets are virtually empty, glistening with rain and swept by icy blasts from the snow-capped mountains. Searching for my hotel, I get lost. The black-and-white mountains tower in the distance, useless to orient me, and I feel as if I might be somewhere else, perhaps Austria or Switzerland. The only thing I recognize is the language, the snatches of Italian spoken by the few people who cross my path. But no sooner do I hear it, no sooner do I grasp the meaning of a word or phrase, than I am a stranger again, mindful of being in a strange land.

· · ·

My mother never finished high school. I don't believe that as an adult she ever read a book from cover to cover. She compensated by imposing on me her aspirations, which were not only educational but social. The child of Italian working-class immigrants, she nurtured an American's naive fascination with British English, synonymous in her mind with aristocracy, upward mobility, cultural refinement—although she was perceptive enough to detect a Cockney accent and dismissive enough to brand it with the pejorative term *Limey*. She named me Lawrence after Laurence Olivier, an actor whose accent had enthralled her. The substitution of *w* for *u* was perhaps her way of insinuating a difference, an unconscious resistance both to the popular films that occupied her imagination and to the class divisions that those films transcended yet maintained.

Her speech was typically filled with colloquialisms and hypercorrections, obscenities and malapropisms. "Excuse my French profoul," she was likely to say, "but he doesn't know his ass from a hole in the ground."

My mother was selflessly devoted to caring for me. But she was also high-strung, riddled with anxieties, subject to panic attacks. Her emotional intensity might happily be expressed as affection, but it could abruptly turn abusive. She was too ready to shout and slap, and I feared her outbursts, furies, violence. As a child I would have a recurrent nightmare in which vaguely familiar people I could not identify performed the most routine household tasks while speaking at the top of their voices, their words too loud to be intelligible yet menacing, horrifically ill-suited to what they were doing. Not until much later did it dawn on me that my dreams were translations of the fear I would occasionally feel in my mother's presence.

In this atmosphere I inherited her nervousness and came to dread her harsh reactions to my speech. She insisted that I absorb standard English, even though it was an ideal that her own lack of education prevented her from ever achieving. One Saturday, when I was about nine or ten, I rebelled: with a piece of charcoal I neatly inscribed a series of obscene words on a brick wall in my grandmother's backyard. *Shit. Bastard. Fuck.* My mother flew into a rage and smacked me across the mouth, her heavy wedding band knocking against a tooth, bloodying my lip.

As I grew older, this scene was repeated with variations, although the hitting gave way to withholding privileges and the rebellious speech acts were reduced to the odd colloquialism or slang, the kind of language used by adolescent friends. Still, I could never anticipate my mother's reactions to nonstandard forms. Once, when she asked where I had spent an afternoon, I replied, "Nowhere, just fooling around." She angrily told me never to use such language again. I was dumbfounded, bereft of the composure (or audacity) I needed to question her response. Exactly what did "fooling around" mean to her? I could not say. Was she disturbed by the suggestion that I was frittering away time better spent doing something more productive? Or did the phrase connote illicit sex to her? Or vandalism? No dictionary could help me understand her translation.

In time my language lost any social or regional marking. I mastered the standard dialect in speech and writing and became an academic, a professor of English. In my work as a translator, however, I find myself constantly challenging this dialect, constantly gravitating toward the most heterogeneous mix of Englishes. My motives cannot be explained solely by an array of theoretical concepts drawn from translation studies. They must incorporate my mother's tongue and her linguistic schooling of me, however abrasive that was, as well as my own tormented love of her.

Yet what do I call "my mother tongue?" Is it her uneducated speech? Or her insistence on the standard dialect? Can it be both?

The translator must always negotiate between divided loyalties. I have kept faith, in my way, with my mother's contradictions.

.   .   .

The warmth of my grandmother's kitchen steamed the windows on winter weekends. Around a huge table, dusted with flour and strewn with metal contraptions, bustled my mother and my aunts. They were making pasta, as they often did on Saturday mornings, cranking out long strands of spaghetti, spooning snowy ricotta onto yellow squares of dough and pinching them closed, shaping neat raviolis. Pots filled with thick red gravy bubbled on the gas stove. It was never called *sauce*, always *gravy*, which I understood as shorthand for a meal centered around pasta. "On Tuesday I'll make gravy," my mother would say. The term *sauce* was used only by *Amerigáns*, as my family referred to people who were not Italian or not of Italian descent.

These culinary rituals constituted language lessons, my first lessons in Italian. The lexicon was untranslatable. It represented an Edenic language in which word and object appeared to be inherently related but were actually linked by my family, by the differences between their recipes and those of other families, especially between the southern Italian cooking that prevailed in my mother's home and the various cuisines on offer outside it. Not only did *noodles* not translate *spaghetti*, but no equivalent existed for *gravy*. It was a color, a smell, a taste that could not be put into other words. But the sensory data could be verified with certainty—whenever we ate pasta.

To grow up Italian American was to be caught in a complicated relationship to Italian. Because I belonged to the second generation born in the United States, after the Second World War, I could learn the language only if I lived for an extended period with my maternal grandparents (who spoke much less English than my father's parents). The more time spent with them the better, because Italian was routinely used as a language of concealment from the children—usually when we were the topic of the conversation—and this obstacle could be overcome only by daily contact with the native speakers. Still, I would not learn standard Italian, only a jumble of dialects that reflected my grandparents' exodus from Foggia to South Philadelphia. I learned civilities, mostly, formulaic phrases, and the words they called me when they pulled me by the hair out of frustration with my behavior. *Gavone* (rhymes with *Stallone*) was the form in which I first heard the word *cafone* (rhyming with *ofay*, it means a provincial person, a boor). *Fungool* was the first Italian obscenity I encountered, a garbled version of "va fan culo" ("up your ass"), although either pronunciation would be certain to raise eyebrows.

Italian was restricted to the home. My parents' generation was obsessed with being American, with assimilating to American cultural norms and trends, so their knowledge of Italian remained rudimentary, intuitive, oral, primarily a means of communicating with my grandparents. My father and mother were native speakers of English who could not read or write Italian. They found distasteful more recent Italian immigrants who lacked a strong command of English, who spoke it with a heavy accent that revealed their origins. My parents called them *greaseballs*.

In the 1960s I attended a Jesuit college prep school whose rigorous academic curriculum was then too conservative, too closely bound to the humanist tradition, to offer instruction in Italian. So I began to learn French, along with the compulsory Latin, and found that declensions and conjugations were just the thing to incite teenage rebellion, more honored in the breach than the observance, at least in the beginning. But soon I got hooked. Studying a foreign language was like assembling a jigsaw puzzle, and translating into my native tongue, the oldest method of foreign-language learning, became routine for me. The mere gratification of solving a linguistic problem kept me reading difficult texts like Tacitus's elegantly concise *Historiae* and Sartre's drama of fantastic torment, *Huis clos*.

It was not until I entered a doctoral program in British and American literatures that I decided to embark on the study of Italian, very painfully, thumbing through a grammar book and a dictionary, struggling to read the great modern writers, Pirandello and Moravia, Ungaretti and Montale. I learned the standard dialect, of course, Tuscan. Italian proved to be a fallow field for me, a site where my literary interests could take root and grow into a new kind of writing, and I immediately began to translate, mainly as a method of reading, so as to understand and interpret the Italian texts.

The memory of those first Italian lessons with my family helped enormously. From them I had absorbed a smattering of lexical items and various speech rhythms, which facilitated the learning process. Yet studying Italian led not to a renewed connection with my past, but to greater distance from it. Because the language no longer served the uses to which my family had put it in my childhood, it seemed to lose its capacity to shut out people, whether the excluded were their own children or some hapless immigrants. It rather opened the door to a new culture, and I began to travel to Italy during summer vacations, particularly spending time in the north, in Tuscany, Milan, Venice, and so avoiding the southern regions of my ancestors.

My parents, however, never visited Italy. Nor did they ever express any wish to do so. Italian admitted me to a world they could never know, ironically reinstating an exclusion I had not anticipated. And with it came a feeling of bad faith, at least initially, as if I had turned against my roots. Although my mother took pride in my newfound relation to Italian culture, she also saw it as snobbish.

.   .   .

"No bazoom, peese," intoned my daughter Gemma at age two and a half, shaking her head, her back pressed against her high chair as if to give added force to her refusal. It was her way of telling my wife and me that she didn't want any chopped basil in her pasta. She was entering her "pale food phase," as we called it, when her preferred meal was either penne with butter or cold noodles with sesame sauce. Anything that marred the pale uniformity of the food was revolting to her. Basil, parsley, oregano, scallions all fell into the category of "dirty bits," in her parlance, and we would have to pick them out. She also had a term for the meals: *noo-noos,* a shortened and infantilized version of *noodles.*

My favorite among her words was *baybels,* which she called *bagels.* Her bagels were certainly Babels. Parenthood meant, in part, a renewed encounter with the biblical curse of disparate languages, although now sugar-coated with cuteness.

Eventually I came to appreciate what was remarkable about Gemma's speech. Her words were renderings of the English dialect spoken on the Upper West Side of Manhattan, her parents' lingo. She was simultaneously inventing and translating. This enabled her to learn our language, but in the process we had to learn hers. We soon found ourselves translating an entire lexicon into forms she could understand and use. It was translation as innovation, shorn of any avant-garde pretensions, driven by the impulse to communicate and to satisfy primal needs like hunger. Given her dependence on us, we jumped at every opportunity to be her translators, believing, somewhat egotistically, that we were teaching her English when she was actually warping ours into weird new forms, broadening the range of Englishes at our command.

This sort of creativity makes children ideal travelers. At a very young age, they become adept at mimicry and quickly adapt to foreign places. Instead of being intimidated by languages they can't understand, they observe how words and phrases are used and imitate them to the letter, relishing the sheer sounds as well as their power to elicit a reaction from elders.

At fifteen months old, my son Jules readily absorbed some Spanish during my tenure as a visiting professor in Barcelona. After we settled into our apartment on the first floor (what would be the second in New York City), he was drawn to the window that looked down into the narrow street where a busy restaurant faced our building. In a couple of days he began to wave frantically and shout "Hola" to people passing by, whether he was standing at the window or being pushed down the sidewalk in a stroller. In the fall we shifted to Italy for a two-year appointment, and after the first year Jules was put into an Italian preschool, a *nido* (or "nest"). He immediately started to speak Italian, the rough-and-ready phrases he picked up from his classmates, enough to carry on a basic conversation and to participate in schoolyard games.

Adults can be so different when confronted with foreignness, especially when it is imprinted on their language. They are inclined to tolerate mispronunciation and misunderstanding in children, but much less so in tourists and immigrants, whether the foreigner is driving a taxi or just asking for directions on the street. The age difference matters. A child's helplessness invites correction that can be taken as offensive by someone older who may be just as helpless in a culture not his or her own.

But more often the age difference means a very different relation to the act of translation. Children, motivated by the will to know, readily become faithful translators of their peers and their elders, ever respectful of the intention with which words are used. Adults, however, can become impatient with words they are forced to translate, regardless of how obvious the meanings may be, as if they expect everyone to speak the same language—theirs—with the same proficiency as they do. This attitude can result in mistranslation, sometimes deliberate, which creates occasions of embarrassment, condescension, cruelty.

My British in-laws would chuckle at my Americanisms, especially when they seemed to deviate from their conservative middle-class etiquette. To an offer of a second helping at supper I once responded, "No thanks, I'm stuffed," which sent them tittering. Their complacent insularity led them to translate what I said into the mild British obscenity, "Get stuffed." They had laughed at my unwitting application of this phrase to myself. My wife instructed me that the proper response would have been something on the order of "I've had sufficient."

I had crashed through her parents' polite reserve. It wouldn't be the last time. I never felt we were speaking the same language.

.   .   .

In *Italian Hours* Henry James remarks that the exquisite "afternoon lights" of Florence betoken the "essential amiability" of its inhabitants. His perception of the colors still holds true, even in this postindustrial age. On clear days, the sky is ice blue, the late afternoon light gilds the buildings, and the sunset bathes Fiesole in a violet glow. Yet when James evokes a Tuscan sensibility ("the sense of saving sanity, of something sound and human"), he indulges in sheer flattery—especially where translation is concerned.

Admittedly, my attitude toward Florence is eccentric. When I lived there at the end of the 1990s, I would spend days browsing in bookshops and leafing through magazines, searching for new Italian writing and new ways of thinking about older works. Italians certainly do these things, particularly writers and literary critics. But not with a translator's sense of what might be worth putting into English, of what might alter the impression of Italian writing in the anglophone reader's mind so as to intrigue, enlighten, give pleasure. A translator can only approach a foreign literature by looking in two directions at once, home and abroad.

Meeting Italian writers has likewise been a schizoid experience for me. On one hand, an enthusiastic admiration for their achievement; on the other, the critical detachment needed to apply the standards of another language and culture—often accompanied by the sobering realization that their Italian success can't be matched in English. Several decades of translating have taught me that the cliché is true: literary translation is simultaneously loss and gain. The loss is irreparable, the gain exorbitant, and both usually go unnoticed by the reader.

Foreign writers sometimes understand these problems. Yet too often they don't because their knowledge of the translating language and culture is limited. William Weaver, the leading anglophone translator of Italian fiction for the latter half of the twentieth century, once told me that the novelist Giorgio Bassani had questioned his use of the word *cot* to render an Italian reference to a child's bed. Bassani's dissatisfaction was based on a dictionary entry that defined *cot* as a shortened form of *cottage*. Still, he deferred to his translator. More willful writers have insisted on controlling the destiny of their works in other languages, regardless of the uncontrollable drift of form and meaning. And copyright law does grant them unlimited and arbitrary power over "derivative" works like translations.

I fell victim to this legal situation shortly after arriving in Florence. Grove/Atlantic approached me for a sample translation from a text by Dario Fo. Translating a Nobel Laureate had never appealed to me, since I much prefer the serendipitous discovery, the engaging writer who has so far remained untranslated. But I found Fo's work attractive, partly because of his political imagination, partly because of his potential impact in English. He demands a writerly translation, an inventiveness that matches his experiments with dialects and thereby challenges the prevalent tendency to render every sort of language into standard usage. Besides, the prize had rankled the New York literary establishment, driving a publisher of many Nobel Laureates, Roger Straus, to declare that Fo didn't write literature. Fo, I realized, carried enough shock value to shake up the canons applied to Italian writing in English and perhaps open them up to different kinds of work.

One rainy afternoon of dismal light I met with Fo's agent in Settignano, just outside of Florence. The text to be translated, *Johan Padan and the Discovery of the Americas,* was a theatrical monologue that retells the story of Columbus's voyage from what might be called a postcolonial viewpoint. The agent and I agreed that an appropriate strategy would be to mix varieties of English, British and American, literary and popular, Shakespearean and slangy. The publisher, too, agreed, and my sample won the commission. Yet a month later another translator emerged to claim ownership of Fo's writing in English—with the author's support. Ultimately I lost the project. Italians use that infamous pun, "traduttore traditore," to underscore a belief that the translator is always a traitor. I couldn't help but feel that here was a case of "autore traditore."

These thoughts weighed on my mind when, during my Florentine sojourn, I traveled to Siena to meet the novelist Antonio Tabucchi. I was invited to speak on translation at a research institute created by the universities of Siena and Toronto. Tabucchi offered to "intervene," as the Italians describe such appearances, by commenting on the English version of his 1994 novel, *Declares Pereira.* He had read my review of it in the *New York Times,* where I expressed admiration for his work as well as Patrick Creagh's translation. I felt honored that he wanted to meet me. Nonetheless, I wondered whether he would praise or blame a translation that had received more attention than his previous five books in English.

The small room was packed. That morning a newspaper had carried a notice with the headline "Tabucchi Speaks." In Italy *Declares Pereira* had catapulted Tabucchi to literary stardom, selling 300,000 copies within a year. I spoke first, arguing that translation never communicates in a direct or untroubled fashion. A translation of a novel may recreate elements of narrative form—point of view, plot, characterization—and even give a sense of prose style. But significant variation occurs because they are recast in dialects, registers, and discourses that are specific to the translating language, producing literary effects that work only in the receiving culture.

To illustrate I presented a sampling of Creagh's choices. His English consists mostly of the standard dialect. But he cultivated a noticeable strain of colloquialism. He rendered "quattro uomini dall'aria sinistra" ("four men with a sinister air") as "four shady-looking characters," "un personaggio del regime" ("a figure in the regime") as "bigwig," and "senza pigiama" ("without pyjamas") as "in his birthday-suit." He also used some British English, rendering "orrendo" ("horrible") as "bloody awful," "pensioncina" ("little boarding house") as "little doss-house," "sono nei guai" ("I'm in trouble") as "I'm in a pickle," and "a vedere" ("to look") as "to take a dekko." Tabucchi looked over my shoulder as I read the examples, apparently surprised.

Although I gave the alternatives provided here parenthetically, I cautioned the audience against treating them as the only acceptable renderings. Creagh's choices are consistent with dictionary definitions, I argued, even if varying the dialect and register. This variation fits the narrative, which is conversational, an official testimony to an unnamed authority. Set in 1938 under the Portuguese dictator Salazar, Tabucchi's novel recounts how Pereira, the cultural editor of a Lisbon newspaper, is radicalized over several weeks, which culminate when he prints an attack on the fascist regime. Creagh's use of slang and

Britishisms alludes to political thrillers of the period, notably Graham Greene's *The Confidential Agent* (1939), which is similarly set during the Spanish Civil War. Through this allusiveness, I suggested, the reader is implicitly invited to distinguish between Tabucchi's left-wing opposition to fascism and Greene's more cautious liberalism.

Then Tabucchi spoke, starting with an allusion to Ortega y Gasset's famous essay on translation. "A translation is never the text," Tabucchi said, "but a path to the text." He contrasted two such paths: one is serviceable, aiming to render meaning, while the other is authorial, whereby the translator vies with the author by giving an interpretation. For Tabucchi, the risks of authorial translation also fell into two categories: a translator might explain, resolving ambiguities and banalizing the text, or a translator might improve, embellishing and departing from stylistic features that the foreign author had intended.

Tabucchi illustrated serviceable translation with his own Italian versions of the Portuguese writer Fernando Pessoa. To illustrate an authorial translation, he cited Creagh's version of *Declares Pereira,* which he felt improved the Italian through choices that were "much more attractive" but "arbitrary." Tabucchi sought to avoid this problem with his next novel, *The Missing Head of Damasceno Montiero* (1997) by examining Creagh's version with a friend and "intervening" where necessary. The novelist wanted to ensure that the translation reflects the several stylistic levels in the Italian, ranging from slang spoken by gypsies to an everyday middle-class language to a more cultured, at times philosophical discourse. These levels, he said, were more difficult to translate than the standard dialect spoken consistently by Pereira.

On finishing, Tabucchi dashed off to give a lecture. I found his talk too optimistic about realizing the author's intended meaning in languages and cultures that weren't his, and too neglectful of the fact that an interpretation always occurs in translation—even when the translator believes himself to be simply transferring the meaning of the source text. I was curious about how Creagh had reacted to Tabucchi's intervention. He was living in Tuscany, so I rang him up when I returned to Florence. Reserving judgment on the changes that Tabucchi had introduced, Creagh said that he no longer considered the translation his and therefore signed it with a pseudonym, J. C. Patrick. The gesture was striking: he clearly felt that he had undergone a Christ-like ordeal. The translation, of course, won't reveal anything about the behind-the-scenes drama. And Creagh never went public about the incident. Perhaps he maintained his silence to protect his career as a professional translator. Between

1965 and his death in 2012, he was prolific, producing some 40 translations of Italian fiction, poetry, travel writing, and art criticism. Yet after the pseudonymous translation appeared in 1999, the steady flow of commissions slowed to a trickle, and he translated only a few more books. In the end, the only reputation Creagh may have preserved was Tabucchi's.

. . .

"Basta così?" asked the woman behind the counter. She was holding a spatula and a knife over an oblong slab of pizza, framing it, waiting for my response. She was asking, "Is this enough?" If I replied, "Sì," she would cut the piece, lay it on a scale, and charge me according to the weight. Hunger dictated my response, naturally. But I enjoyed this opportunity to engage with her, so I would avoid laconic answers and say either "Un poco meno, per favore" ("A little less, please") or "Vorrei più che quella" ("I'd like more than that"). Depending on her mood and the size of the crowd, she might come back with a quip like "Non ha fame oggi?" ("Not hungry today"?) or "Rinunciate al suo regime?" ("Going off your diet?"). Here, I thought, you can find immediate satisfaction, whether your goal is an Italian meal or a brief exchange with an Italian (or both).

Located in Rome near the Piazzale Flaminio, the shop offered pizza "a taglio," literally "by the cut," although like other New Yorkers I was inclined to say "by the slice." Still, I couldn't bring myself to translate the phrase into a familiar experience. No pizza joint in New York bore the slightest resemblance to this Roman place.

For one thing the pizzas were baked in rectangular pans, but none of the Italian patrons was likely to call them "Sicilian," as I used to do while growing up in South Philadelphia. My maternal grandfather worked in a local bakery, a family-run business that produced not only Italian breads but pizzas. An immigrant from Foggia, he was Roman by birth, bearer of the venerable surname of Rutigliano, which might not only refer to a town in Puglia but derive from a Latin word, *Rutuliani,* alluding to an ancient Italic tribe that figures in Virgil's *Aeneid* (they fought against Aeneas's Trojan army, that is to say, on the losing side). Even though Grandpa had never advanced beyond a handful of English words and always uttered them with a thick accent, he, too, came to describe as "Sicilian" the rectangular pizzas he would make for other Italian Americans, including his own family. Not until I traveled to Italy as an adult did I realize that the term masks significant culinary differences.

Another difference was the variety of toppings at my pizza a taglio. I found the customary *margherita,* recognizable by sight but unusual in taste, much more savory than the tomato-and-cheese pies back home because of ingredients like bufala, mozzarella made from water buffalo milk. The *pizza rossa,* a thin crust smeared with tomato sauce, I recognized as a Roman staple but virtually impossible to find in New York. The two pizzas I favored were rarities, available every day but in limited quantity. One was a crust sprinkled with tomato sauce and olive oil and then layered with arugula, mozzarella, and smoked salmon, the last three ingredients uncooked, a sort of Italo-Nordic salad of a pizza. The other was stuffed, two crusts between which were wedged thin slices of grilled eggplant lightly dusted with crushed red pepper, a mixture of sweetness and heat.

My pizza a taglio couldn't really be called a pizzeria. That suggests a sit-down restaurant, whereas this was purely take-away, containing just a counter that stretched the width of a room about 20 feet square. Most of it lay empty till lunchtime, when it filled with customers who spilled out onto the sidewalk. A university campus up the block brought droves of students; nearby banks, offices, and stores brought employees; and the crowd grew dense. When I joined it, I quickly abandoned any American-bred notion of private space and inched closer to the counter to grab the attention of the help and call out my order.

I was a neighbor for a while, living in an apartment whose rear window looks onto the street behind the shop. On warm days the back door was left open, and I could see the pizzas being assembled and cooked, the aromas wafting toward my room, making work increasingly difficult. My spoken Italian had markedly improved, and my Italian look enabled me to pass for a native. Passing gave a narcissistic pleasure, I suppose, but I was blindly pursuing something else. It was partly a search for roots I never had. But because I was living alone after my marriage had ended, I was also looking for a sense of belonging, although comforted by the anonymity of just being a neighborhood face that shop owners might acknowledge with a nod. I wanted to translate myself into a foreign community, even if my accent, occasionally deciphered by natives as vaguely Germanic, set me apart. (Once, when I told a taxi driver my destination, he shot back, "Jawohl!") But I didn't really want to belong: I couldn't bear another identity at the time. I just wanted to pass, unquestioned, unsure of who exactly I might become.

. . .

A Mediterranean winter, cold but mild, the sun a yellow smudge in a gauzy sky. I am standing at the counter of a quiet café in Barcelona, a customer here and there at the tables. I want a certain kind of Spanish coffee: a shot of espresso served in a small cup, whether ceramic or glass, which is then filled to the brim with hot milk. No foam (that'd be Italian, *un macchiato*), just milk. But first I must decide which language to use, whether to speak Castilian or Catalan, whether to order "un cortado" or "un tallat."

Although both words would be understood, the barman's reaction might differ. Castilian would be met with a blank expression and business as usual. If I use Catalan with a barman reared in Castilian, possibly fed up with the chauvinism invested in Catalan, he might grimace. A Catalanist might smile, especially if he detects my accent, pleased to encounter an anglophone sympathizer with a culture that suffered brutal repression under Franco's regime, a speaker of the globally dominant language who thinks enough of a minor tongue to take up its cause—by speaking it. Although both words refer to the same object, their meanings diverge.

I have been studying the language and culture of Catalunya, developing a taste for its poetry and painting, its food and drink. I have relied on a number of guides who were helpful and understanding, sometimes more. My closest informant used to be a woman born in the American South who had lived in Spain longer than in the United States and held dual citizenship. She saw herself as a Barcelonesa, in fact a Catalana, commanding native proficiency in Castilian and Catalan. I, a newcomer, lacking an assured fluency in any language but English, can never shake the feeling of being on the outside.

Faced daily with translating between languages whose prestige and power vary with my interlocutor, I could pause to question the conditions of every speech act. But I don't, conscious that I'd never get my shopping done, never buy a newspaper or stamps, never take my shirts to the laundry, never order a meal in a restaurant without having second thoughts. Instead I notice how English surrenders its role as the unmoved mover of meaning, the relay point of every word and phrase, and begins to switch with Castilian and Catalan as the means by which the world becomes intelligible to me. Imagine the three languages as electrical circuits strung vertically along a ladder, the cultural hierarchy in which they are positioned. At every unpredictable switch among them, I am rushing to make sense, climbing up and down, up and down, as in a gag from some early talkie. To be an anglophone open to the bilingualism of this culture is to lose any complacency that might still inhere in my relationship to English.

The barman walks over. "Hola, bon dia," he says. Not "buenos días." He is speaking Catalan, so I follow suit. "Un tallat, si us plau." I give the words my best pronunciation, clipped but rounding the final dipthong in the phrase for "please"—"sis plow." He turns to operate the machine and places the little cup of chocolate-colored liquid before me. His gestures are routine, inexpressive. I realize I've passed, he's taken me for Catalan, or I've been accepted, any peculiarity of accent overlooked.

I sip the coffee, struck by how a connection with another person is built on a series of translations that can easily fail, usually because the parties involved have different ideas of what constitutes a faithful translation. These differences won't necessarily prevent communication, but they can preempt or destroy a relationship. They can also create a possibility that did not before exist, the possibility of a new life that, under favorable circumstances, might unfold with wonder and hope. It depends on taking a chance, choosing to be faithful to a different language, or the difference one hears in it. As I had done with the barman's.

When the cup is empty, I say, "Moltes gràcies," and start for the door. It's then that he flashes a smile. "Adéu," I respond and head back into the cold.

Note

1. Portions of this essay have appeared in a somewhat different form in the *Times Literary Supplement* (2000) and in *City Secrets Rome* (Kahn and Kahn 2011).

Works Cited

Venuti, Lawrence. 2000. "Letter from Florence." *Times Literary Supplement* (20 March): 14.

Venuti, Lawrence. 2011. "Pizza Rustica." In *City Secrets Rome: The Essential Insider's Guide*, edited by Robert Kahn and Fiona Kahn, 114–16. New York: Fang Duff Kahn.

A Portrait of the Translator as Laborer

A Reflection on Rodolfo Walsh's "Nota al pie"

Rosemary Arrojo

> I find increasingly that it is fiction and, at times, autobiography,
> rather than translation theory *per se* that probes
> the wondering as well as the wandering of translation.
> —Carol Maier, "The Translator as *Theôros*"

The reading of fiction on the theme of translation, rather than merely confirm or echo the arguments and conclusions of philosophers and translation studies scholars, can illuminate certain issues that are only rarely explored in more conventional scholarship.[1] It can bring insights, for instance, into the psychology involved in the power relationships that are usually at work in the composition and the production of translations. To the extent that stories about translations or translators make such relationships visible and tend to reveal conflicting viewpoints on such visibility—as represented, for instance, by the different voices that are woven together in fictional plots—they constitute invaluable material for a reflection on the ways in which translations and translators have been viewed and treated throughout history. It is my goal here to address what seems to be a recurrent theme in contemporary fiction about translation: the tensions between different characters usually representing, on the one hand, the "establishment"—or the established power of the "original" or of what it represents—and, on the other, the difference, or the dissidence associated with the translator's agency. I focus on "Nota al pie" ("Footnote"), a poignant story by the Argentine Rodolfo Walsh, first published in 1967, which explores the footnote as a metaphor for the marginality of the translator, whose voice, if or when it is allowed to be heard, must come from and remain at the bottom of the page. Walsh's characterization of the translator as an oppressed laborer freelancing for a publishing house in Buenos Aires—presumably from the mid-1950s to the mid-1960s—will allow me to reflect on issues of visibility and power and how they can be associated with the fundamental question as to what and whom translations and translators ultimately serve.

Walsh's Split Narrative

In "Nota al pie," we are introduced to León de Sanctis, a lonely and unhappy translator who has just killed himself in the cheap boardinghouse where he lived. Ironically, as the story opens, we are told that the self-effacing translator, who spent most of his life perfecting the art of being invisible, "undoubtedly wanted" Otero, his boss at La Casa, the publishing house for which he worked, "to come and see him, naked and dead [. . .] and that is why he wrote [Otero's] name on the envelope containing the letter that might explain everything" (69).[2] Otero has indeed come to the boardinghouse to identify León's body at the request of the police and is guided by the elderly housekeeper to the shabby bedroom where the dead translator lies covered by a sheet. She hands him León's letter, a letter that Otero does not open "because he wants to imagine the dead man's version," and, as we are informed in the very last line of the first page, Otero does imagine "its general tone of lugubrious apology, his first sentence of farewell and regret" (69). At this point a footnote is inserted, dividing the text into two narratives: while in the main body of the text, the omniscient narrator allows us to learn about Otero's take on León and what has happened, at the bottom of the page, in the footnote—which occupies more and more space on each page up to the last one when it actually takes over and replaces the main narrative—we are given access to the translator's suicide letter and his own version of the facts.

The story's split narrative provides an eloquent illustration of the hierarchical dichotomies that oppose the "establishment" to the margins, or the main body of the text to the footnote, as well as the employer, represented by Otero, who holds the almost exclusive power to establish what can be read and how it should be translated, to the subservient translator, who is expected to be invisible and blindly serve the publisher's interests. Furthermore, as Walsh's story seems to suggest a clear connection between La Casa—literally "The House" or "The Home"—and the country itself, this is a dichotomy that also reflects some key aspects of the complex relationship that opposes the elite to the working class or, even, the authoritarian state to the Argentine people. Appropriately, these two opposing worlds find their representation in the language and the style that give us access to Otero's thoughts in the main narrative and to León's letter at the bottom of the page. While Otero's perspective is presented in an elegant, controlled form of traditional prose that can be associated with the conventions of highbrow literature, rich in insightful descriptions and subtle associations, León's letter is simple, emotional, and often touchingly naive.

In the main body of the text, we learn that, according to Otero, being invisible, "erasing" one's personality is in fact the "hardest of all the secrets" a translator needs to learn: "to be unnoticed, to write like another and not let anybody know that" (75). While the translator must accept a passive role in the production of translations, it is the publishing house's "mission" to "nourish the dreams of the people and build a culture for them, even against themselves" (76). According to Otero, in the beginning, León was "innately loyal" and seemed to understand the heroic "sacrifice" inherent in La Casa's mission (76). However, just like the housekeeper, Otero does not seem to know much about the translator who managed to go unnoticed for so long. Together with Otero we learn from the housekeeper—a simple, older woman also hardened by relentless work and loneliness—that León was poor but paid his rent on time, and did not disturb anybody even though at night one could often hear the noise made by his typewriter in the room he shared with another boarder. In the last few months he got sick and seemed sadder and more reserved and did not want to leave the bedroom. Then he just went mad (71–72).

Her reminiscences of León brings to Otero's mind some of the translator's "eccentricities" such as his insistence on delivering a handwritten assignment just a couple of months before, alleging some vague problem with his typewriter (72). We also learn that in the last few months León was no longer welcome in the editor's office as the translator would generally bring annoying questions and complaints, often expressing a surprising "aversion" toward "certain types of books"—the same kind he used to enjoy at the beginning—as well as a "secret (and laughable) desire" to influence La Casa's editorial policies. At other times he would mention his desire to maybe start writing his own stories, or his wish to work on "the great classics of all time" series, a promotion that Otero considered to be "undoubtedly risky" considering León's background (82).

As he reminisces about his working relationship with the translator, Otero reveals himself to be incapable of empathizing with León and his plight. Indeed, the central issue that informs the development of the main narrative is the process through which Otero comes to terms with his potential role in León's death, a process that begins with his awareness that he has come to the boardinghouse most of all "to be at peace with his own conscience" (70). For Otero, since "nobody can live with the dead," we must "kill them inside ourselves and reduce them to an innocuous image that will forever be safe in our memory" (71). In the end, after he formally identifies the body, Otero concludes that he can now see things clearly: everything that happened was undoubtedly León's own fault. His suicide was indeed the solution to which only a mediocre man might resort, a man whose tendency to be melancholy and always question the status quo also reflected the chaos of their times as well as "the metaphysical malady that was destroying the country" (84).[3] As far as Otero is concerned, if he had to be blamed for anything, it would only be for, as usual, being too good and too soft and not forcing León to change his ways and return to the right path (85–86).

At the bottom of the page, León apologizes for not having finished the last translation assignment he received from La Casa and explains why he was unable to type his manuscripts in recent months: after spending the last of his money to treat a serious bout of sinusitis he was forced to pawn his typewriter, which he never managed to reclaim (72). At the same time, he tries to make arrangements to pay for his rent and burial expenses counting on the money he should be paid for the 130 pages of the unfinished, handwritten translation he left on his desk and with whatever could be obtained from the sale of his pawned typewriter (75). He also apologizes for the "abuse" of asking Otero to help him with such arrangements and expresses his gratitude and his affection by leaving his old dictionary, his only personal possession, to the editor (77–78). Furthermore, León's letter briefly describes his difficult childhood as a destitute orphan, then his job as a manual laborer at a tire shop and his efforts to improve his lot. After several years studying English at night at a Pitman School,[4] he managed to find employment as a freelance translator of detective fiction at La Casa (83). Soon, though, León realized that he worked more hours and made less money than he did fixing tires (86, 90) and, after a few years, as science fiction began to replace detective stories in the publishing house's catalog, he became increasingly aware of his painful role as a servant to the "imbecile" authors he was assigned to translate (94). In the end, alone and physically and emotionally drained after years of continuous hardship and total dedication to an activity of which he could no longer be proud, León decides to end his life. He blames only himself for his decision and has no complaints about La Casa (94).

A Subversive Footnote

A footnote could arguably be used as an appropriate metaphor for the marginal, ambivalent position generally occupied by translators divided between the demands of invisibility prescribed by tradition and their need to be heard and participate in the virtual dialogue with readers. To the extent that it betrays the presence of the translator as an active participant in the writing and/or reading of someone else's text, even if it is at the bottom of the page, the translator's footnote breaks the illusion of the transparency of translation and of the translator's invisibility and, consequently, also the fantasy of the author's "original" as a closed, stable object, identifiable as some sort of reliable presence. At the same time that it is expected to separate and protect what belongs to the author and the "original" from the translator's commentary or supplement, the translator's footnote is, thus, also a reminder of the incompleteness and the instability of any text, always open to uninvited or unexpected interventions.

In "Nota al pie," Walsh potentializes the basically subversive character of the footnote by employing it as an effective device first to challenge and, then, slowly but surely invade and take over the main text.[5] As the central focus of the plot, Walsh's footnote is fundamental not merely for what it actually says but, more importantly, for what it does. Since it makes the translator visible to us, the readers, the footnote allows León's letter to confront what is being narrated in the main body of the text at the same time that it brings us the narrator's take on what is being narrated. Although León's letter tells Otero that he had no complaints about La Casa, when this letter is intercepted by the narrator and inserted as a footnote into the very line in which we learn that Otero will not read the translator's message, it functions as part of the narrator's strategy to empower the dead translator, turning his suicide letter into a compelling amendment to Otero's perspective in the main narrative—a perspective that is, for the editor, the "original," established version of the facts. Thus, as León's letter becomes the narrator's footnote, or the latter's "message" to his readers, it ends up telling a different story, suggesting that León's tragedy could also be associated with the general, heavily hierarchical regime of La Casa, characterized by centralization of power, authoritarian editorial policies, adverse working conditions, and the silencing of the oppressed, under which there was hardly any room for the translator to grow and thrive.

The narrator's use of the translator's unopened letter as an invasive footnote is particularly meaningful when we consider that footnotes were unacceptable in the translations produced for La Casa, as León painfully learned after receiving Otero's feedback on his very first assignment, a lesson that made the translator decide to forever give up his visibility on the pages of his translations and stay away from that "abominable device" (88). Just as Otero's visit to the boarding-house at the request of the police forces him to acknowledge the presence of the translator's body lying in his shabby room and the dreary working-class environment in which he lived and did his translations, León's letter is made visible despite Otero's refusal to open it, allowing the subaltern translator to speak—at least to us—and present his side of the story. Ironically, as the dead translator becomes visible, he is finally given the opportunity to reveal the misery of his life and the behind-the-scenes of the translation activity that sustained La Casa. As a vehicle that restores and brings forth León's repressed voice and gradually takes over the whole page, the narrator's footnote is particularly efficient in destabilizing the asymmetries that generally define the dynamics between the main text and its margins or between the editor and the translator—and, one may arguably infer, also the Argentine elite and the working class—at the same time that it offers a somewhat hopeful sign of resistance promising the empowerment and the rise of the oppressed.

The Translator as Laborer

As we learn from the last few lines of his suicide letter, after 12 years devoted to the publishing house, León found himself in a more dire situation than when he had begun. He was alone, exhausted, and felt that his efforts only served the useless authors and the escapist fiction he was assigned to translate. After having translated 130 books, 80,000 words each, six letters per word, that is, after 60 million strokes on the typewriter keys, all he had was two outfits (one for summer, the other for winter), one pair of shoes, an old dictionary, and no accomplishment of which he could be proud (96).

His tragic end provides a moving contrast with the sheer joy with which he started his career, when translation represented the promise of a better life away from poverty and the rigors of manual labor. In fact, as he came to understand later on, his initial enthusiasm for his work as a translator was not merely associated with the opportunity to replace English originals with Spanish versions, but with the enticing possibility that he could actually "translate" himself into someone different (86). While León's trajectory—from the tire shop and a less than adequate formal education to his first translation assignment—may seem unrealistic, at least in some contexts, it does reflect some fundamental aspects of a profession that is still largely underestimated worldwide and whose protocols are generally defined by those who commission rather than those who actually produce translations. It is in this context that, for León, becoming a translator also involved the development of basic skills that had to be learned on the job and under the guidance of the editor.

When he received his first translation assignments—of detective fiction by minor authors—León could barely contain his enthusiasm, bordering on "fanaticism," with which he went about doing his work (84). For him then, translation was a labor of love: since no word was "definitive," he used to prepare several drafts and write countless notes in the margins, reading and rereading his originals as if they were great literature, always in search of new nuances and subtleties (84). He also became a ferocious reader of contemporary detective fiction recommended by Otero, and, later on, of major literary figures such as Coleridge, Keats, and Shakespeare, even if he could not fully understand them, so as to better prepare himself to do his work, which he saw as a true form of creative writing (86, 89, 93).[6] The translator's attitude and work habits obviously clashed with the publisher's more pragmatic views and from the start Otero urged León to work harder and to produce more. While for León translation represented a combination of intellectual endeavor and creative writing, for Otero it was just one of the stages in the process of mass producing the cheap innocuous books that were compatible with the publishing house's agenda. Under Otero's guidance León applied himself to curbing his authorial impulse—and all the care and dedication as well as the pleasure and pride that it involved—and finally managed to translate a 300-page-long novel in 15 days and, after a while, five pages in one hour (92, 94).

As León attempted to depersonalize his work, he also began to question where his own transformation had actually taken him. Although his external transformation was clearly visible—he was now frailer, had softer hands, and needed prescription glasses—León's greatest transformation was internal: he felt more and more apathetic and exhausted (90, 94). His disenchantment seemed to come from the realization that even though he had somehow managed to translate himself into an intellectual and appeared to have an easier life than his fellow boarders—all of them manual laborers—he was at least as alienated from the product of his labor as they were from theirs, with the painful difference that the translator's work involved a type of investment in and a relationship with what he produced that was much more personal. As León explained in his letter, even though his fellow boarders seemed to think that he was privileged and maybe even envied him, they certainly could not know what it meant "to feel inhabited by another, who [was] often an imbecile: to lend your head to a stranger and only recover it when it [was] worn out, empty, devoid of ideas, useless for the rest of the day" (94). While manual laborers were required to "rent their hands," the translator had to "rent [his] soul" and was thus a truly "used man," an expression that, according to León, translates the word *Yung-jen* ("servant," in Chinese) (94).

While León's own experience taught him that the translator had to lend his head and his soul—his mind and his individuality—to the authors and texts he translated, La Casa generally treated translation as a mere replacement of words. It was basically this gap between these different conceptions of translation that gradually undermined León's enthusiasm as well as his work ethic to the point that one day "he began not to pay attention, to get distracted, to skip words, and then sentences," and to simply omit any particularly difficult fragment, focusing instead on counting the words of his translations, as he probably used to count tires in his previous job, in order to calculate the meager remuneration he was entitled to receiving (96). In the end it was León's inability to reconcile the complex nature of the translator's work—which "nobody around him could truly understand" (94)—with the limited role it seemed to play in the general economy of La Casa that made it difficult for him to continue to live. Caught up in a system where there was no room for self-expression or for any relevant reflection on the dismal reality surrounding him, León was not only invisible and impotent as a translator and as an intellectual, but socially isolated as well. Working as a freelancer, he had no peers, no colleagues, no one with whom he could discuss his work or exchange ideas, with perhaps the exception of his old dictionary, which he fondly called Mr. Appleton in the "conversations" they used to have while he worked (79). In the highly stratified social structure that serves as the story's backdrop, the translator felt he did not have much in common with the "rough and small-minded" laborers among whom he lived in the boardinghouse (73), just as the editor kept distant from the translator whose background and education seemed to qualify him to take on only minor genres such as detective stories and science fiction.

Finally, in Walsh's representation of the translator as a social and professional pariah, the translator's invisibility can also be related to the paternalistic structure defining labor relations in the story, a structure that, among other things, prevented León—who saw Otero as a father figure, a benefactor—from recognizing the role played by the editor and the publishing house in the mechanisms that made the system work for the elite (and, ultimately, also for the state), and from acknowledging his own role as an important component of such mechanisms. Consequently, as his enforced invisibility also seemed to blur his vision of his own context, what León failed to see, as a translator working for La Casa, was that he was actually much more of a servant to them than to the authors he had learned to despise.

"The Dead Man Who Speaks"

Rodolfo Walsh's representation of the translator as a subservient laborer is further enriched when we take into account his commitment to the struggle of the oppressed in Argentina in the 1960s and 1970s. Born in the province of Rio Negro in 1927, Walsh was a prolific translator, a prominent journalist and author, as well as a passionate political activist when the state "unofficially" ambushed and executed him in Buenos Aires in 1977. His execution occurred one day after he began the clandestine distribution of his "Carta Abierta a la Junta Militar" [Open letter to the military junta], which marked the first anniversary of the coup d'état that had overthrown the elected President Isabel Perón in March 1976. In the "Letter" Walsh denounces the horrendous crimes perpetrated by the military, giving special emphasis to their economic policies, in the name of whose enforcement they justified their heinous treatment of the working class, which constituted an "even greater form of atrocity that punishe[d] millions of human beings with planned destitution" (Walsh 2007:22). As we read Walsh's

"Letter" against the background of Leóns in "Nota al pie," it is chilling to realize how the representation of the oppressed translator who could no longer remain invisible is not only reflected but deeply inscribed in the courageous "Letter" that also announced its author's own death.

In "El muerto que habla" [The dead man who speaks], published on the thirtieth anniversary of Walsh's assassination, Alan Pauls describes him as "someone possessed by a compulsive need to speak" and who cherished the power of language as a form of "testimony and testament" that could change the status quo. And this is a compulsion that, as Pauls argues, was directly related to death and mortality: Walsh would not stop speaking or, rather, writing because he knew his time was limited and the enemy was always nearby (Pauls 2007). In an interview given to Ricardo Piglia in January 1973, Walsh elaborated on his faith in the power of language. He redefined the typewriter as a highly effective weapon—"with paper and a typewriter you can move people to an incalculable degree" (Piglia 2001)—a weapon that for him had a precise target: to give voice to the voiceless living under the repressive regime in Argentina. In the same interview Walsh also mentioned his disillusionment with traditional fiction, which no longer played the subversive role it once had and his decision in the late 1960s to abandon bourgeois literature and to explore other forms of writing that would speak more directly to and for the people (Piglia 2001).

Walsh's best known book, *Operación Masacre* [Operation massacre], first published in 1957, exemplifies the kind of committed writing he was interested in pursuing in the early 1970s. Anticipating by almost a decade the narrative strategies of Truman Capote's *In Cold Blood* (1966), Walsh's nonfiction novel has been recognized as the inaugural text of a new genre that combines investigative journalism and the techniques of fiction writing (Foster 1984:42), a genre that he masterfully crafted in order to bring to light the story of a horrific massacre that "officially" had never happened.[7] Considered to be "perhaps the most sophisticated example of Latin American documentary narrative in the service of sociopolitical awareness," Walsh's text utilizes the techniques of fiction to "enhance the texture of truth and the density of human experience" and "demands to be read as a socio-historical document" (Foster 1984:44).

As one of the last stories Walsh ever wrote, "Nota al pie," published ten years after *Operación Masacre,* seems to have helped him realize he should devote his life and his writing to the oppressed, reconnecting him with his literary activism. In fact in León's characterization and trajectory, readers can recognize echoes of Walsh's own biography. For example, in the early 1940s a teenage

Walsh moved to a boardinghouse for laborers in Buenos Aires and found work, among other things, as a dishwasher and a window cleaner until 1944, when he was hired as a proofreader and then as a translator of detective fiction by Hachette, the well-known publishing house. From 1946 to 1953 he translated some 20 books of detective fiction by popular authors such as Ellery Queen, one of the authors León used to read in his journey to becoming a better translator. Obviously, however, unlike his character, Walsh did fulfill his dream of becoming an author, and in 1953 published his first book, *Variaciones in Rojo* [Variations in red], a collection of detective stories whose protagonist and main crime solver, Daniel Hernández, is also a proofreader (Molina and Goldoni 2011:227). In the end, also unlike León, Walsh finally managed to turn his typewriter into a powerful weapon and to make a difference with his writing.

Fiction as Theory

Rodolfo Walsh's "Nota al pie" is a superb illustration of the power of fiction as a privileged locus for reflection and, thus, for theory and theorizing, particularly in a context of oppression and inequality. In its felicitous combination of autobiography, philosophical insight, and enthusiastic activism, and in line with Walsh's most important work, the story constitutes a memorable space for the exploration of the hierarchical opposition between the elite and the subaltern as it is transformed into an inspiring plot, in which the silenced translator's voice is finally heard and becomes an optimistic reminder of the possibility of resistance and empowerment for the margins. Besides offering us a moving glimpse into the life and death of an oppressed worker and aspiring intellectual in the difficult years of the Argentine history of the 1960s, "Nota al pie" provides us with a sensitive portrait of the translator that transcends the more specific context in which it is presented.

Even though "Nota al pie" invites us to imagine what it might have been like to be a translator caught up in the limiting mechanisms of a cultural industry that was fully committed to the interests of an authoritarian state, Walsh's stirring characterization of the translator as a subservient laborer, forced to be alienated from the product of his work and to repress his creativity, brings to mind the aspects often ignored about translators and their activity, regardless of their context and circumstances, i.e., the fact that translators are, inescapably, the writers and the authors of their translations and, thus, directly and intimately invested in how "originals" are composed in other languages. As Walsh's story exposes the contrast between the powerful editor's views and the humble translator's, as well as the conditions in which their work is developed, it provides readers with a wealth of material for reflection on the precarious organization of the profession, about which, as León appropriately remarks, nobody seems to know much. And it is precisely because translation is still largely viewed as an innocuous replacement of words that it can generally (and unapologetically) be used to serve interests that are not necessarily the translator's. Thus the story underscores asymmetrical relations of power even in contexts that are allegedly more democratic than the specific Argentine background depicted in Walsh's story.

"Nota al pie" is not merely telling a story: it constitutes a space for reflection on the practice of translation and on the translator's (in)visibility, a reflection that is also an eloquent form of activism. As Walsh's narrator openly takes a stand and actually forces the translator to be visible right before our eyes and to take over the main narrative, the character seems to be playing a role that is quite similar to that of contemporary translation studies scholars who are committed to a form of theory that is also inseparable from activism. Lawrence Venuti, for example, whose name is widely associated with what could be considered the central focus of contemporary translation studies—the recognition and exploration of the translator's visibility and its consequences—sees the "motive" of his well-known book, *The Translator's Invisibility: A History of Translation,* as making "the translator more visible so as to resist and change the conditions under which translation is theorized, studied, and practiced today" (2008:13). More specifically, as he declares in the opening page of another book, his project is precisely "to expose" the "scandals of translation" that are "cultural, economic, and political"; these scandals basically refer to the marginal status of the translator's activity, which "is stigmatized as a form of writing, discouraged by copyright law, depreciated by the academy, exploited by publishers and corporations, governments and religions institutions" (1998:1). Venuti explicitly states that perhaps "the greatest scandal of translation" is that "asymmetries, inequities, relations of domination and dependence exist in every act of translating, of putting the translated in the service of the translating culture" (1998:4).

Although both fiction, as represented here by Walsh's story, and scholarly texts on translation, such as Venuti's, may in fact address similar issues and even lead to similar conclusions, we cannot simply collapse the usual distinctions between literature and theory. They are after all different genres, shaped by different goals and conventions, and are usually addressed to different readers with different motivations and in different contexts. However, in spite of such differences, the reading of stories about translation can certainly enrich our reading of scholarly texts on the topic just as the reading of such texts can make readers interested in translation more attuned to the ways in which translators are actually represented in fiction. An intertextual dialogue between Venuti's comments briefly mentioned above, for example, and Walsh's story might help readers of "Nota al Pie" to better contextualize and deepen their understanding of the implications and consequences of Leon's precarious status as a professional and the absurd demands imposed on the translator by the publishing house and the power relations they represent.

At the same time, however, it seems fair to conclude that perhaps because of the ways in which we are generally expected to treat fiction—as a multilayered network of texts and textual relations that may include the author's biography, context, influences, and overall work—a story like "Nota al pie" can offer us a portrait of the translator that is also multilayered and, thus, potentially more nuanced than the kind of investigation of the translator's role that we usually find in scholarly texts. Moreover, because the construction of fictional characters tends to rely heavily on psychological and emotional elements and to elaborate on how they feel or react, both consciously and unconsciously, explicitly and implicitly, the reading of fiction usually promotes a closer, more personal relationship between readers and texts. Therefore, as readers, we are likely to get more involved with characters like León and Otero and, arguably, be more personally touched or impacted by them and what they represent than by the sound, rational arguments of our most lucid theorists on, say, the translator's invisibility or the power relations that constitute translation. After all, it is fair to assume that it might be quite difficult for us to find a more unforgettable or more poignant representation of the translator's (in)visibility than Walsh's image of León's covered dead body, whose disturbing presence must be acknowledged by the editor and is, thus, also made concretely visible to us, the readers, by the rising, invading footnote that takes over the page, overwhelms the "original," and literally blurs the limits between the author's and the translator's voices.

Notes

1. This text relies on material previously introduced in a paper presented at the 2009 meeting of the American Comparative Literature Association (ACLA) at Harvard University and further elaborated in a presentation delivered at the International Association of Translation and Interpreting Studies (IATIS) Conference that took place in Belfast, Northern Ireland, in July 2012.

2. All translations are mine, except where otherwise noted.

3. The background against which Otero makes his comments about León and the country's "malady" seems to reflect the Argentine context of the early to mid-1960s: oppressive labor policies, social unrest, and the growing authoritarianism of the government that resulted in the "Argentine Revolution," the misnomer given by the military to the establishment of a dictatorship in 1966. For an appropriate contextualization of the Argentine history between the mid-1950s to the mid-1980s, as well as the cultural responses it produced, see Foster (1995).

4. The "Academias Pitman" constituted a school franchise first established in Buenos Aires in 1919 whose goal was to teach basic skills such as typing and shorthand to aspiring secretaries and bank clerks. Its heyday coincided with Perón's first term as president (1946–52), and their courses, which usually lasted just a few months, were "a lifeline for laborers and low-middle class workers who aspired to ascend socially" (Toro 1999).

5. Readers familiar with the work of Jacques Derrida will probably associate Walsh's footnote with one of the French philosopher's first texts ever published in English, "Living on Borderlines," which appeared more than ten years after the publication of "Nota al pie." In his essay Derrida uses the footnote as a text in its own right, which he turns into a space devoted to an ongoing reflection on the visibility of translation and on its inextricable relationship with the "main" text, and which also allows him to establish a dialogue with his potential translators.

6. Readers familiar with Jorge Luis Borges's views of translation as a legitimate form of creative writing might recognize some echoes of his vision in León's initial approach to translation. I am thinking, for example, of Borges's comment about the concept of the "definitive text," which, as he suggests, "corresponds only to religion or exhaustion," in the words of his translator, Eliot Weinberger (Borges 1999:69).

7. The clandestine event took place in 1956, when a group of innocent citizens were summarily executed by the police in the outskirts of Buenos Aires because they were allegedly plotting to overthrow the government. Six months later, after learning that some of the victims had actually survived the massacre and were in hiding, Walsh set out to investigate and then write their stories. For details, see, for example, Foster (1984).

Works Cited

Borges, Jorge Luis. 1999. "The Homeric Versions." In *Selected Non-Fictions,* translated by Eliot Weinberger, 69–74. . New York: Penguin.

Capote, T. 1965. *In Cold Blood.* New York: Random House.

Derrida, Jacques. 1979. "Living on Border Lines." In *Deconstruction and Criticism,* edited by Harold Bloom, Paul de Man, Jacques.Derrida, Geoffrey Hartman, and J. Hillis Miller, 75–176. Translated by James Hulbert. New York: Seabury Press.

Foster, David William. 1984. "Latin American Documentary Narrative." *PMLA* 99(1): 41–55.

Foster, David William. 1995. *Violence in Argentine Literature: Cultural Responses to Tyranny.* Columbia: University of Missouri Press.

Maier, Carol. 2006. "The Translator as *Theôros:* Thoughts on Cogitation, Figuration, and Current Creative Writing." In *Translating Others,* Vol. 1, edited by Theo Hermans, 163–80. Manchester: St. Jerome.

Molina, Sergio, and Rubia P. Goldoni. 2011. "Posfácio." In *Variações em Vermelho,* by Rodolfo Walsh, 227–38. Translated by Sergio Molina and Rubia P. Goldoni. São Paulo: Editora 34.

Pauls, Alan. 2007. "El muerto que habla." *Suplemento Especial, Radar,* "30 años sin Walsh" (25 March): 12. Available at: www.elortiba.org/walsh3.html (accessed 25 October 2014).

Piglia, Ricardo. 2001. "Rodolfo Walsh." In *Grandes Entrevistas de la Historia Argentina (1879–1988),* edited by Sylvia Saitta and Luis A.Romero. Buenos Aires: Punto de Leitura. Available at: www.elortiba.org/walsh.html (accessed 25 October 2014).

Toro, Alberto G. 1999. "Pasado y presente de una academia que hizo época." *El Clarín.* Available at: http://edant.clarin.com/diario/1999/05/30/e-04401d.htm (accessed 10 October 25).

Venuti, Lawrence. 1998. *The Scandals of Translation: Towards an Ethics of Difference.* New York: Routledge.

Venuti, Lawrence. 2008. *The Translator's Invisibility: A History of Translation.* 2nd ed. New York: Routledge.

Walsh, Rodolfo. 2007. "Carta Abierta a la Junta Militar." In *Recordar y entender: a 30 años de la "Carta Abierta a la Junta Militar,"* edited by Edgardo Vannucchi, 7–13. Buenos Aires: Ministerio de Educación, Gobierno de la Ciudad de Buenos Aires.

Walsh, Rodolfo. 2008. "Nota al pie." In *Un Kilo de Oro,* 69–96. Buenos Aires: Ediciones de la Flor.

Walsh, Rodolfo. 2009. *Operación Masacre.* Buenos Aires: Ediciones de la Flor.

Memoir as Translation, Memory in Translation

Christi A. Merrill

If I were to write my own version of the time I spent with Mangalesh, it would start in New Delhi in 2000, with him handing me a slim volume titled *ek bar ayowa*. This was my first trip back to India since the 1994–95 school year when I had gotten so sick I thought my days in India were completely behind me. His book had been published in 1996.

"You should translate it," he suggested as he handed me a signed copy. He added something characteristically mirthful and self-ironic about the circumstances of the publication. A publisher friend had urged him to write about his three months on the International Writing Program, and he had agreed only because he thought there wouldn't be much to say.

This was a version of the joke he used to repeat a decade earlier when we first met in Iowa City: a poet gets up and writes a poem and then spends the rest of his day doing what he was meant to be doing all along. Nothing. "Why aspire to be a novelist or short-story writer?" he would tease me. "Too much work."

That was when I was still writing fiction and before I had started taking classes in literary nonfiction. I realized more acutely then as we spoke in 2000 that the phrase "literary nonfiction" didn't translate well into Hindi, the language we used with each other. Even writers who worked in English argued about what this new kind of writing should be called and what its rules were. If I had read it already I could have argued with Mangalesh that the very book he was handing me was a wonderful example of "literary nonfiction." Maybe together we could have come up with a better phrase in Hindi than my clunky literal translation of a phrase that didn't work that well in English either.

I tried instead to explain the difference between fiction and literary nonfiction, and why it wasn't enough just to say "prose" (*gadya*): With fiction you had to work harder to make the details of real life believable, and with nonfiction you had to work harder to make the details of real life poignant. I didn't want to tell him that I was tired of turning in thinly veiled autobiographical accounts of my life to workshop classes and being told the stories were completely implausible. At least labeling them nonfiction made my classmates concentrate their comments on matters of craft.

Later, as I started to read his book, I realized Mangalesh was right. I should translate it. And not only because it was written by a friend. I was interested in the challenge: How to render his very particular perspective? That entailed figuring out a way of signaling the generic cues of a work that played by a different set of rules than the ones an English-language reader might expect, as well as recreating in English the sense that the intended reader was a Hindi speaker, someone far away from the world of soy crops and workshop etiquette. Even the title intrigued me for the way it suggested the ephemerality of travel, the American Midwest suddenly rendered exotic, fairytale-ish. I knew right away what the English version should be: *Once, Iowa*.

Translating the entire book would later prove to be more of a challenge. That day Mangalesh told me that the publisher at Three Essays Press was interested in bringing out the English translation. Even though it really wasn't three essays, he joked, at least it was short enough to be considered for the series. Mangalesh didn't know then that his joke would be on all of us: however short the hoped-for manuscript, the publisher certainly has had to wait a long time!

. . .

Of course, the biggest difference between fiction and literary nonfiction is the question of what some might call factual accuracy, what Joan Scott (1991) discusses in terms of "the evidence of experience," but what I like to think of as fidelity. I use the word purposely to emphasize the comparison with translation. With literary nonfiction people invariably seem to assume that we have an original to compare the work to—real life. What they don't seem to realize is that in this case the original is an event with as many unreliable narrators as there are witnesses. That is only the beginning of the complexity, as the Rigoberta Menchu controversy (Arias 2001) teaches us. Part of what seemed to rankle her critics was how very effective Menchu's *testimonio* was (1984). There seemed to be an assumption that matters of craft were antithetical to considerations of accuracy. On what basis do we ascertain whether someone's version of her life is faithful?

Rather than assuming craft and fidelity to be in tension, the eighteenth-century Swiss philologist Johann Jacob Breitinger (1977) sees them as integrated and thus intimately connected. His discussion (1977:23) of translation, which, not incidentally, he considers to be "a very useful exercise" in helping to cultivate "good taste in the rhetorical arts . . ." (23), offers important insight into the demands made of literary nonfiction, especially that a first-person narrative be judged in terms of its "equivalence" with real life:

> A good translator must have mastered to perfection the nature, the constitution, and the ways of the language he wants to translate into, and he must take great pains to incorporate them into his translation as best he can, especially so that when he is forced to deviate from his original because of a certain idiom in it: this is the only way in which he can give his translation the character and appearance of an original. A translator should also be careful in his work, because he is faced with the disadvantage that the reader who knows both languages will put copy and original side by side and will be able to find out how closely he has hit his mark or how far he has fallen short of it, whereas it is not so easy to decide in the work of the original writer whether the mistakes in his writing are caused by a lack of ability to think or by lack of knowledge of the language. (26)

In the case of Mangalesh's memoir I recognized Mangalesh's ability as a prose stylist precisely because I was there at some of the scenes he described. I was fully aware of how closely he had hit his mark. And we might say, in the way Benjamin (2004) notes that the original comes into being through translation, so too I only began to be aware of this particular mark after reading Mangalesh's version of this memory we shared. How much would my own version of events influence the resulting translation? How much should it in order to be considered faithful?

Of course questions of fidelity are particularly delicate when working "*between languages and cultures*" (to quote the title of the book on the subject edited by Anuradhna Dingwaney and Carol Maier [1995], which has influenced me greatly). I soon discovered that much of what I learned in my PhD work focusing on translation and postcoloniality applied readily to the issues I began encountering with travel writing in general and with Mangalesh's memoir in particular. Both the translator and the travel writer were crossing borders, and reporting back on that crossing in a manner that involved selecting from a host of competing priorities. Invariably when these border crossings are discussed in postcolonial scholarship, it is to demonstrate how complicit translators and travel writers are in these colonial projects, their personal perspectives shaped by and speaking to an implied audience back home. Mary Louise Pratt (1992:201) offers a devastating characterization of the empire-bolstered authority of this writerly stance, summed up most tidily and ironically with the phrase "monarch of all I survey." She and others convincingly show how writers of this ilk assume a clear-cut distinction between an inside circle of "us" here at home looking down on "them," those locals who inhabited the landscapes there, far away. When I started to write my own essays about my years living in India, I wondered: Was there a more ethical way of writing about another place that didn't succumb to and therefore neatly reinscribe these colonial hierarchies?

At first glance one might assume that Mangalesh's memoir neatly flips the colonial hierarchies, but only if one reads it in fairly reductive the-empire-writes-back terms. It is true, he is a postcolonial subject writing about the West. But as soon as you start reading his prose you start to notice patterns familiar from Victorian travel accounts, especially his approximation of a confident insiderness, which lays down a clear distinction between the audience he is writing to and the natives he describes. He undermines that air of superiority with his own self-deprecating humor and also with his focus on Iowa, which in the American landscape represents rural guilelessness, a far cry from the stereotype of America as the invincible West.

By the time I started translating Mangalesh's memoir, I was a professor and regularly teaching a course titled "Writing Home from Away" that called into question the very notions underpinning old-fashioned travel writing. I included memoirs of people like Sara Suleri (1989) and Michael Ondaatje (1982), who had grown up in South Asia (in Pakistan and Sri Lanka, respectively) and who were settled in North America, writing about their childhoods from afar. I also put on the reading list accounts by Western writers of South Asian heritage like V. S. Naipaul (1964) and Suketu Mehta (1997), who use their descriptions of visits to India to grapple with tough questions of identity, as well others like Santa Rama Rau and Meena Alexander (1993), who describe growing up in Africa as Indian citizens. Sometimes I assigned the writing of men involved in nationalist struggles, such as Gandhi (1948), Tagore (1962), and Ambedkar (1993), to show how time spent abroad can render home unfamiliar upon return. I also brought in accounts by South Asian writers describing trips elsewhere, such as Amitav Ghosh's (1993) rich discussion of his time in Egypt, *In an Antique Land*.

I taught Ghosh's book both in literature seminars and in my writing courses because he experiments with the form of travel writing in such interesting ways. I published an article (2007) arguing that Ghosh uses both irony and references to translation (in this case from Arabic) to call into question our assumptions about what we share with the implied author. Ghosh makes fun of his narrator as a way of reconsidering his own authority, thus undermining the very assumption that his account could represent the Egyptian locals to an English-speaking reader with complete fidelity. I felt fully convinced of my own theories in this regard and even proffered my own analogies in passing between Ghosh's experiments and Dabral's prose.

But when I started reading further and experimenting with strategies for rendering Mangalesh's Hindi into English, I found myself more taken aback than I had expected when I was forced to grapple with the fact that one of the locals being described to the author's faraway audience was me, the would-be translator:

> There was a party at the home of the International Writing Program Director, Clark Blaise. He's a writer and novelist. The walls of his house were covered in Indian miniatures. Most of them in the Rajasthan style. Quite a few *originals* among them. Some with actual gold, even. This party was the first chance I had to meet people face-to-face. I saw poet and translator Daniel Weissbort and was filled with happy memories. . . . Daniel introduced me to a tall, skinny, large-laughing girl: Christi Merrill. She greeted me with a full namaskar, like an Air India stewardess. Christi speaks good Hindi. That is, whatever she knows, she speaks with full confidence. She is studying at the university and teaching at the same time. She has already translated the short stories of Vijaydan Detha. Rajasthan is very dear to her. She doesn't drink booze. She doesn't eat meat. She will translate my poetry here. I kept speaking in Hindi to her. Told her that she was more Indian than I was. Whoever she saw at the party she smiled at. Here people like to either always be happy or at least appear to be.

This is the first time I have drunk so much beer since coming to America. It was as if Clark had opened a beer factory in his house. As soon as my beer was finished, I'd smoke a cigarette, and as soon as the cigarette went out, I'd start to drink another beer. In the midst of all this, Christi Merrill or Rovena Torvallis would come over and flash me their coke can or some other soft drink like sprite. To show me that, look, we don't do those kinds of intoxicants. Altogether the night was like a wave. The writers and poets who had come from African countries were laughing even more than they were drinking. As if they were having some sort of contest with the Americans. (My translation from Dabral 1996:16–17)

I knew as I worked on the scene that Breitinger's theories of equivalence were not applicable here. I didn't want my translation to be mistaken as an original: I wanted readers to notice an explicit distance between Mangalesh's memory of that evening and my own.

I knew it was silly. I couldn't properly explain to myself what disconcerted me so much about his description of me, which is, on the face of it, attentive and affectionate in its humor. All I knew was that I cringed every time I tried to translate the paragraphs, the way I used to cringe back when I was a free-lance writer transcribing audiotapes of myself talking in Hindi in my interviews with puppeteers, hand-block printers, and potters.

·   ·   ·

The party he describes was early on in my time at Iowa. Later I would learn about the importance of the narrator's perspective in literary nonfiction, that there could be a difference between what the narrator notices and what the character experienced at the time. That what distinguished a work of non-fiction as literary weren't the raw experiences themselves but how they were presented. This notion was confusing even for my writing students who were otherwise quite sophisticated and committed to the idea of being writers. I remember their reaction to Joan Didion's essay "Goodbye to All That" (1994), which is mostly about trying to make a new life as a 20-something in New York City and being so overwhelmed the narrator couldn't leave her apartment. She describes lying on the living room floor, feeling despondent, watching the long, yellow curtains lap at the open window, in and out, not able to go outside to shop for food, or look for a job, or do much of anything. My students argued with me about whether the power of the story came from her writing or what happened to her. "I could write like that if I also had a glamorous life in New York!" one of my students blurted out, and the others nodded in agreement. They didn't think being from Iowa was anything to write about.

Mangalesh thought living in Iowa for three months was something to write about. But it wasn't the fact of his being there that made the read so engaging. What I particularly liked about the book in general was how different some familiar details of Iowa City seemed in his words—how he drew attention to aspects of life I had taken for granted. It reminded me of something my friend Marilyn Abildskov described in one of Carol de Saint Victor's legendary travel writing seminars: "I would go anywhere with this writer, just to see what she sees." In my memory she was referring to Jan Morris (1984), but it could just as well have been in reference to Bruce Chatwin (1987) or Pico Iyer (1997) as far as I'm concerned—when you read a scene you imagine it in more than three dimensions, and they put their finger on something that seems so true and yet you hadn't known it was true before reading their work. But what aspect of Dabral's version of me was a true something or other that I should be faithful to?

.   .   .

Of course my memory of the evening is different, by degrees that some might consider unimportant. I'm not calling his version unfaithful, you understand. And I want to make clear that the differences I notice between his version of the evening and mine in retrospect wouldn't be an issue at all if Mangalesh and I hadn't become friends, if he hadn't included that cameo of me in his memoir, and if I hadn't been asked to translate it. I'd like to think I have a fairly expansive understanding of truth when it comes to literary nonfiction. I'm not acting like those hurt friends or family members who are shocked to discover what that quiet writer in their midst really thought about them. I recognize that this is Mangalesh's memoir, his memory, and that he's narrating this scene to a Hindi-speaking audience. But as I think about embarking on a translation of the whole book and publishing it under his name with me as the faithful translator, part of me wants to include a long defensive footnote or create a hyperlinked text explaining my side of things. Here I'm faced with a slightly different problem from the one Venuti (1995) described so aptly as the translator's invisibility. I'm visible here, as a character, one I do not wish to be.

I said some garbled version of this once to Harish Trivedi, whom I first met through Mangalesh and who has since become a friend and colleague I see regularly at conferences. Harish smiled and said it was precisely Mangalesh's naïveté that made his narrative so charming. He said this to me in English in such a way that conveyed he was not naive like Mangalesh, that he understood that America in general and Iowa in particular were more complex than Mangalesh had expected, and that Harish recognized that realities were more nuanced than these simplistic stereotypes. But then he recounted Mangalesh's sketch of me and began laughing helplessly, looking away because he was having so much trouble getting the image out of his head. I saw in an instant that there was something in Mangalesh's description that he saw in me still. And here I had hoped I had outgrown this caricatured version of myself.

I wish I had been familiar enough with Mangalesh's travel account to argue with Harish that day we spoke about it. I think I remember him using the Hindi word *bhola,* even though we were mostly speaking in English, to describe Mangalesh's innocence, his emotional vulnerability, the sense that he is laying bare for others an authentic and genuine feeling anyone sensitive enough and unguarded enough would experience. Once I actually read *ek bar ayowa* I could see how affecting the narrator's sincerity becomes, especially when paired with a place that itself strikes one as genuine, unpretentious, unguarded. Why Iowa? Mangalesh explains in a short opening chapter called "Before Iowa" (*ayowa se pahele*) how he got the chance to go to America on the International Writing Program, how he promised an editor friend that he would keep a diary, and how he planned to write about each city he visited. He admits, "At one point I thought I would write a memoir of all the places I had visited in America while the memories were still fresh but except for Iowa I never had time in the other cities to keep up my daily diary" (Dabral 1996:12).

His focus on Iowa is one of my favorite things about the book. He doesn't offer an overt critique of the ways Iowa is discussed in the American national news, but his awareness of it certainly was one of the things that struck me as being especially astute, especially after I myself had lived there all those years, always with the feeling of being an outsider myself, albeit to a different degree. The patronization of Iowa becomes noticeable during the Iowa caucuses every four years, and in the ways same-sex marriage debates are recounted: even in Iowa they think this black man can become president! Even in Iowa they favor marriage equality! In all cases this performance of innocence is strategic. It allows the outsider to feel superior and in the process makes room for having one's thinking about these norms be changed. In his writing Mangalesh seems to understand the exoticization of rural areas, the feeling of being peripheral in your own country's imagination.

. . .

The truth is that if I were to write my own essay about my time in Iowa with Mangalesh, I would have a completely different focus and might not even mention the party that night. And if I did include the party, I would find some way of bringing my fiancé's mother into the scene, even though in all actuality she wasn't physically present that night. (This raises another issue: Should such writing be considered fictional or nonfictional if I describe a presence that hovered there only in my imagination?)

I should explain. The night I met Mangalesh I had recently become engaged to a filmmaker I had met while living in India, after years of clandestine assignations and elaborate subterfuges. My fiancé wanted to keep our engagement secret from his mother because he knew she would be devastated by his marrying out of caste. In the meantime, and just in case, my fiancé had impressed upon me the importance of reputation (he used the word *maryada,* which I have since noticed translated as the provocative "honor") so that stories wouldn't get back to her someday and confirm all her worst suspicions about foreign women. He told me this was out of concern mostly for me, that I'd be much happier in my new married life if I could find a way to get along with his mother. This required mastering a whole set of rules, some of which were already familiar to me from my years of being a student in India. But this took them to a whole new level.

By the time I met my fiancé, I had already lived in India long enough to understand the particularly negative connotations of alcohol. The teenage children of the family I lived with my first year in India would ask me repeatedly, in complete disbelief, "People in your country drink liquor in church?" There was no distinction in Hindi between wine and hard liquor. It was all *sharab.* I pointed out to the boy I lived with that his Brahmin family made drinks with *bhang* at holidays, which even the grandparents drank, and no one seemed to think that was horrible. Later I came to discover that opium was a regular part of my fiancé's life growing up—it was offered to esteemed guests with elaborate ritual, and it was something his mother gave him in small doses for a cough or upset stomach—but alcohol was for her and everyone she knew a substance beyond the moral pale. I wasn't much of a drinker anyway, so it didn't seem like such a hardship. But other judgment calls were more difficult to make. I could not have imagined curtailing my life so much that I wouldn't have a career, or travel on my own, or go to parties where men and women commingled and alcohol was served. I figured I could let down my guard more or less once I was back in America, in Iowa—that is until I met a poet from Delhi who I realized was perfectly capable of reporting my antics back to people who might say something to my fiancé's mother.

As I was introduced to Mangalesh, I imagined her floating just behind his head, spitting in disgust at the sight of me. This is the *bahu* you bring me? I could imagine her gesturing at me emphatically, not with just one but with all her fingers outstretched. This was the woman who snuffed when she first met me, "At least she doesn't wipe her ass with paper like most of them."

Back in the late 1980s, I hadn't yet learned to speak the local dialect, so I hadn't understood her quip. I just knew she looked me up and down from behind her veil, muttered something indistinct, and that everyone in the room except me laughed uproariously. I didn't trust my host's translation at the time: "She said you are very beautiful."

"Then why did everyone laugh?" I asked. He tried answering with vague platitudes about the difficulties of translation. It was the way she said it, or something along those lines. I hadn't yet gotten involved with the man who would become my fiancé. He was the one who later told me what she had said. At least he provided me with a translation I found credible, however disconcerting. Years later after we had gotten engaged, then broken up, then gotten re-engaged, and then broken up for good, he contacted me when he heard I was very sick to see if there was anything he could do. I said no but appreciated his concern. He sighed and told me his mother had finally agreed to let him marry that foreign girl—even though she was never really sure which foreign girl he was in love with—when she saw how miserable he was to lose her. Years after it was too late, he mourned. By then I no longer had it in me to try.

Perhaps what makes me cringe most about Mangalesh's portrait of me is to see how much trouble I was having reconciling my two lives and to realize how impossible it would have been to ever be good enough to erase her suspicions of me. I can imagine several of my feminist friends in India shaking their heads in fond consternation, repeating a version of Mangalesh's comment, "You're more Indian than we are!" But my attempts all seemed like a farce then. I couldn't muster the calm upper-caste confidence of Bharati Mukherjee, who had figured out which of her Indian ways she wanted to keep with her in the United States. What I see in my prim stiffness is my own inability to marry these traditions in a way that I was comfortable with. This was only one scene among many that made me sure that my former fiancé and I were trying for a version of a future together that just wasn't possible.

I couldn't have shared any of these thoughts with Mangalesh, not that evening and not in subsequent years. As close as we became in the fall of 1991, we rarely talked about anything private, except when he made jokes about his high phone bills. He missed his family so much he would make drunken calls to them every night, and later he told me that he had used up so much of his stipend that he barely had money to buy presents for them. When I think about his time in Iowa, I think too about how he insisted I read my English translations of his poetry when he was invited to read in front of a live audience broadcast on the local public radio station. He admitted first to me in private and then on stage that he stuttered in English but not in Hindi, so preferred reading his own poems in Hindi and having me read the English translations.

Once he was in front of the audience he went on to thank me publicly in English for the translations and for lending him my old down coat, which was keeping him so warm. That's the version of me I would still want others to see.

. . .

If I were to write my own version of the time I spent with Mangalesh, I would be sure to include the week in 1995 when I stayed with his family in Delhi on my way back to graduate school in Iowa, after being very sick with hepatitis. I was too weak to stand for more than a few minutes at a time and still had trouble keeping food down. His wife cooked simple rice and dahl meals especially for me, without hot spices or oil, and Mangalesh took time off work to bring me to specialists, drawing on personal favors to get opinions from doctors he really trusted. "Those physicians are at the top of the field," he told me as we visited one medical center after another. "They know what they are doing." His assurances underscored a confidence I sensed in their competence and kind concern that made me hopeful when they contradicted the dire warnings in the previous pathology reports. It was the first moment when I started to think that perhaps I wouldn't die as soon as all that.

He and his wife teased me the next time they saw me about how emaciated I had looked, so skinny and weak I didn't even have enough in me to laugh. This was in 2000, during my first visit back after being sick. I happened to be in Delhi the week he received word that his latest book of poetry had been selected for a national award from the Sahitya Akademi. We had already made plans for me to come to his home and see his family, and I declined his offers to stay on for the spontaneous night of drinking with fellow poets. His wife said in her characteristically cheerful and straightforward way that she understood why I might be worried about traveling back to my hotel room unaccompanied and offered—in part as consolation—that it's not very fun to listen to a bunch of people talking into their drinks when you yourself don't drink. She seemed to be speaking from her own experience but she didn't say it in a way that felt like a complaint.

Meanwhile Mangalesh admitted that he wasn't looking forward to the evening very much either and observed wryly that he had spent nearly triple his award money celebrating his award with his friends night after night. He and his friends ended up going through the bottle of Johnny Walker I had brought him duty free. "I don't have the liver for this kind of fame!" he laughed.

By this point I had already started distancing myself from my previous overdone insistence on not drinking and all the associations that seemed to come with it. I realized strangers were going to make the same assumptions about me whether I drank alcohol in front of them or not. Later, reading Mangalesh's description of me made me see how much of a strain it had been to live between these two sets of rules with no role I could inhabit easily. If I were to write a commentary of the scene in Iowa City where Mangalesh and I first met, I would point out that I was laughing at this disconnect, even there in that moment, so much so that the role I inhabited turned into a parody. It's not clear whether Mangalesh shares the joke in his telling or whether he is laughing at me. But then again, it's not clear how much Dabral, the implied author, is laughing at his former self's innocence and gullibility. He is both the sensitive, self-effacing Third World citizen with a stammer and the lauded, confident cosmopolitan poet and editor.

If my overarching goal for the translation (which I will publish someday) is to have this authorial self-irony come alive, then it only follows that my aim for the scene in which I appear should be to allow myself as translator some distance from the character I was then and to let myself laugh at her with all the affection and understanding the implied author does. If I am going to be faithful to anything, it is less to my own version of the memory than to my reading of Mangalesh's memoir of the scene all these years later.

Works Cited

Alexander, Meena. 1993. *Fault Lines.* New York: Feminist Press of the City of New York.

Ambedkar, B. R. 1993. "Waiting for a Visa." In *Writings and Speeches,* Vol. 12, edited by Vasant Moon, 663–91. Bombay: Education Department, Government of Maharashtra.

Arias, Arturo, ed. 2001. *The Rigoberta Menchu Controversy.* Minneapolis: University of Minnesota Press.

Benjamin, Walter. 2004. "The Task of the Translator." In *The Translation Studies Reader,* 2nd ed., edited by Lawrence Venuti, 75–85. New York and London: Routledge.

Breitenger, Johann Jacob. 1977. "Equivalence." In *Translating Literature: The German Tradition from Luther to Rosenzweig,* edited by Andre Lefevere, 23–27. Assen and Amsterdam: Van Gorcum.

Chatwin, Bruce. 1987. *The Songlines.* New York: Viking Press.

Dabral, Mangalesh. 1996. *ek bar ayowa* [Once, Iowa]. Panchkula, Haryana: Adhar Prakashan.

Didion, Joan. 1994 "Good-bye to All That." In *The Art of the Personal Essay,* edited by Philip Lopate, 681–88. New York: Anchor Books Doubleday.

Dingwaney, Anuradhna, and Carol Maier, eds. 1995. *Between Languages and Cultures: Translation and Cross-Cultural Texts.* Pittsburgh, Penn.: University of Pittsburgh Press.

Gandhi, M. K. 1948. *An Autobiography: The Story of my Experiments with Truth.* Translated by Mahadev Desai. Washington, D.C.: Public Affairs Press.

Ghosh, Amitav. 1993. *In an Antique Land.* New York: A. A. Knopf.

Iyer, Pico. 1997. *Tropical Classical: Essays from Several Directions.* New York: A. A. Knopf.

Mehta, Suketu. 1997. "Mumbai" *Granta* 57 (Spring): 97–126.

Menchu, Rigoberta. 1984. *I, Rigoberta Menchú: An Indian Woman in Guatemala.* Edited by Elisabeth Burgos-Debray. Translated by Ann Wright. London: Verso.

Merrill, Christi A. 2007. "Laughing Out of Place: Humour Alliances and Other Post-colonial Translations in *In an Antique Land.*" *Interventions: International Journal of Postcolonial Studies* 9, no. 1: 106–23.

Morris, Jan. 1984. *Journeys.* New York: Oxford University Press.

Naipaul, V. S. 1964. *An Area of Darkness.* London: A. Deutsch.

Ondaatje, Michael. 1982. *Running in the Family.* New York: W. W. Norton.

Pratt, Mary Louise. 1992. *Imperial Eyes: Travel Writing and Transculturation.* New York: Routledge.

Rau, Santa Rama. 1945. *Home to India.* New York and London: Harper and Brothers.

Scott, Joan. 1991. "The Evidence of Experience." *Critical Inquiry* 17, no. 4: 773–97.

Suleri, Sara. 1989. *Meatless Days.* Chicago: University of Chicago Press.

Tagore, Rabindranath. 1962. *The Diary of a Westward Voyage.* Translated by Indu Dutt. New York: Asia Publishing House.

Venuti, Lawrence. 1995. *The Translator's Invisibility: A History of Translation.* London: Routledge.

"The Other Adventure" with Bioy Casares

Notes toward a Literary Memoir

Suzanne Jill Levine

I.

Jorge Luis Borges often remarked that his close friend and collaborator Adolfo Bioy Casares led him to write in a more classical manner, away from the self-conscious Baroque *ultraísta* pyrotechnics of his early essays, poems, and stories. Borges was being generous to the younger man perhaps, because even before the time when, at age 30, he and the 17-year-old Bioy Casares met, Borges was already casting doubts on *el ultraísmo* and the avant-garde fervor of his own young years.

I begin with mention of a classical style because it is not easy to define the subtleties involved in translating Bioy Casares. Except when he and Borges were camping it up with their Bustos Domecq parodies, Bioy wrote in a spare style that followed his meticulous tendency toward tight narrative forms (stories, novellas, short novels). It is easier to examine the translation of loudly "untranslatable" "baroque" texts because the problems are more visible, tangible, notably knotty. Bioy Casares's style gives the appearance of transparency; however, there is almost always an opacity in his "less is more" approach to language. His reader and certainly his translator must catch the understated nuance or register of the words and phrases he uses; he had a keen ear for colloquial speech, and his narrators and characters invite the reader's laughter at unexpected moments, either because of wry depictions of clumsy behavior or because their utterances are unintentionally buffoonish.

In brief, the challenge is to transmit his humor. A recent description of Jean-Philippe Toussaint's comic mode by Tom McCarthy would serve also to depict Bioy's humor: "Toussaint's writing is comic in a very formal sense—the sense in which, for example, Bergson used the term. For Bergson, comedy entailed a tendency toward the mechanical. People, gestures and events become like automata—compressed, sprung, interlocked and endlessly repeating" (2008:11). Kafka's sense of absurd lurks here; the Czech's black humor in the following phrase (cited by McCarthy) would be totally in line as well with Bioy's world: "In the fight between you and the world, back the world."

Similarly I once wrote about the "Kafkaesque" feel of Bioy's characters:

> Their elliptical, matter-of-fact manner of communicating bewilderment makes the reader both laugh at and sympathize with these bunglers who don't quite have a grip on reality but are doing their best. Bioy could be considered a Kafka with a light touch, and his protagonists often remind one of the bungling, well-meaning, and often justifiably paranoid characters in silent slapstick comedy. Like Kafka's exasperatingly banal dialogues, spoken language in Bioy Casares' stories becomes an empty rhetoric which veils a sinister or tragic reality; the cliché becomes emblematic of insidious alienation; it is, of course, essential for the translator to capture the nuances of these local commonplaces. (Levine 1994:xiv)

Such "commonplaces" pertain to realism, one might think, but Bioy's fictions, whether or not they begin on a realist note or are marked with a realist register, slip imperceptibly into what finally feels like a dream.

II.

What Borges meant by Bioy's "classicism" needs to be understood, I believe, not only in terms of an economic verbal style but also in terms of T. S. Eliot's impersonal figure of the poet. The modernists' reaction to romanticism shaped the engagement of Borges and Bioy with literary practices, among them, translation. Together Borges and Bioy were dubbed "Biorges" by Emir Rodriguez Monegal, literary critic of the Latin American Boom era of the 1960s and 1970s; they invented a third (fourth and even fifth) writer when they collaborated. That Bioy was considered (outside of their circle of friends) for many years to be an invention not of Morel but of Borges—that is, a fictional character who appeared on the first pages of "Tlon, Uqbar, Orbis, Tertius," for example—made him impersonal or quasi-anonymous almost in the literal sense of being invisible, certainly for the first decades of his existence as a writer. As a member of the upper classes, he seemed to cultivate this invisibility because, among the elite circles of River Plate culture, self-promoting professional writers were seen as crass merchants, a value system that sealed his aforementioned fate as the inhabitant of an unreal world. When he was awarded the prestigious Cervantes Prize in 1990, in his late seventies, Bioy Casares didn't seem to be quite at home with all the hullabaloo, and was so nervous about giving a speech that his voice trembled the entire time. He would always be a writer more comfortable at his desk than in the public sphere.

III.

Your life should resemble a description of your life.
—Adolfo Bioy Casares

Bioy's diaries of his conversations with Borges from the 1940s to the 1980s (recently published posthumously) certainly expose a different Bioy than the reserved image he cultivated in his lifetime. Be this as it may, it was in any case the latter Bioy Casares, the polite upper-class charmer, dazzled me in equal parts with his wit and elegant good looks.

With Emir Rodriguez Monegal I met Bioy (as he was called by his friends) in the summer (though in Buenos Aires it was winter) of 1971. The Uruguayan literary critic—whom Bioy would later refer to with affectionate praise as being "muy criollo," very gaucho—was bringing me and another young North American scholar, Alfred MacAdam, also visiting Buenos Aires that summer, to meet these writers who were already legends to both of us. I was even younger than Alfred, and extraordinary impressed to be in the ample Buenos Aires apartment with high ceilings and dark wood shelves with books from floor to ceiling. It was on the top floor of a beautiful building, in the very best Recoleta neighborhood, which belonged to the wealthy Ocampo family into which Bioy had married, and each floor was the home of one of the various Ocampo siblings. We were met at the door by a maid in uniform, who led us from a shadowy foyer into the book-lined salon, where we were invited to take a seat, and that the "señores" would be with us momentarily. Years later, another Uruguayan, the journalist Mauricio Muller, a wry wit himself, remarked to me that of the famous trio—Bioy, Borges, and Silvina—Silvina Ocampos was by far the most clever and interesting.

Bioy entered first, with a quick athletic step. He was a slight man with a V-shaped torso (he had been an active horseman and tennis player), white hair and thick eyebrows, smiling blue eyes, a strong, sensual mouth, and dressed in a stylish gray suit and vest like a British gentleman. The saying goes that the Argentines speak Spanish like Italians, eat like Frenchmen, and dress like Englishmen. This adage fit Bioy like a glove, except that his speech had a "criollo" lilt, native-born, refined, not like the Italianate speech of recent immigrants who spoke the local Italianate slang *lunfardo,* which Bioy and Borges would caricature in their Bustos Domecq creations. I don't remember Silvina's entrance but rather remember her already seated in an armchair, a striking apparition in an elegant pantsuit, a short, sharp-featured woman with jangling bracelets—in her hand the ice in the glass of whiskey also jangled—and a notably nasal voice, an intonation common among the "rancid" Argentine aristocracy.

I recall very little, unfortunately, from that initial meeting except that Bioy, a famous lady-killer, definitely took note of me in the typical half-paternal, half-flirtatious way that an older man might look at a young woman, that the conversation was lively with humor and literary allusions, and that Alfred and I listened intensely as Emir and his two literary friends resumed a dialogue that had been interrupted some years back. That evening or the next morning, Bioy called our hotel to invite Emir and me to dinner at their apartment with Silvina—and added "Borges will join us." Emir was then working on his biography of Borges; I had already met the great guru a year earlier in the United States, when he came to give a lecture at Yale University.

Life has its highs and those 12 days in Buenos Aires were certainly a peak experience. As Emir's consort I was meeting the cream of Argentina's intellectual and artistic life: the filmmaker Torre Nilsson and his sparkling wife; the writer Beatriz Guido; the journalist Homero Alsina Thevenet, who could imitate Groucho Marx even better—if this is possible—than Guillermo Cabrera Infante; the brilliant and witty Jose "Pepe" Bianco, former editor of *Sur* magazine; lively Luisa Valenzuela and her mother Luisa Mercedes Levinson, both of them novelists. We also spent time with that new young and exciting novelist Manuel Puig, with whom by then I had a friendly and playful connection as his translator, and we were beginning to work on our next project, the translation of his second book, *Boquitas pintadas.* I now look at these names and observe sadly that almost all these vivid individuals are inhabitants of the irretrievable past.

. . .

Bioy was ironic yet could be a compassionate observer of his own failings as well as those of others, that is, the fragility of love, the ambiguity of human relations, the futile efforts. He was a stoic—Marcus Aurelius was one of his "guides"—and his view of humanity, which filtered through in our conversations, was that we're all more or less hopeless clowns, in the same boat as it were, so let's try to have at least some humility about our large aspirations and our little catastrophes. "One man's dream is another man's nightmare," he said to me once, and his relationship with the striking Elena Garro, Octavio Paz's first wife, was exemplary of this adulterous story as well as the aforementioned aspirations and catastrophes. The memoir by Garro's daughter traces Bioy's experiences and character as a man skeptical about himself as well as the rest of humanity, envisioning men and women as creatures who irrevocably repeat their behaviors, much like his miscellaneous sketch of a rusty automaton-like monkey mechanically riding a bicycle.

IV.

The Selected Stories of Adolfo Bioy Casares, which I published in English with New Directions, was the result of a collaboration over many years with Bioy as well as with Emir. Commissioned in the early 1970s by Emir to translate a story by Bioy called "The Myth of Orpheus and Eurydice," about a Peronist incident in 1953 in Buenos Aires, I sent the translation to Bioy in hopes that he would approve. He wrote me a delightfully encouraging letter that came all the way to New Haven from "Rincon Viejo, Pardo," the Casares family ranch "Old Corner" in the town of Pardo, where in the late 1930s he had written his famous novella *The Invention of Morel.* Here is the relevant excerpt (my translation):

Rincon Viejo, Pardo, March 8 1972

My Dear Jill:

Thanks for the letter and for the translation. About the latter, great suspense for the moment: to be elaborated on later.

I hadn't answered you until today, because for a time that has seemed immemorial I have spent my season at Mar de Plata lying face up, dedicated to examining, in all its details—which have struck me as sinister—the ceiling. It was nothing, lumbago; but, what a lumbago! That finally ended with a single injection, applied after fifty useless ones upon the advice of the father of my daughter's literature professor. There's nothing like literature.

The lumbago interrupted the progress of a short novel, *Los desaparecidos de Villa Urquiza* [published as *Dormir al sol* in 1973 and translated by me in 1978 as *Asleep in the Sun*] that I had begun with great hopes. But there is always something to be gained, as a Mexican general once said, and if I suffered over not writing (incredible as this seems), I spent who knows how many hours a day thinking about the little novel. As I watched it grow, not without fear of forgetting in the future, the novel and I became more intimate. Now I understand that before the lumbago, like an irresponsible chap, I was going to write about something of which I was completely ignorant.

Back, finally, to your translation. I wouldn't like to be unfair with anybody but I think, Jill, that it's the best that's been done with a text of mine. In general, the task of the translator consists in simplifying a text by weakening it, so that a mystery remains in evidence: Why did someone write (of course for this question there is never any answer) and why did someone else take the trouble to translate? Any author who doesn't want to abandon right there and then his profession should abstain from such depressing readings. With "The Myth of Orpheus and Eurydice" the danger, for me, is one of pride. I assure you that I have caught myself in the mirror, reading your pages with a beatific smile . . . , which could only correspond to the phrase: "How well I write!" "The Myth of Orpheus and Eurydice" does not read like a translation but as an original written with confidence, with intelligence, and with grace.

As if I believed that those merits were also my own, your translation stimulated me to confront the continuous difficulties that fetter me in the composition and writing of "The Disappeared. . . ."

This gratifying letter, the reader can readily understand, was an immense boost of encouragement to the young translator I then was. It is also interesting to note how translation stimulated his own writing, particularly in the context of Bioy's sense of himself as a somewhat invisible writer: the fact simply of being recognized through translation was in itself a stimulus to a man who was a consummate practitioner of courteous criollo modesty, or, more precisely, self-effacement.

. . .

These brief reminiscences about Bioy Casares feel appropriate, in the realm of communicating vessels, to this celebration of Carol Maier's admirable career. Having had the pleasure of collaborating with Carol on two beautiful and poignant books by Severo Sarduy, *Christ on the Rue Jacob* and *Beach Birds,* I got to know Carol in the intimate realm of her work process. She is a meticulously creative translator, and shares the modest spirit of Bioy and all creative people whose love for their work matters much more than the image of themselves in the literary marketplace.

Works Cited

Bioy Casares, Adolfo. (1940) 2003. *The Invention of Morel,* translated by Ruth L. Simms and preface by Suzanne Jill Levine. New York: New York Review of Books Modern Classics.

Levine, Suzanne Jill. 1994. "Introduction." In *The Selected Stories of Adolfo Bioy Casares,* edited and translated by Suzanne Jill Levine, vii–xv. New York: New Directions.

McCarthy, Tom. 2008. Review of Jean-Philippe Toussaint's *Camera* (Dalkey Archive Press). *New York Times Book Review* (21 December 2008): 11.

Paz Garro, Helena. 2003. *Memorias.* Mexico, D.F.: Oceano.

What Is Red?

Reclaiming the Art of Interpreting

Moira Inghilleri

Introduction

In recent decades, questions of visibility and agency have increasingly emerged as a central focus within translation and interpreting research. Scholars in the field have responded in different but related ways to the ethical dilemmas that translators and interpreters encounter in negotiating the tensions between the demands of their tasks and their complex personal and professional, local and global, cultural and institutional allegiances. This recognition of the visible negotiation and creative interpretation that are required in different types of translation and interpreting activity has been a continuing theme in Carol Maier's immense contribution to the field.

In 2006 at the International Association of Translation and Interpreting Studies conference in Cape Town, South Africa, Maier gave a keynote address in which she spoke about the conflictive situations in which translators and interpreters find themselves and the cognitive and emotional effects on them in their role as "intervenient beings" with respect to the stories, real or fictional, they tell and the individuals, real or imagined, they represent. In a published version of this paper, Maier (2007) elaborates on this experience of intervenience. She relates the story of an experienced Chilean interpreter, one of her students, who writes about the "shattering effect" an interpreting assignment involving a young abused mother who had attempted suicide had on her:

She wrote about being "haunted" for a long time by the young woman and her situation. A mother herself, she could feel the other woman's "pain, her helplessness." She realized that together they were trapped in the same system that has few real solutions to offer an abused woman and that she herself was unprepared to handle "the emotional aspects of interpreting," which left her feeling distraught, especially since she knew "that emotional involvement is a deterrent to the quality of the interpretation" (2007:3).

Maier connects the emotional response this student experiences and the professional dilemma it causes her with the "many forms of abrasion" that translators face. She recalls different descriptions of this experience by translation and interpreting scholars, among them Antoine Berman's account of the translator's "ambivalence," Douglas Robinson's "rather devastating portrait of the translator's 'pandemonium self'" (3), and Dirk Delabastita's and Rainier Grutman's "list of the main affective and unconscious components of the translator's subjective experience" (3).

In their introduction to an issue of *Linguistica Antverpiensia* entitled "Fictional Representations of Multilingualism and Translation," Delabastita and Grutman summarize the type of components that are sometimes found in fictionalized accounts involving multilingual encounters and experiences where the focus is on the subjective, emotional, and experiential dimensions of translators and translation and their impact on individuals or communities (2005:22–23). Two of these components, trauma and identity, are particularly relevant to the issues Maier raises regarding the question of how translators and interpreters cope with the immense task of revoicing or rewriting other people's trauma and of how they maintain an emotional equilibrium as a result of these experiences. Figuring out the answers to these questions in a particular encounter inevitably compels individual translators and interpreters to confront the boundaries of their own understandings, beliefs, prior experiences, and, importantly, their ethical positions, particularly bearing in mind that it is often individuals and groups of individuals with the least powerful voices who are most dependent upon translators and interpreters to represent them capably, making sure that their understandings, beliefs, experiences, and ethical positions are recognizable to others, thereby avoiding misrecognition.

According to Axel Honneth, the expectation of recognition involves the guarantee of three basic principles: self-trust (the right to basic self-confidence), self-respect (a sense of authorship over one's life), and self-esteem (the right to live in a semantic-symbolic environment that enables a rich self-interpretation), each of which is necessary to achieve individual autonomy (Honneth and Anderson 2005). In situations where these conditions are not met, whether over a prolonged period of time or as a result of specific instances of injustice, individuals come to feel disrespected and humiliated, or in more extreme cases to "view their own feelings with suspicion, and to distrust their own desires" (2005:134). Translators and interpreters often find themselves in actual or fictionalized situations standing by and standing in for individuals who have lost and are attempting to reclaim self or mutual recognition.

In my contribution to this volume, I wish to further explore the view, elaborated more fully elsewhere (Inghilleri 2012), of interpreted contexts as instances of language in action; dialogic encounters in contact zones that contribute to the formation of worldviews, opinions, values, and beliefs, formed and transformed in interaction and through the intervention of different social environments. This perspective forcefully calls into question a representational view of language, a view that has historically informed both translation (particularly of nonliterary texts) and interpreting theory and practice. Such theorizations of language tend to privilege aspects of formal discourse at the expense of more productive insights about the immediate interpretive aspect of communication, its capacity to transform cognitive understandings and permit individuals to develop new perspectives drawing from their conventionalized modes of thought.

In this essay I use the medium of visual art and the work of two artists, Kazimir Malevich and Mark Rothko, to illustrate the ways that privileging formal discourse can limit rather than enhance the representation of meaning, particularly emotive meaning. Like other forms of art, spoken language is a crucial, creative, and interactive means through which individuals engage thought and express complex feelings. This is an observation that Carol Maier has often acknowledged in her writing, and so with this in mind, the central task of this paper is to reclaim interpreting as art.

Reclaiming the Art of Interpreting

Franz Pöchhacker has traced the differentiation established between translation and interpreting studies to the early nineteenth century and Schleiermacher's distinction between art and scholarship on the one hand (associated with literary translation) and commerce on the other (linked to interpreting and technical translation). He quotes Schleiermacher's description of interpreting as "a merely mechanical task that can be performed by anyone with a modest proficiency in both languages, and where, so long as obvious errors are avoided, there is little difference between worse and better renditions" (qtd. in Pöchhacker 2004:53). This distinction between literary translation on the one hand and interpreting and technical translation on the other persisted through the development of translation studies and interpreting studies, contributing to a lack of awareness of any perceived ties between the translation of written and spoken language despite the many linguistic, cultural, ethical, and ideological issues common to both. The view of interpreting as a "commercial transaction" in more than one language helped sustain the view of an interpreter as an impartial and invisible channel between two linguistic systems capable of achieving unproblematic linguistic and cultural equivalence for the primary purpose of purely transactional communication. Interpreted dialogue was viewed solely as a means to an end rather than an end in itself.

Much of interpreting theory and practice continues to operate on the assumption of an ideal sender-receiver, context and culture-neutral model of communication, in which thoughts are transferred from a speaker to a hearer and back again. Variations on this view, while allowing interpreters a degree of interpretation of utterances based on contextual and cultural knowledge, ultimately remain loyal to the view of languages as comparative linguistic *systems*. This can be directly traced to the evaluation inherent in Saussure's initial distinction between *langue* and *parole*, later reproduced in Chomsky, where parole/performance is seen as largely irrelevant to the proper workings of the language system. Even in situations where cultural mediation is accepted as a legitimate part of communicative practices, the competence deemed necessary is usually conceived of as a set of prescriptive, pragmatic rules, similar in kind to rules of grammar. Consequently, breakdowns in interpreted communication are usually attributed to one or more of the participants' inability to use language appropriately—to choose a word, syntactic form, or utterance—based on rules of linguistic competence, i.e., lexico-grammatical knowledge, or rules of communicative competence, i.e., cultural or contextual knowledge. The assumption is that where rules of competency are mastered and the appropriate choice selected, more successful translation, i.e. greater equivalence, can be achieved. On this assumption the interpreter serves as a mere channel to ensure that a concept being transferred from one speaker to another becomes the "same" concept in both linguistic systems. It is not surprising that so much of the early focus of interpreting research until a few decades ago focused on psycholinguistics, neurolinguistics, and the cognitive skills required of interpreters. If interpreters are viewed primarily as "conduits" for communication (a view that persists to this day), then it stands to reason that issues to do with memory, meaning assembly, perceptual segmentation, and information processing would become the central concerns of interpreting research (for examples of this early focus, see parts 1–3 in Pöchhacker and Shlesinger 2002:25–202).

Although there have been important developments that have challenged the centrality of cognitive aspects of interpreting, a consequence of this early work can be seen in the continued absence of a strong perception among translation and interpreting scholars of the significant overlaps between the spoken texts that interpreters translate and the written works, particularly of fiction, that translators translate. The similarities between "the play of signifiers" in literary texts and "the signifiers in play" in interpreting contexts have gone largely unnoticed. The association of literary translation with art and scholarship helped free that domain to explore a more creative and experimental relationship between signifier and signified that was not, as it was in interpreting research, tied to a strict representational view of language. For the literary translator this relationship could also operate as a site of cultural and political transformation. The "cultural turn" in translation, for example, challenged literary translators to operate against their own constraints, including the constraint of fluency. Translators themselves came to be seen as potential vehicles for dissent aimed at recognizing less powerful voices and, ultimately, achieving greater social and cultural equality. Literary translation could thus claim an ethical function— represented in terms like *foreignization, resistance,* and *abusive fidelity,* which opposed existing norms of fluency, domestication, and ethnocentric violence. Literary translation came to be seen as providing a means for understanding the present in dialogue with the past and with other cultures. The emphasis in postcolonial theories on contact zones, asymmetrical power relations, and the ideological over the aesthetic further revealed translation as an activity involving far more than contact between languages.

But, of course, interpreters, like translators, also translate and must "interpret" narratives of trauma, illness, poverty, torture, and conditions in war zones, as well as multilayered corporate, medical, scientific, and, indeed, literary, discourses. In both cases semantic uncertainty is involved as are strategic manipulations, webs of interlocution, cultural and textual grids, and overt or covert political agendas. Though a good deal of interpretive "prospecting" may be involved in the reading of a written text, the challenge is even greater in the reading of a spoken utterance given the cognitive demands on interpreters. In both types of text, however, meaning must be determined against a background of prior uses, present communicative objectives, and a spectrum of accumulated beliefs about who the interlocutors are and what their communicative behavior signifies. The demand on interpreters of spoken texts to remain "impartial" and "objective"—two words repeatedly found in their codes of practice—can therefore be no more straightforward than it would be for translators of fictional texts insofar as for both there is a presumption of faithful practice. Even "abusive fidelity" does not necessarily imply that any interpretation can count as valid or appropriate.

A Challenge to a Representational View of Language

Another unfortunate consequence of examining interpreting processes and products primarily through a representational view of language has been that the underlying function of interpreting has come to be viewed as one of establishing the sameness of a world beyond language. This view reinforces a conception of language as a "unity" intervening between the self and some nonlinguistic reality, culturally or universally given, which it is the task of language to represent (see Rorty 1989:3–22). Since Wittgenstein, critiques of such systems- or rule-governed models of language have centered on their inability to account for the flexible and innovatory nature of communication and for their limitations in explaining the dialogic or dialectical nature of communicative practices. Acts of translation, whether of spoken or written language, are equally dialogic and dialectical in nature. Putnam suggests the following:

> One can understand the assertion that a translation fails to capture exactly the sense or reference of the original as an admission that a better translation scheme might be found; but it makes only an illusion of sense to say that all possible translation schemes fail to capture the "real" sense or reference. Synonymy exists only as a relation, or better, as a family of relations, each of them somewhat vague, which we employ to equate different expressions for the purposes of the interpretation. The idea that there is some such thing as "real" synonymy apart from all workable practices of mutual interpretation, has been discarded as a myth. (1981:116)

Putman's comments recall Wittgenstein's notion of "family resemblances": the idea that there is no essential core in which the meaning of a word is located and which is, therefore, common to all uses of that word; on the contrary, words acquire meaning in interaction with others, not in isolation or by being paired with other words, experiences, or things. For Wittgenstein language-games were ways of acting based on habits, instincts, and emotions. In his argument against the possibility of a private language, Wittgenstein (1963) asserted that it is impossible for speakers to know whether they are using the words of their language "correctly" or the "same" with reference to a sensation or an object or an experience, for no language can refer to a sphere of private things. The influential language philosopher Donald Davidson has similarly argued against adhering to this distinction between determinate realities and a set of words or concepts that may or may not be adequate to them. For Davidson, all attempts to describe the "truth" of utterances through notions of conceptual schemes fall back on the same erroneous assumption that languages organize or fit something like an objective "reality" or sensory experience (1984:183–98). Ultimately, however, the meaning of words is determined by their communicative purpose in particular contexts of use. In interpreted interactions, the search for "workable practices of mutual interpretation" includes questions such as the following: What is at stake for individual participants in an interpreted event? What are the professional, ethical, political, social, or personal risks involved in the interaction? Is there a potential for conflicting views over what may be reasonably meant or understood by an utterance in the particular situation? What ethical, political, or social factors may lie behind a claim that one participant's understanding of an utterance is reasonable or that another's should be challenged?

To produce workable mutual interpretations, interpreters, like translators and all language users, use more than their cognitive and linguistic skills. They participate in the world as communicating social agents in contexts that may foster ambiguity, contradiction, misunderstanding, and different forms of real or symbolic violence and betrayal. In situations where evidence of some form of trauma is present, there is an added obligation to minimize disrespect, humiliation, or mistrust between individuals, while maximizing the possibility that communicative objectives are met; finding, discarding, and clarifying meanings can be a particularly daunting task. There are no guarantees that interpreters will evaluate accurately what is at stake in an interaction, just as there is no certainty that their judgments will produce a positive outcome. Fallibility is a part of and must be written into our understandings of the socially constituted social and ethical spaces interpreters inhabit. The greater the visibility of inter-preters within these spaces, the more that is revealed about the ethical impera-tive inherent in their role: to minimize misrecognition and maximize the pos-sibility that communicative objectives are met, that is, to find the best words to represent the meanings expressed while, as Maier suggests, "altering the sur-face in ways that have more than 'superficial impact'" (2006:3). The struggle to achieve the right level of impact to best represent the profound emotions be-hind sometimes "unspeakable" experiences is an aim that many visual artists wishing to convey human complexity in figurative art, and the burden they feel in attempting to do so, share with interpreters. An Iraqi interpreter explains as follows: "I would do my best to be that person who's in the session with the cli-nician, and not just by speaking the language but also by trying my best to feel his feelings, and putting myself in the situation, being in this country, alone, nobody around, they are totally blind and deaf and they need somebody who can represent them, and convey the accurate message" (Inghilleri 2012:84).

At one point in their lives, both Malevich and Rothko rejected representa-tional art because it became an inadequate means for them to express them-selves. For both, the situated process of signification itself became the subject, the same subject that hovers in the air in all interpreted dialogue where mean-ing is struggling to escape.

Kazimir Malevich (1878–1935): Transcending the Object

In 1919 Malevich wrote in his *New Systems in Art:* "People are always demand-ing that art be comprehensible and never make the effort to adapt their own minds to comprehend it; the most cultivated socialists have taken this path, and require of art what a shopkeeper requires of a sign-painter, that he rep-resents the goods for sale as accurately as possible" (qtd. in Néret 2003:13).

My first encounter with the Ukrainian-born Russian artist Kazimir Mal-evich was at an exhibition at the Metropolitan Museum of Art in New York in 1991. The Malevich exhibition portrayed his journey from figurative art toward the realization of his aim to develop an abstract art of "pure sensa-tions"—what he would call "Suprematism"—only to be compelled to return to figurative painting in response to political intimidation by the Soviet state, which deemed the social realist aesthetic to be the only genuine proletarian art. Malevich's origins in rural Ukraine exposed him to local peasants with whom he felt a deep kinship; he explored their working lives in his Neoprimitivist paintings, borrowing from Russian traditional art forms such as icon painting and folk art: "consecrating the labourer's poses" while aspiring to reduce forms, and therefore nature, to "cones, cubes and spheres" (Néret 2003:21). Malevich explained his stance in 1933:

> I perceived a link between peasant art and that of the icon: the art of the icon is the superior form of peasant art. I discovered in icons the spiritual side of the peasant epoch. I understood the peasants through the icons. I perceived [their] faces, not as those of saints, but as those of simple men. Knowledge of the icon had convinced me that the point is not in the study of anatomy and perspective, not to render nature in all its truth, but to gain an intuition of the nature of art and artistic realism. (qtd. in Néret 2003:21–22)

His 1912 painting *Peasant Woman with Buckets and Child* (Figure 1) illustrates this aim perfectly.

At around this same time Malevich, together with Russian literary figures, issued a "futurist manifesto" repudiating conventional meaning and form, coining the term *zaum*, meaning "beyond reason" or "beyond the mind," to describe their semantic inventions in which the aim was to invent new words and illogical combinations of sounds (Bowlt 1990:180). Malevich's Suprematist program originated during this period. Suprematism was "aimed at redirecting viewers' attention to what mattered most in art—not the material things it reproduced but the feelings it expressed" (Chave 1989:190). Malevich likened the innovation of Suprematism to "getting behind a painted face in the theatre: we can't recognize the actor as his true face is hidden, but like a piece of art the actor doesn't require a face at all—all he feels on stage is his experience behind the mask. His face is hidden and is unnecessary" ("Looking at Art That Enrages").

This sentiment is expressed in the painting *Black Square* (Figure 2), perhaps Malevich's most "iconic" painting. Indeed, when it was first publicly displayed at an exhibition in 1915, it was hung high, like an icon across a corner (Néret 2003:49). It was later placed on the wall above Malevich's body as it lay in state in his Leningrad apartment in 1935.

Much has been written about this painting. In addition to being seen as among the most uncompromisingly abstract paintings of its time, it is generally considered to express Malevich's repudiation of the material world, evoking instead a spiritual one unmediated by any recognizable object. It was the ultimate expression of an objectless world. Malevich would explore this idea further in a series of Suprematist works he called "pictorial" or "painterly" realism—"painting as its own objective" (qtd. in Néret 2003:61), which included works in which planes of color appear isolated as independent forms suspended on a white background, representing an extranatural infinite space. He described this form of realism in the following way: "There is creation only where a form appears in the painting that takes nothing from what has been created in nature, but which develops pictorial volumes without repeating or modifying the primary forms of objects of nature" (61). This thinking is conveyed in *Self-Portrait in Two Dimensions* (1915) (Figure 3) and in *Painterly Realism of a Boy with a Knapsack* (1915) (Figure 4).

Malevich was careful to point out that in looking at these paintings, one should not look for the forms their titles suggest. In these paintings, he instructs the viewers, "real forms have been looked at by myself primarily as heaps of pictorial volumes devoid of form, on the basis of which a pictorial painting has been created that is nothing to do with nature" (51).

By the 1920s Malevich and his idealist Suprematist art came under increasing attack from conservative artistic groups that promoted naturalistic paintings on the theme of the worker's role in society as the only genuine proletarian art. In 1930 he was imprisoned for three months and interrogated about the "ideology of existing trends" (Joosten 1990:19). By 1934, when the first All-Union Congress of Soviet Writers met in Moscow to adopt Socialist Realism as the exclusive style for Soviet writers and artists, Malevich had already begun to produce paintings more reminiscent of his earlier work as a response to growing pressure (20). His 1933 self-portrait (Figure 5), one of his last paintings, is representative of this later work, which he described as "supra-naturalism," a style in which, as Néret suggests, "the timeless beings that he represents belong to another world, a future world from which Big Brother has been banished, and they seem to communicate with coded gestures that they alone understand" (2003:88–89). In several of these paintings, including *Self Portrait*, Malevich paints a small black square in the lower corner, thereby imbuing these superficially representational works with Suprematist allusions.

For Malevich what mattered most in art was the emotion it conveyed not the objects it represented. He was convinced that eliminating the "object" was the only means for the artist to express pure feeling. He believed that the pursuit of representational art and its traditional techniques and subjects revealed

Figure 1: Kazimir Malevich, *Peasant Woman with Buckets and Child* (1912)

Figure 2: Kazimir Malevich, Black Square (1915)

Figure 3: Kazimir Malevich, *Self-Portrait in Two Dimensions* (1915)

Figure 4: Kazimir Malevich, *Painterly Realism of a Boy with a Knapsack* (1915)

Figure 5: Kazimir Malevich, *Self Portrait* (1933)

Figure 6: Mark Rothko, *White Center* (1957) (© 1998 Kate Rothko Prizel & Christopher Rothko/Artists Rights Society [ARS], New York)

Figure 7: Mark Rothko, *Red on Maroon*, 1959. (Tate, London/Art Resource, NY. © 1998 Kate Rothko Prizel & Christopher Rothko/Artists Rights Society [ARS], New York)

Figure 8: Mark Rothko, *Black on Maroon*, 1959. (Tate, London/Art Resource, NY. ©
1998 Kate Rothko Prizel & Christopher Rothko/Artists Rights Society [ARS], New York)

artists' *inability* to depict what he described as the "truth," and this, according to Malevich, was not art.

Mark Rothko (1903–70): Ending the Silence

Malevich's predicament involved the unresolvable tension between the spiritual and the political—he became a kind of aesthetic prisoner within a system that did not allow him to speak his deepest language. His only defiance was the minute black square, the Suprematist sign, in the corner of his socialist realist paintings, a wink to the knowing. Rothko's predicament had more to do with emotional pain than with spirituality, more with existential anguish than with ideological concerns. But interestingly, like Malevich, Rothko's interest in abstraction was also about its greater capacity to express feeling. As he stated with reference to his art, "squares were not squares but all my feelings about life, about humanity" (O'Doherty 1988:164). And also like Malevich, Rothko's rejection of representational art meant reaching a deeper level of human communication.

Russian-born and Jewish, Rothko's work was deeply affected by the events of the 1930s and 1940s and the sense of social crisis and conflict that defined these decades, including the Second World War and its aftermath. His earlier figurative paintings often conveyed his concern for the human condition in the twentieth century in the mundane acts of everyday life. Following a period in which he experimented with painting mythological fantasies, he gradually and reluctantly, according to him, became disappointed with representations of figures on a canvas and concluded that they could not express depth of feeling. He put it this way:

> The solitary figure could not raise its limbs in a single gesture that might indicate concern with the fact of mortality and an insatiable appetite for ubiquitous experience in the face of this fact. Nor could the solitude be overcome. It could gather on beaches and streets and in parks only through coincidence, and with its companions, form a tableau vivant of human incommunicability. I do not believe that there was ever a question of abstract or representational. It is really a matter of ending this silence and solitude, of breathing and stretching one's arms again. (Rothko 1947/1948)

Rothko did not wish to be constrained by the idea that human experience had to be expressed in art through outward appearances, by describing or depicting individual people, as in portraiture. Modern art, he felt, had discovered the potential of a "portrait" of an idea. The art historian Anna Chave has noted that figures were never actually removed from his paintings; his rectangles and his colors acted as substitutes for figures, "things in the artist's eye," not voids: iconic signs and conceptual representations (Chave 1989:116). She suggests that any of his paintings can be described as having a portrait-like aspect (118), as in his *White Center* (1957) (Figure 6).

Rothko's paintings can be said to be iconic in a more strict semiotic sense the same way that Malevich's paintings are in a religious sense. In both, the relationship between the image and its referent is not one of simple correspondence; the relationship itself, if one is to be discerned at all, is more abstract. Rothko's rectangles and colors are intended to project ideas; they are, as Malevich suggested about his own paintings, "heaps of pictorial volumes" that do not aim to offer any type of assurance or evidence of an origin in nature. The well-known British art critic David Sylvester, in his review of an exhibition of Rothko's work in London in 1961, astutely observes that

> The evocative quality of the form, the seductive charm of the colour become irrelevant when the paintings are confronted. These paintings are beyond poetry as they are beyond picture-making. To fantasise about them (as the catalogue does), to discover storm clouds or deserts in them, or sarcophagi, or aftermaths of nuclear explosions, is as corny as looking at Gothic architecture and thinking of the noon-day twilight of the forest. These paintings begin and end with an intense and utterly direct expression of feeling though the interaction of coloured areas of a certain size. They are the complete fulfilment of Van Gogh's notion of using colour to convey man's passions. They are the realization of what abstract artists have dreamed for fifty years of doing-making painting as inherently expressive as music. More than this: for not even with music, where the inevitable sense of the performer's activity introduces more of the effects of personality, does isolated emotion touch the nervous system so directly. (Sylvester 2001:64–65)

Sylvester's references to color are significant here. Rothko usually mixed his own paints. Beginning with the priming, the painting was built up using layers of color that were so thinned that the pigment just barely adhered to the surface. The layers were applied quickly with a light touch, which gave a transparency and luminosity to the painting ("Looking at Art That Enrages"). Through these areas of color he induced viewers to feel a deep connection with his paintings, to develop a symbiotic relationship with them (Chave 1989:104), not as a result of the color relationships alone, but because of the intensity of feeling these relationships evoked.

What Is Red?

In 2009 I attended a performance of a play about Rothko entitled *Red* (2009), written by John Logan. The play takes place in 1959 in Rothko's New York studio during the period that he was painting a series of murals commissioned by the Seagram's Corporation, two of which are included here: *Red on Maroon* (1959) (Figure 7) and *Black on Maroon* (1959) (Figure 8).

The play is constructed as a dialogue mainly about art between Rothko and his young assistant, named Ken, in the play. During Scene Two of the play, in the midst of one of their conversations, Rothko stops abruptly and stares at one of the as yet unfinished murals. The intense exchange between the two that follows reveals a lot about the relationship between color and human emotion for Rothko. As the exchange begins, Rothko gazes at one of the murals (Logan 2009:22–26).

> *He tilts his head. Like he's listening. Like he's seeing something new in the painting.*
> R: Bring me the second bucket.
> K: Are you really going to paint?
> R: What do you think I *have* been doing?
> *Ken retreats. He watches Rothko closely. Rothko dips the five-inch house-painter's brush into the paint. He's ready. Then he stands there frozen. Just his eyes move craftily over the canvas. Paint drips. Ken is breathless. Rothko is coiled. He tilts his head, studying, adjudicating. He considers the color of the paint in the bucket. Needs something.*
> R: Gimme black number four and the first maroon.
> *Ken brings some powdered pigments in old jars. Rothko instructs, still barely moving. His eyes dart from the bucket of paint to the canvas.*
> R: A pinch of black.

Ken adds a bit of black pigment, stirs it carefully.

R: Just that amount again.

Ken adds a bit more, keeps stirring.

R: Twice as much maroon.

Ken adds some maroon pigment, keeps stirring.

Rothko is unsure. He looks at the painting. The moment is passing. He is getting desperate.

R: (*To himself, frustrated.*) Come on . . . come on . . . come on . . . What does it need?

K: Red

R: I wasn't talking to you!

Tragically the moment has passed for Rothko. He FLINGS the paintbrush away. It splatters. He spins on Ken.

R: DON'T YOU EVER DO THAT AGAIN!

He rages, stomping restlessly around the room.

R: By what right do you speak?! By what right do you express an opinion on my work? Who the fuck are you? What have you done? What have you seen? Where have you earned the right to exist here with me and these things you don't understand?! "RED?!" You want to paint the thing?! Go ahead- here's red-!

He clumsily slings packets of various red paints at Ken.

R: And red! And red! And red!—I don't even know what that means! What does red mean to me? You mean scarlet? You mean crimson? You mean plum-mulberry-magenta-burgundy-salmon-carmine-carnelian-coral? Anything but "red!" What is "RED?!"

Rothko stands, getting his breath collecting himself.

Ken picks up the packets of paint from the floor. Rothko prowls, discontent. Pause.

K: I meant Sunrise.

R: Sunrise?

K: I meant the red at sunrise. . . . The feeling of it.

R: (*Derisive*) Oh "the feeling of it." What do you mean the feeling of it?

K: I didn't mean red paint only. I meant the *emotion* at sunrise.

R: Sunrise isn't red.

K: Yes it is.

R: I'm telling you it's not.

K: Sunrise is red and red is sunrise. Red is heartbeat. Red is passion. Red wine. Red roses. Red lipstick. Beets. Tulips. Peppers.

R: Arterial blood.

K: That too.

Rothko thinks about it.

R: Rust on the bike on the lawn.

K: And apples. . . . And tomatoes.

R: Dresden firestorm at night. The sun in Rousseau, the flag in Delacroix, the robe in El Greco.

K: A rabbit's nose. An albino's eyes. A parakeet.

R: Florentine marble. Atomic flash. Nick yourself shaving, blood in the Barbasol.

K: The ruby slippers. Technicolor. That phone to the Kremlin on the president's desk.

R: Russian flag. Nazi flag. Chinese flag.

K: Persimmons. Pomegranates. Redlight district. Red tape. Rouge.

R: Lava. Lobsters. Scorpions.

K: Stop sign. Sports car. A blush.

R: Viscera. Flame. Dead Fauvists.

K: Traffic lights. Titian hair.

R: Slash your wrists. Blood in the sink.

K: Santa Claus.

R: Satan.

R: So . . . red.

K: Exactly.

Rothko gazes thoughtfully at his painting

R: We got more cigarettes?

The reflective semantic process vividly portrayed in this exchange is akin to what interpreters experience in their struggles to do justice to others' thoughts, to get each shade of meaning exact against a background of alternative shades of meanings. Words create for interpreters what color and form created for Rothko: structures of feeling. What happens in this exchange is similar to the kinds of challenges interpreters face trying to find the right words to represent others' powerful emotional experiences. At first Rothko is enraged by Ken's attempt to "interpret" what he wants to say: one can imagine the same indignation and incredulity felt by individuals who must rely on interpreters to express their feelings. Rothko's words—"What have you done? What have you seen? Where have you earned the right to exist here with me and these things you don't understand?!"—recall the quiet yet perceptible desperation in people's faces as they listen, without comprehending, to an interpreter re-tell their stories of trauma and displacement.

Such stories are frequently made up of apparently simple statements like "No, it happened Tuesday at lunch time, it was getting dark, before not after our papers were taken from us," which require a number of reflective linguistic decisions on the part of the interpreter: What is "lunch time" (dinner, supper, tea)? What are "papers" (official, forged, stolen/documents, passports, birth/marriage certificates)? What is "taken" (seized, collected, stored, reviewed)? This information forms part of a narrative that must stand up to critical scrutiny by a government official, an immigration judge, a lawyer, a doctor. This implies that such decisions are also situated in some drama of context.

Rothko was particularly aware of the relationship between the immediate environment and viewers' experience of his work, particularly the spacing and the lighting. In a letter to a curator at the Art Institute of Chicago about an upcoming solo exhibition, he advises her on the installation of his paintings:

> Since my pictures are large, colorful and unframed, and since museum walls are usually immense and formidable, there is a danger that the pictures relate themselves as decorative areas to the walls. This would be a distortion of their meaning, since the pictures are intimate and intense, and are the opposite of what is decorative, and have been painted in a scale of normal living rather than an institutional scale. (qtd. in Weiss 2000:345)

Many interpreters are similarly aware of the dangers of the environments in which "intimate and intense" stories are told about experiences of wars, forms of persecution and abuse, and emotional and physical trauma, what for them, tragically, has come to constitute "normal living." They are witnesses to the distortions of meaning that occur in environments of "institutional scale" where much is at stake: that is, where the linguistic signs of common currency are not sufficient to reveal crucial and relevant detail, and there may be a predisposition toward ethnocentric violence and assimilative tendencies.

The Seagram paintings are considered Rothko's first formalized attempt to shape and control the experience of viewing his paintings in a specific room. They have been described as evoking "a frame or portal" and "comprising a drama of entry and exclusion, one that is ultimately claustrophobic in its denial—through the intense opacity of Rothko's application of paint—of a realm beyond the wall" (qtd. in Weiss 2000:318). With his Seagram murals, Rothko claimed that one of his inspirations was Michelangelo's Laurentian Library in Florence. He said "After I had been at work for some time, I realized that I was much influenced subconsciously by Michelangelo's walls in the staircase of the Medicean Library in Florence. He achieved just the kind of feeling I'm after—he makes the viewers feel that they are trapped in a room where all the doors and windows are bricked up so that all they do is butt their heads forever against the wall" (qtd. in Seldes 1996:44).

Rothko's wish to share his "dark visions of man's mortality" with the intended viewers of his murals was said by him to have a malicious intent (Seldes 1996:44), though in the end the murals ended up in a variety of places, different from the ones for which they were originally intended.[1] It is interesting to consider that Rothko's murals were as susceptible to misrecognition as the stories of individuals seeking refuge of one kind or another. Though the consequences are undoubtedly different, distortions in the intended meaning of a Rothko painting or a refugee's story are possible because the socially, politically, and historically motivated structures of feeling they represent are always subject to elimination, assimilation, or alteration, whether willful or not. Instances of interpreted interactions where misunderstandings or misrepresentations do occur become ethical matters for interpreters, who might choose to submit to their contingent status in relation to more powerful interlocutors, or to challenge the constraints of form (and norms) so as to allow the surface of stories to have more than a "superficial" impact, as Carol Maier (2007) suggests. Interpreters are acutely aware of the difficulties involved in making the meaning of one individual's words clear enough to another in a given context, especially in the face of opposing communicative objectives and imbalances of social or discursive power. Yet they occupy a unique position in the mutual knowledge-building that plays a central role in achieving meaningful dialogue. This does not imply that they have special access to what individuals mean; it does suggest, however, that as the "channels" of communication, they can best facilitate the development of mutual understanding, if not shared perspectives, by being able to ask the right questions of both parties in the dialogue.

The exchange between Rothko and Ken, launched as the result of one question—"What is RED?"—initiates a productive exploration about the range of possible feelings the color can invoke. It is a dialogue that begins in conflict and frustration on Rothko's part and ends with his contemplative "So . . . red," to which Ken calmly responds, "Exactly." The resolution to their question is that there is no resolution—that words, like figures on a canvas, cannot represent anything exactly, when that means faithfully or accurately. Maier's student was troubled by her reaction in her role as interpreter to a young woman's story of abuse because "she knew that emotional involvement was a deterrent to the quality of an interpretation." But what are the words interpreters live by if not emotional expressions of feelings and lived experiences? What Malevich and Rothko wanted to be able to demonstrate in their paintings was that it is "emotional involvement" that makes us human. Interpreters want to be able to demonstrate the same with their words. The limitations imposed on their use of language are as intellectually and historically contingent as the dominance of figurative art was in Malevich's and Rothko's time. Yet in 1920 Malevich wrote, "What, in fact, is the canvas? What do we see represented on it? Analyzing the canvas, we see, primarily, a window through which we discover life" (qtd. in Anderson 1968:125). If interpreters can start to see words more like open windows, they just might stop feeling trapped, like Rothko in Michelangelo's Library, "in rooms where all the doors and windows are bricked up so that all they do is butt their heads forever against the wall" (qtd. in Seldes 1996:44). Reclaiming interpreting as art might just help interpreters and those whose worlds they represent to see and be seen more clearly.

Note

1. Rothko is quoted as saying that he had taken the Seagram job with "strictly malicious intents. I hope to paint something that will ruin the appetite of every son-of-a-bitch who ever eats in that room" (Seldes 1996:44). Originally intended for an upscale restaurant inside the Seagram Building in New York, he eventually refused the commission, returning the money after dining there with his wife "horrified by the ostentatious setting," where the murals were to be displayed (Seldes 1996: 345). The final series of Seagram Murals are now displayed in three locations: London's Tate Modern, Japan's Kawamura Memorial Museum, and the National Gallery of Art in Washington, D.C.

Works Cited

Anderson, Troels, ed. 1968. *K. S. Malevich. Essays on Art, 1915–1928*. Vol. 1. Translated by Xenia Glowacki-Prus and Arnold McMillin. Copenhagen: Borgen.
Bowlt, John E. 1990. "Malevich and the Energy of Language." In *Kazimir Malevich 1878–1935*, Exhibition Catalogue, 179–86. Los Angeles: The Armand Hammer Museum of Art.

Chave, Anna C. 1989. *Mark Rothko, Subjects in Abstraction.* New Haven, Conn.: Yale University Press.

Davidson, Donald. 1984. *Inquiries into Truth and Interpretation,* 183–98. Oxford: Clarendon Press.

Delabastita, Dirk, and Rainier Grutman. 2005. "Fictional Representations of Multilingualism and Translation." *Linguistica Antverpiensia* 4: 12–24.

Honneth, Axel, and Joel Anderson. 2005. "Autonomy, Vulnerability, Recognition, and Justice." In *Autonomy and the Challenges to Liberalism: New Essays,* edited by John Christman and Joel Anderson, 127–49. Cambridge: Cambridge University Press.

Inghilleri, Moira. 2012. *Interpreting Justice: Language, Ethics, and Politics.* New York and London: Routledge.

Joosten, Joop M. 1990. "Chronology." In *Kazimir Malevich 1878–1935,* Exhibition Catalogue, 5–21. Los Angeles: The Armand Hammer Museum of Art.

Logan, John. 2009. *Red.* London: Oberon Books, 2009.

"Looking at Art That Enrages, Part 1: My Five Year Old Could Do That!" Available at: www.artsbigpicture.com/enrageone3.htm (accessed 21 December 2013).

Maier, Carol. 2007. "The Translator as an Intervenient Being." In *Translation as Intervention,* edited by Jeremy Munday, 1–17. London: Continuum.

Néret, Gilles. 2003. *Kazimir Malevich and Suprematism 1878–1935.* Translated by Chris Miller. Köln: Taschen.

O'Doherty, Brian. 1988. *American Masters: The Voice and the Myth.* New York: Random House.

Pöchhacker, Franz. 2004. *Introducing Interpreting Studies.* New York and London: Routledge.

Pöchhacker, Franz, and Miriam Shlesinger, eds. 2002. *The Interpreting Studies Reader.* New York and London: Routledge.

Putnam, Hilary. 1981. *Reason, Truth, and History.* Cambridge: Cambridge University Press.

Rorty, Richard. 1989. *Contingency, Irony, and Solidarity.* Cambridge: Cambridge University Press.

Rothko, Mark. 1947–48. "The Romantics Were Prompted." *Possibilities* 1 (Winter): 84. Available at: http://teifidancer-teifidancer.blogspot.com/2009/12/mark-rothko-romantics-were-prompted.html 3 (accessed 21 December 2013).

Seldes, Lee. 1996. *The Legacy of Mark Rothko.* Cambridge, Mass.: Da Capo.

Sylvester, David. 2001. "Rothko" (1961). In *About Modern Art,* 2nd ed., 64–65. New Haven, Conn.: Yale University Press.

Weiss, Jeffrey. 2000. *Mark Rothko.* New Haven, Conn.: Yale University Press.

Wittgenstein, Ludwig. 1963. *Philosophical Investigations.* Oxford: Basil Blackwell.

Interview with Carol Maier

Julie Boéri

Conducted in Barcelona in October 2011, this interview resulted from several years of thought-provoking exchanges between Carol Maier and me as we worked together as coeditors of *Compromiso Social y Traducción/Interpretación— Translation/Interpreting and Social Activism* (2010).

JB: Carol, you are known primarily as a literary translator and scholar, but you have recently addressed interpreting with a specific focus on situations of friction and conflict. Could you tell us how you have moved from focusing on literary translations toward looking at accounts of interpreters in situations of conflict?

CM: As you note, I have little experience as an interpreter, and the experience that I do have is not recent. That experience made a great impression on me, though. For instance, when my children were in elementary school, I worked closely with a family of Cuban exiles. Some of the work involved interpreting, and most of the work involved situations of cultural conflict, in particular with the numerous medical situations encountered by a young adolescent boy, an overprotective mother, and a father in need of extensive dental work. In all of those situations I saw interpreting as not a question of simply passing messages back and forth; it required explaining cultures and, for the interpreter, also perceiving quickly the discomfort, dislocation, and tension experienced by the person for whom I was interpreting.

Several years later that experience remained in my thoughts when I taught undergraduates at Bradley University in Peoria, Illinois. Although I did not teach interpreting, I arranged for and supervised student internships with the Illinois Migrant Council. The scarcity of interpreters and need for interpreters were great, and the students were often called on to interpret. The first semesters I taught at Kent, I also had the experience of working with interpreting, since Kent's MA program originally included basic instruction in interpreting. During my second or third year, my colleagues and I decided that we could not effectively teach both translation and interpreting at the same time, given the limits of our program, our faculty, and our facilities. On the basis of those semesters, however, I was able to experience firsthand the difference between the work of interpreters and translators. I should also mention here my belief that both the frequent interaction between German and English when I was growing up and, during my high school years, extensive experience as an accompanist and with two- and three-piano collaborations contributed significantly to my sensitivity to the sound, rhythm, and intimations of words spoken and sung.

When I wrote my keynote speech for the IATIS [International Association of Translation and Intercultural Studies] conference in 2006 [see Maier 2007], intervention was the theme of the conference; consequently, I began to think about what became a meditation on the translator as an intervenient being. That preparation prompted me to look at accounts by translators about translation. I also wanted to include interpreters, and I was fortunate to find striking accounts of interpreters in both fiction and in nonfiction, and they interested me a great deal. In addition, even though we were no longer teaching interpreting in our program at Kent, many of the MA students, especially the international students, were actively doing interpreting work, and some of them had spoken with me about their experiences. One of the students in particular had been interpreting for domestic violence situations. She and I talked about the emotional upheaval she had experienced when the interpreting required her simultaneously to witness and interpret that situation without trying to intervene in ways that would have violated professional codes of interpreting. It was clear to me that she had experienced what might be called a form of posttraumatic stress, seeing that she had participated in a troubling abusive situation but was not able to intervene beyond the terms appropriate to and limited by her role as interpreter.

Also at the time I was writing the paper, reportage about interpreters in Kuwait, Iraq, Afghanistan, and Guantánamo began to appear in the media, as did the first examples of what would be many books and testimonies on the part of both military personnel and interpreters. I well recall reading, for example, Erik Saar's and Viveca Novak's *Inside the Wire: A Military Intelligence Soldier's Eyewitness Account of Guantánamo* [2005] and Kayla Williams's and Michael E. Staub's *Love My Rifle More Than You: Young and Female in the U.S. Army* [2006] and the strong impression they made on me. Reading comments by American soldiers who had served in Iraq, who spoke about some of the things they had witnessed, even if they were not specifically recounting incidents in which they had intervened and even when they were not interpreting, also gave me an increased understanding of the interpreter's role in situations of strife and of how their work might affect them long term. The same is true of material published soon after I finished my talk: George Packer's 2007 *New Yorker* article "Betrayed," for example, and his play by the same name that premiered in New York early in 2008. It is also important to note here that Moira Inghilleri's [2008] work on Bourdieu and what she referred to as interpreter agency in zones of uncertainty, along with other scholarship on related topics in *Translation and Interpreting Studies,* had begun to appear shortly before.

JB: What, in your view can be gained from exploring these accounts? Are the kinds of dilemmas faced by interpreters in any way different from those faced by literary translators?

CM: With respect to literary translation, it would depend on the material one was translating, but, as you know, analyzing a translation is very different from analyzing an interpreting situation, and in my talk I did not analyze interpreting situations and I had not been in the situations of conflict to which I referred. But what I think can be gained from awareness of those accounts on the part of the general public—and I believe this is very important—is a respect for the tension and danger to which interpreters, whether North Americans or not, are subject. I would stress the "or not," because at the time I was working on my talk, coverage in the media was beginning to shed light on the jeopardy in which their work for the U.S. government was placing Iraqi translators. Both the general public and students in particular should realize the complexity of the issues involved in such interpreting situations.

JB: You have mentioned your IATIS keynote speech in which you proposed the term *intervenience* rather than *intervention.* What led you to this choice?

CM: You are asking me two questions, I believe. One of them has to do with the idea of intervenience and how it differs from intervention. I believe that two things led me to use *intervenience.* First, intervention is most often seen as negative and I believe it is important to recognize that one can intervene in ways both helpful and hurtful. Also, I was looking for something that would describe the role of the translator and/or interpreter as an individual, no matter the activity in which that person was engaged. In addition, I did not find the thought of an intervening being either appropriate or felicitous, especially to refer to a way of being. Second, an intervenient being—and I was happy to find out that adjective in the dictionary—is one who intervenes as part of her makeup, part of her profession, and also part of her being itself. I liked *intervenient* as an adjective because it reminded me of the individual as an individual, it included what an individual does but also the *way* she conducts herself; it refers not so much to the product of her activity as to the doing—the praxis—as it were.

JB: This deliberate choice highlights our duty as scholars to reflect upon the mediation inherent in the prisms we use to explore those accounts. What impact do those prisms have on our understanding of interpreters' positioning and dilemmas?

CM: I think it can be useful to think of oneself as intervenient but I also find it useful to consider the ways that a prism limits or deforms one's perspectives. We were talking earlier about metaphors and prepositions. I recall that we ended up discussing one of each in particular. One that is very common, which we discussed with respect to the book about *compromiso,* commitment, and social intervention, is that of the conduit. The limit of this metaphor has been addressed quite often in translation studies scholarship, but I don't believe that either readers of translations or even many translators are much aware of how misleading it is even to suggest a clean passing through.

When a person is interpreting and talking, he or she is intervening all the time and in ways that might not even enter her (or our) thoughts. The more I learn about neuroscience, for instance, the more I realize that every single part of your organism, every single tiny cell, is an integral part of your thinking, which indicates a material intervenience that only recently has entered discussions about translation.

With respect to prepositions, we spoke of *in* as opposed to *among. Between,* as I discussed in the paper, is a restrictive, bifurcating term, which is why I prefer the Spanish preposition *entre* to the English *between.* English does offer *in* or *among* but *entre,* which includes both, permits the distinction between *two* and *many;* and the danger of *in* is its polarization of one and the other. Maria Tymoczko [2003] has written very well about this in one of the first articles to explore in depth the danger of the *between*. I recall the effect of reading Tymoczko's article and my subsequent rethinking of the title of the collection about language and culture that I coedited with Anuradha Dingwaney [1995], especially our efforts to make the *between* more nuanced. Simply by using the word *between*, however, we were inevitably polarizing whatever entities we discussed and not acknowledging that whenever you have things between, you have two things whose embedded nature is easily overlooked. Whereas when you think in terms of *among*, you are led to think about more than two, prompted to recognize that polarities are in fact not clear polarities at all, but multiplicities, multidimensional. So, I believe that although changing thought and language is difficult, by endeavoring to make even small changes in terms and reminding oneself to adhere to those changes, in one's teaching, for example, we can influence thought.

JB: In other words *intervenience* would refer to a state of mind and body, intellect and emotion. Might neuroscience offer insight into points of contact between those two long-held dichotomies? So far, discussions about translation and neuroscience have approached interpreting primarily with respect to the brain with an interest in uncovering what happens cognitively in the black box of the individual interpreter.

CM: The link you mention is inevitable, but here I speak very hesitantly because I do not have a background in neuroscience nor do I work with cognition. I do think about this topic a great deal, though, and I believe that the more translation studies can learn from and be studied in light of neuroscience, the better. You mentioned focusing only on the brain of the individual, in this case, the interpreter. I would make two comments here: I believe that you were suggesting that cognitive research would involve focusing on the brain of a person who is doing the interpreting. In truth, however, in order to study fully an interpreting situation, it would be necessary to study the brain of every person involved. And an understanding of the interaction of different brains would require the most sophisticated understanding of what happens in the brain, and the brain as it interacts with the body from which it is inseparable.

I continue to write about this in my journal, although the language I have for doing that is limited, and the writing is somewhat stalled until I've read enough for my understanding and, consequently, for my language to expand. My goal is to be able to write in a more nuanced and vital way about translating as an organism—the body as organism. I used the word *vital* deliberately, because I want to move beyond metaphor, to materialize metaphor, if I may be permitted to use the verb in that way, because the act of translating affects one's organism, one's digestion, for instance, one's posture—it is a physical, material experience, every aspect of it is not abstract but vital. In addition, the effects of translation on your organism as you translate will affect those of your reader. When you interpret, the activity of interpreting itself on your organism will affect the organism of the person or persons with whom you're speaking. This is not merely a question of body language, but beyond or within it, to an extent and in ways in which we're not familiar, much less conversant.

I can't start my career over again and become a neuroscientist in addition to being a literary translator and perhaps also a psychoanalyst, but in truth one would need to have a wide range of knowledge in order to discuss translation in depth and in full.

JB: Your comments about intervenience as part of one's profession and of one's way of being seem to bring professional ethos and self into the equation of the interpreter's behavior. How might this work in practice in the process of interpreting?

What about interpreters' intervenience beyond the realm of intermediation? Some interpreters go public about what they experience during the process of interpreting while some others are reluctant to do so. Why is that? Are interpreters still intervenient beings when they choose not to describe their experience?

CM: Again, you've asked two different questions, and I hope I won't lose my train of thought, but I believe I can come at an answer by commenting first on literary translation. Many literary translators reflect on the process, as do many writers of both fiction and nonfiction, and they're more accustomed to writing about their reflections, even to fictionalizing their reflections in novels or in poems that in some way concern translation. But with respect to interpreters, the notion of visibility, public scrutiny outside the profession or the classroom, the situation is different. Only recently has there been that sort of scrutiny and accompanying reflection on the part of interpreters; their work is often highly confidential, if not classified. Recent conflict in the Middle East and the crucial, often contested role of interpreters has brought to light the often conflicted role of interpreters, whose work has placed them in unexpectedly challenging and dangerous situations, prompting them to question and reflect on the limits and limitations of codes of ethics that had long seemed adequately inclusive.

JB: Yes, there is now an agenda for recovering lost stories of interpreting that may shed light on present stories. The recovery of and reflection on accounts by interpreters require the collaboration of the media and the interest of an audience. There are signs, with the media coverage of interpreters' experience in Iraq, Guantanamo, and Afghanistan, that such audience interest is on the increase. How might we build on that interest and raise public awareness to the invaluable contribution that translators make to society and the dangerous conditions under which they often work?

CM: Two things occur to me. First, yes, of course there are signs, but if despite those signs there is reluctance on the part of interpreters to have their work evaluated or made public, that reluctance may arise from the fact that interpreters most often come into the news when they've made a mistake that sparks interest but also anger. How many times in important high-level discussions—I'm thinking in terms of political security, for example—one hears not about what a good job an interpreter did, about how the interpreter might have facilitated this or that agreement or treaty, but about a gaffe or error that led to an important miscommunication? This sort of publicity would make anyone reluctant to face scrutiny or to reflect openly on ambiguity or ambivalence.

JB: What a double-edged sword hangs over the interpreter! She's tolerated when communication flows but held responsible for any communication breakdown. This paradoxical view of interpreters as a "necessary evil" does not do justice to the added value that an interpreter brings to an exchange. To what extent can codes of ethics contribute to or constrain the construction of a culture of public reflection through such limiting prisms?

CM: This would be the second part of my response to your last question, and we've been talking about it the last few days as we presented our book: the role of social commitment, and the advantages and disadvantages of codes of ethics when an individual finds herself in a situation of conflict. Because codes of ethics don't truly cover all situations. There're not nuanced enough. And so, on the one hand they give an interpreter a guide, a set of guidelines, but on the other hand, when the situation becomes very difficult and very complicated, they can actually limit one's behavior because of being too prescriptive and/or not sufficiently inclusive of varied situations. We have also been talking about ways that instruction and classroom situations could prepare students better for such situations so as to give them tools for thinking their way through moments of uncertainty when conventional codes are inadequate, to enable them to go forward with the most complex and nuanced perspective possible.

JB: Yes, workshops, for example, dealing with concrete situations of conflict or communication clashes enable students to look at real situations that are not often reported or that in effect are erased by codes of ethics that represent interpreters as invisible. It is encouraging to see that there is growing resistance to this sort of code on the part of both professional interpreters and those in academia. Scholarship in this area—for example, studies about the work of interpreters on the ground in situations of conflict—is truly useful. It complements training initiatives such as the ones you mention.

CM: I agree, but it's also important to recognize that codes of ethics do play an important role in providing guidelines. The challenge is to be aware of the limits they inevitably place on one's thinking. With respect to the classroom, then, it's a question of training students or oneself to know when the codes are limiting and how to think past or around them when they don't cover a given situation. Here, as you mentioned, is a place for workshops, for analyzing actual and imagined situations—small groups of people talking about how they would deal with uncertainty and devising alternatives to solutions not addressed by conventional codes. You offer students multiple solutions and talk about the pros and cons of each, so that when they have to make a decision quickly, they have had plenty of practice in thinking in a complex manner under pressure.

JB: Thank you for answering these questions, Carol.

CM: My thanks to you for prompting me to think further about the relation between translation and interpreting and the potential conflict in both forms of contact.

Works Cited

Boéri, Julie, and Carol Maier, eds. 2010. *Compromiso Social y Traducción/Interpretación—Translation / Interpreting and Social Activism.* Granada: ECOS.

Dingwaney, Anuradha, and Carol Maier, eds. 1995. *Between Languages and Cultures: Translation and Cross-cultural Texts.* Pittsburgh: University of Pittsburgh.

Inghilleri, Moira. 2008. "The Ethical Task of the Translator in the Geo-political Arena." *Translation Studies* 1(2): 212–23.

Maier, Carol. 2007. "The Translator as an Intervenient Being." In *Translation as Intervention,* edited by Jeremy Munday, 1–16. London: Continuum.

Packer, George. 2007. "Betrayed." *The New Yorker* (2 April). Available at: www.newyorker .com/magazine/2007/04/02/george-packer-betrayed (accessed 25 October 2014).

Packer, George. 2008. *Betrayed: A Play.* London: Faber & Faber.

Saar, Erik, and Viveca Novak. 2005. *Inside the Wire: A Military Intelligence Soldier's Eyewitness Account of Life at Guantanamo.* New York: Penguin.

Tymoczko, Maria. 2003. "Ideology and the Position of the Translator: In What Sense Is a Translator 'In Between'?" In *Apropos of Ideology: Translation Studies on Ideology—Ideologies in Translation Studies,* edited by María Calzada Pérez, 181–202. Manchester: St. Jerome.

Williams, Kayla, and Michael E. Staub. 2006. *Love My Rifle More Than You: Young and Female in the U.S. Army.* New York: W. W. Norton.

Author Trouble

Translating the Living, Translating the Dead

Kelly Washbourne

Books are the ghosts of living writers,
and dead writers are the ghosts of books.
And maybe *this* is immortality . . .
—Rodrigo Fresán, *Kensington Gardens* (translated by Natasha Wimmer)

Someone said: "The dead writers are remote
from us because we *know* so much more than they did."
Precisely, and they are what we know.
—T. S. Eliot, "Tradition and the Individual Talent"

I Trade with both the Living and the Dead.
—John Dryden, "Dedication of the *Æneis* (1697)"

Translation entails collective authorship. The collaborative roles of the author and translator, however, intersect with some of the major unresolved issues in translation. But what should it matter if an author being translated is living or dead? Clearly our figurations of both kinds of author diverge. The way we see our relationships and collaborations and our notions of authorship that govern these interactions and interventions color our translation processes and products. In this essay I look at some of the narratives that have been constructed about the translated author, as well as the strategic constraints involved in translating each kind of author. I also situate my reflections within the debates over biographism and the author's extraliterary bearing on a text's meaning. Although the sparse work that has been done on this topic is largely—perhaps unavoidably—anecdotal, I attempt to shed light on the figurations of authors and authoring that shape the conditions for translating. Rather than focusing on translating living and dead languages, synchronic and diachronic translation, or the legal frameworks governing these acts—which are by now well understood—I focus instead on the problems of authorship, authority, agency, and aura that these author types, the living and the dead, can pose.

Translating the Living

> I am destined to perish, definitively,
> and only some instant of me may live on in him . . .
>   —Jorge Luis Borges, "Borges and I"

By themselves, living or dead, writers are simple enough. Writer-translator collaborations, however, are complex relationships. Let's consider the living first. One of the prevailing metaphors of translating a living author is that of *translation as negotiation* (Pym 1993; Eco 2004). But the metaphor often applies to *texts,* or if we read the metaphor as a framing of *translation and opposition,* *negotiate* is understood as the translator *maneuvering around an obstacle.* The obstacle in this case can be both textual and personal: "living authors can be useless, difficult, demanding, or unreasonable" (Wechsler 1998:205). Negotiation neatly encapsulates the give and take, the *territorialization* of the act of translation occurring with both text and author. We tend to think of negotiation as a freely entered arena for claims and counterclaims in which all parties have full information, equal stakes, and equal bargaining power. But note how closely allied *negotiation* and *power imbalances* are conceptually and metonymically (e.g., *war negotiations*) on the macrotextual level in translation, as Burton Raffel illustrates. "Two languages *contend for dominance* in translation. It is a *struggle* that occurs all along the *disputed text,* and each language *must yield* points to the *more forceful* configurations of the other. . . . If we wish to escape this strange romance involving 'fidelity' and 'liberties taken,' a field of warring identities and the erotics of *power,* we must conceive the translator's art differently . . ." (Raffel 1988:36–37; emphasis added). How curious, then, the ideal of friendly working relations with one's author if all the while a war is on!

Tensions appear at the level of canon as well. Do living writers have translational priority over the dead? Does death perform a more rigorous threshing and winnowing of the canon than life does? Do we not see a bias or preference for novelty in American publishing practices, therefore contributing to an erosion of eminence that comes with age? (The counterpart of this, paradoxically, is true as well: an aura can accrue to *certain* dead writers, as it can to certain living ones.) Although publishing houses on the whole do not have a stated bias toward the living (what Maud Ellmann [1990] calls "vivocentrism"), most, it seems, do make a distinction or else use what we could call the "contemporary/classic" or "modern/ancient" euphemism.[1] Modern writers often see the binary oedipally. "Ancient" or "classic" may also be a distancing, segregating strategy in a crowded market.

At times the living and the dead appear to cohabit and even share space without rivalry or enmity. Michael Bérubé describes one publisher's catalog with metaphors suggesting a department of social services, a soup kitchen, or a transient hotel: "The Dalkey Archive . . . works the side of the street populated by great dead writers down on their luck and talented living writers who've been cut from the backlist" (1998:137). In at least some instances, the recent death of a writer is read cynically by critics commenting on the marketability of a "tragic" figure. Roberto Bolaño's mythologization is a case in point (see, for example, Castellanos Moya 2009).

A working definition of *author-translator collaboration* helps orient our discussion. A translator and author can be said to be collaborating when the following conditions are met: first, when they are working with some metatextual, dialogic heuristic (i.e., the text alone cannot collaborate, and there must be give and take between author and translator as at least nominal coequals in problem-solving); second, when they are working toward a rewriting across some language barrier (*barrier,* if you like); and third, when they have some consensual goal of producing a work for some relatively defined new readership.[2] Minimally, there must be *something outside the text*—an intentionality, a method, and a goal—turned interpretively onto the text for collaboration to happen, properly speaking. Collaborative writers have "a working sense of shared authorship, shared authority, and shared intellectual property" (Lunsford and Ede 1994:434). Similarly de Kock writes, "both writers have to *give up* their exclusive claim to the text" (2003:348).

Thus, though it may seem obvious, the dead can "collaborate" insofar as they do not release their claim on a text, but they cannot collaborate insofar as they cannot engage in metatextual analysis nor assume a joint editorial function toward completing some *real communicative task,* namely, the translation at hand. In this sense philological notes left behind after death—"How to Translate Me When I'm Dead"—would not constitute collaboration. We do well to try to define collaboration strictly, since the boundaries quickly blur. Do I "collaborate" if given carte blanche by a writer whose sole contribution is tacit approval? Is it the same sort of collaboration if I revise a previously rejected draft of a translation from another translator? And what of an author whose sole contributions are overwritten by an editor? And then there are male-female collaborations, collaborations in unequal power relations, or collaborations on a work where there are as many as 17 translators of vastly different statuses (as in the proto-crowdsourced 1717 edition of Ovid's *Metamorphoses*).

Of course the complexity of collaboration extends beyond the tensions involved and reveals that the translator's subjectivity is ultimately rooted in community, Loffrado and Perteghella note:

> Collaboration . . . sits at the heart of "creative" translation, demonstrating how creativity is not an individualistic concept. A collaborative project, either a translator working together with a source text writer or with other translators, turns out to be an important translational moment displaying the richness of each subjectivity as it simultaneously enters into relationships with the text and with language, creating intriguing intertextual configurations; collaborations ultimately allow us to see how the people involved are all contributors, that is co-writers. (Loffrado and Perteghella 2006:8)

Two poles of translator collaboration can be said to be subtypes of collaborative authorship. At one pole there are experiences of the kind Suzanne Jill Levine recounts in *The Subversive Scribe,* which are "closelaborations" (2009:xiii), making the translator a "co-conspirator" in shaping the text and, in turn, affecting subsequent source texts, as in Levine's work with Guillermo Cabrera Infante. This phenomenon, though revolutionary in literature, is taken for granted in the social sciences—it is called the *decentering* method, whereby the translation (for example, of a research instrument) reveals points for *improvement in the source,* which in turn affects the translation, effectively bidirectionalizing text production.[3] We can also conceive of this type of collaboration as editing—creating a new edition—via translation, giving the lie to the myth of the fixed, stable source text.[4] Certain self-translations (e.g., those of Samuel Beckett) and exceptionally thorough revisions (e.g., those of Isaac Bashevis Singer) done by authors would fall at this end of the continuum, as would the assumption of the leading role by the translator, as described by Matthew Howard (1997).

At the other pole lies the now-proverbial cautionary tale in translation studies of Milan Kundera's participation in the translation of his works, which by most accounts was censorial, prescriptive, and unilaterally negotiated. Lest anyone think the violent imagery used by Raffel is anomalous, consider, for example, Kundera's prohibition in the introduction to *Jacques and His Master*: "Death to all who dare rewrite what has been written! . . . Castrate them and cut off their ears!"(Kundera 1985:9, quoted in Heim 2007:83). When Kundera's *The Joke* finally appeared in translation, in its fifth iteration, the translator's name did not appear on the title page, reflecting the author's continued dissatisfaction or possibly the translator's attempt to be disassociated from the project. Filipina Filipova characterizes the author's silencing of the translator as a divine punishment for a blasphemous act, a kind of expulsion of the translator from Paradise: "The Author has finally killed the Translator for the latter's inability to produce a copy in the Author's image and likeness" (2011:4).

These extreme cases of translation actually have an important commonality at their root: a relationship conferring authority. While editors, publishers, patrons, and other agents of translation complicate these models, translators at these two poles are fundamentally *given or denied authority for their approach to translation from a single living source*. It may seem strange to align these distant poles, but they have more in common in this sense than they would have with translations, say, authorized by spirit-channeling (see Robinson 2001), translations defended as resistant based on an ideology (for example, so-called abusive translation; cf. Lewis 1985), or translations in which a patron or commissioner has determined a specific audience and mode of reception (an adult novel turned into a children's book, or a short story turned into a script, for example). In other words, in this paradigm the translator's role expands or contracts according to *what a living author (de)authorizes*. Such authorization may even come in the form of denial—that is, an author's refusal to join world literature and leave behind the local, the regional, and the national.[5]

Seven Factors That Can Limit Effective
Collaborations with Living Authors

According to one practitioner, collaboration produces "the doubling of af-terthoughts: one or the other of the collaborators is bound to . . . find some-thing [in the text] that does not sound quite right and, given the existence of a partner in the enterprise, to feel a moral obligation to communicate his new hesitancy . . ." (Keeley 2000:40). The inverse of the coin is that this aes-thetic and ethical dialectic can be altogether missing: "with the dead there is no one to convince. More than that: there is no one to say that one mustn't" (Halkin 1983:84). Let us now look at some unexamined assumptions about collaborating, along with the potential pitfalls. I leave aside ideal collabora-tions, should they exist.

1. *Readers tend to read translations of living writers naively as endorsements, as possessing what textual criticism calls* authority.[6] A translation of a living writer, read reductively, ascribes authorial intention to the author and, by extension, *explicit* approval of the translator's choices. We might call this the *haunted translation fallacy,* the tacit belief in a living author's spirit transmi-grating into and pervading a work. The reader in this mode thinks: If a text is translated in a given way, it is because the author wanted it that way, and the result is a "halo effect." In other words, the naive reader thinks that the living author *willed* the text. It is an illusion, naturally, and an overestimation of the author's role in translation (the author actually chooses very few words of the target text). This reading may derive in part from the reader's orientation toward the Romantic vision of the single author. Arguably, multiple author-ship—as with translations—complicates the idea of the single author, as well as the idea of the text as a transparent record of a consciousness, making the author-function visible as a verbal construct. The interactions between an au-thor and a translator, moreover, usually have only the text itself as testimony; only the paratext (the translator's introduction, notes, and so forth, or, less commonly, a writer's account of working with the translator) reconstructs a relationship and implies joint authorship.

The reality is that the translator's microstrategic choices and their impact on the propositional content and literary effect of the whole often escape the author's attention or are beyond his or her ability to see or foresee, particu-larly when a given work might be translated into 20 languages. The reader who is intimately familiar with the work in the source language, however, is likely to have a stronger orientation toward the source text's authority and may condemn perceived departures in the target text *even if the author has explicitly authorized them.* The burden to describe or defend translation choices falls even more heavily on the translator when this kind of reader is involved. These two kinds of reader, of course, pale alongside the most naive reader of all: one who expects or insists upon the illusion of transparency—that is, *unmediated access to the writer and his or her thoughts* (cf. Venuti 1995).

2. *Living authors can answer some kinds of questions that no one else can, but no solutions can "close" a work or prove definitive.* Authors are indispensable in addressing questions of denotation, allusion, regionalism, intertextualities with their other works, roman à clef "insider information," archival parallel texts, and other matters of historical or text-production specificity. In an essay on the late Giovanni Pontiero's collaborations, Peter Bush notes that Pontiero would write to author Daniel Moyano for him to be a "possible provider of privileged insights into the meaning of obscure phrasing. However, there is no implication at all that Moyano as the originator of the text is the final arbiter of meaning or of the translation. The author is one source among many and it is the professional, experienced translator who is calling the shots" (Bush 1997:118). The author's translational savvy, of course, affects the extent of the author's role. Few living authors can or do work as obligingly and sympathetically with their translators as Umberto Eco, who writes: "The problem . . . is to make translators aware of allusions, that, for many reasons, might escape them. For this reason I usually send my translators pages and pages of notes about my various undetectable quotations—and suggest to them the way in which these quotations can be made perceptible in their own language" (2004:117). While translators have been known to use the cachet of the author's name as collaborator to lend ballast to their project, the translator is usually the one taken to task when readers and critics reject a translation strategy or result, even when it is the product of an author's or editor's decision rather than the translator's choice. The author *can* at times be implicated, however. When a Jorge Luis Borges–Norman Thomas Di Giovanni translation collaboration fixed an inconsistency in the Spanish source text, it was met with protest, at which point Borges asserted his right to alter his own texts however he liked (Kristal 2002:14). Perhaps we can moderate this point to say that writers can close or alter texts, or offer definitive readings,

but readers may reject those readings in deference to the text as an autonomous source of authority. Consider the outcry from film enthusiasts when certain directors update, recut, colorize, or otherwise manipulate their films from the past. The sense of ownership in such cases has shifted.

What separates a good translation from a competent one, or from a great one, may not be in the writer's control. Sirkku Aaltonen argues in her essay, "The Translator in the Attic," that there is a mixed message, an ambiguity, surrounding authorial control over meaning: "A writer cannot claim to 'possess' one reading of the text although copyright law suggests that this is possible" (2000:109). We must ask where the authority of an author comes from. Who should have the last word on how a writer is translated? If one says, "the author," then we can test that hypothesis with the following reductio ad absurdum: any self-translating writer could never be held accountable for a poor translation because he or she could authorize the self-translation's success merely by pronouncing it successful.

3. *As a rule authors are not the ideal readers of their work in the target language of the translation.* Authors are often not the best critics of their own work, either in the source language or the target. In Isaac Asimov's science fiction story "The Immortal Bard" (1954), Shakespeare is brought back to life. He anonymously enrolls in a Shakespeare class, which he flunks. We can read the classic tale as a parody of the interpretation industry but it also has face value: there is no reason to believe that every Shakespeare is a Shakespearean scholar, as is often assumed.

4. *Not all writers have experience working with translation or translators.* For those writers being translated for the first time, there can be a sense of blindness. So great is the honor of being translated that the translation itself—its messiness, its heartbreaks, its elusiveness, its *work*—is secondary. Others, however, have a healthy "critical distance" (Weinberger 2002:115) and experience reading themselves in translation as familiarity-in-strangeness. Still others cannot warm to themselves as an alienated voice or they realize their weaknesses when they see the text as a translator sees it.[7]

In working with inexperienced or unrealistic writers, a translator bears the burden of *client education,* because the first client in the product chain and the first reader in the quality chain is the author-collaborator. For example, the author may think "Why does this translator ask so many questions? He must not be very competent. . . ." Experienced translators, of course, work from the opposite assumption, namely that good queries make for informed choices. Alternatively, an author may have naive ideas about translation, thinking that translation is not an act of creating or recreating but an act of rediscovering his or her preexisting voice in the target language, one that must simply be found and that will be recognized when heard.

5. *Affinity and friendship with a living author do not necessarily result in good translation.* Note this excerpt from an interview with a female Chinese author Xue Xinran (Pellatt et al. 2010:128–29; Xinran is her "nom de plume"):

> Interviewer: So far all your translators have been women. Would you have a man to do your translation work or would you rather stay with women, because you feel they empathize better?
>
> Xinran: For me, getting a male translator? No way! The reason is that I believe, even if we try very hard to understand each other, physically and mentally we are completely different selves.

A number of presuppositions can be plumbed here. First, there is the "natural" assumption that close identity between author and translator will be superior (an assumption demolished in Borges's story, "Pierre Menard, Author of Don Quixote" [1962]). Moreover, we see here the gendered imperatives legitimating representation.

In the interview with Xinran quoted above, the author asserts the existence of an identity for both author and translator, independent of the text, that is gender-based and relevant to translation ("we are completely different selves").[8] Xinran's remarks reveal a presupposition seldom made explicit: It is the *writer* who is explicitly adhering to and enforcing a norm of identification.

Mutual respect, understanding, and kindred spirit in translation collaborations are commonly extolled. Pontiero relates the intimate nature of the duties tied to the translator's task: "writers frequently betray certain insecurities which transform the translator into confidant, psychiatrist, and even guru" (1997:64). But what does the mythos of the agreeable author or translator say about the translation itself?

The translation process under such conditions may be pleasant, but is it more rigorous? In *The Translator's Invisibility* Lawrence Venuti casts a withering gaze at what he calls simpatico, the identification and sympathy shared by author and translator, which to this day dominates ideas about translation.

With simpatico he warns us "the translation process can be seen as a veritable recapitulation of the creative process by which the original came into existence; and when the translator is assumed to participate vicariously in the author's thoughts and feelings, the translated text is read as the transparent expression of authorial psychology or meaning" (1995:274). In other words the simpatico model enacts a pragmatics of the intentional fallacy: *If I can just see how the writer goes about her day, I can inhabit her knowingness and project her voice.* The problem, as Venuti concludes, is that the simpatico voice is "always recognized as the author's, never as a translator's, nor even as some hybrid of the two" (1995:274). A corollary: *Author-translator dissent—or different world-experience—does not doom a translation.*

6. *Collaboration may complicate or dilute a translation, whatever the collaborative relationship, and play havoc with a translator-author's own literary voice.* Literary history is littered with empathetic collaborations that nevertheless were perceived as a threat to the development of the translator's writing. Gertrude Stein's translation of George Hugnet's "Enfances" is an example. We can see the misshaping influence the translation exerted on her own style and habit of thought: "[The translation] left Stein unsure of her own voice. . . . Translating 'Enfances' required her to follow the words, the forms, the mind of another, already formulated. The fact that Hugnet's poems were inappropriate for her ways with words merely dramatized what under any circumstances would have been difficult. The discrepancy between her voice and his in 'Enfances' left her disabled" (Dydo and Rice 2003:322).

7. A corollary of the previous point is that *writers often don't have the skills in the target language to collaborate* on a microtextual level. This inability can create a barrier, or a diffusion of authority. Translators have received correspondence from authors that make this all too clear ("My daughter spent a year in the United States, and she wonders if your use of 'enamored of' is correct. See her list of questions attached.")

T. S. Eliot's prefaces to his translation of St.-John Perse's *Anabase* from French leave a suggestive trace of this dynamic and of how it affects the internal balance of power in the collaboration. The 1959 version of the poem features three prefaces by Eliot, from 1930, 1949, and 1958. In the 1930 preface, by far the longest, Eliot lavishes encomiums and offers justifications of the writer's method, sequences, and poetic logic. The prefatory words end with a kind of letter of introduction to the "half-translator": "The author of this poem is, even in the most practical sense, an authority on the Far East; he has lived there, as well as in the tropics. As for the translation, it would not be even so satisfactory as it is, if the author had not collaborated with me to such an extent as to be half-translator. He has, I can testify, a sensitive and intimate knowledge of the English language, as well as a mastery of his own" (Eliot 1959c:11–12). In the preface to the revised edition (1959a), we meet a chastened, confessional Eliot with a new authorial agenda:

> When this translation was made, St.-John Perse was little known outside of France. The translator, perhaps for the reason that he was introducing the poem to the English-speaking public, was then concerned, here and there, less with rendering the exact sense of a phrase, than with coining some phrase in English, which might have equivalent value; he may even have taken liberties in the interest of originality, and sometimes interposed his own idiom between author and reader. (1959a:13)

Eliot argues that the aim of his translation was "only to assist the English-speaking reader who wishes to approach the French text" (ibid.). He concedes the need for improvement, and then identifies the impetus for it: "the translation may still serve its purpose. But at this stage it was felt that a greater fidelity to the exact meaning, a more literal translation, was what was needed. I have corrected not only my own licences, but several positive errors and mistakes. In this revision I have depended heavily upon the recommendations of the author, *whose increasing mastery of English has enabled him to detect faults previously unobserved . . .*" (1959a:13; emphasis added; see also Folkart 2007:ch. 6). By the third edition Eliot's preface consists of a mere three lines: "The alterations to the English text of this edition have been made by the author himself, and tend to make the translation more literal than in previous editions. T. S. Eliot, 1958" (1959b:15). Placed in dialogue, these prefaces dramatize the birth of an author's critical consciousness, which coincides proportionally with the translator's progressively reduced role. The author begins as a "half-translator" and emerges as an editor, an autonomous reader of himself. What would Eliot's strategy have been had the author always known English well? We'll never know, but we can surmise.

Translating the Dead

> You might think that translating the dead gives you a whole lot of freedom
> ... [but] in fact there are crowds of people looking over your shoulder. ...
> Translating a dead man means stepping very warily through a minefield
> littered with the debris of another time and another translation.
> —Richard Philcox, "On Retranslating Fanon"

I prefer my authors dead. Every translation conference features some variation on this remark. What is the source of its humor? Perhaps the quip is funny for its ghoulish irreverence and for its inversion of the perceived author-translator power hierarchy. Perhaps it exorcizes translators' fears and misgivings about live authors (the living are an unreasonable lot; the living thwart literary license; the living are contingent, unproven), whether or not these feelings are warranted.

Jacek Laskowski has proposed a tripartite typology in reference to playwriting: "Translating the famous dead, the dead obscure, and the living" (Laskowski 1996). For the "dead obscure," getting translated is a problem. In this sense we might consider translating the dead as a form of *advocacy translation.* For the "famous dead," the immortals, the problem is that of *retranslation.* Instead of constructing an image, the translator must reconstruct one, and position the text within the constellation of already existing translations. A dead writer, then, can have multiple "source texts," as Laskowski explains.[9] Geoffrey Wall's introduction to his *Madame Bovary* illustrates this point. He argues that:

> [t]ranslating afresh the already translated classic text, the translator is drawn into dialogue with his or her precursors. Though I was working on different principles, and though I found I eventually disagreed with some of their most cherished effects, I have profited from the *posthumous conversation* of three previous translators . . . (Wall 1992:xlii; qtd. in Salama-Carr 2000:8; emphasis added)

Wall's statement introduces us to the trope of communication with the dead, here represented as a (two-way) conversation. An important observation can be made: the living party in this conversation is the most privileged for she can see the farthest. However, the benefits of existing translations are often offset by burdens, including the following: What claim do older translations have on the new one? Can a translator afford to ignore them for fear of "contamination"?

One of the two poles of translating the dead is suggested by the epigraph to this section. Translating the dead is claustrophobic, hazardous. It is claustrophobic because of the vested interests that have accumulated and the claims that have been staked; it is hazardous because those interests have constructed a sacred image, an aura. The posthumous accrual of an aura is often cultivated by the executor of the author's literary estate, who can be, in Eliot Weinberger's words, "the author's only strictly fundamentalist reader; the one who believes in the absolute inviolability of every word the author wrote. Some of them . . . refuse to allow any translations whatsoever, for they are blasphemies against the sacred scripture" (1998:235–36n2). In this conception the executor is not so much a reader as a conservator or, less generously, a tomb guardian. At the other pole of dead writers lies the orphan awaiting adoption: "All they have, if they are lucky, is a translator. And they cannot even defend themselves against him" (Halkin 1983:88). Plato has Socrates say something similar about writing in the *Phaedrus:* "when [speeches] have been once written down they are tumbled about anywhere among those who may or may not understand them, and know not to whom they should reply, to whom not: and, if they are maltreated or abused, they have no parent to protect them; and they cannot protect or defend themselves" (n.p.).[10] Pairing writing with orphanhood, of course, expresses anxiety about posterity, the fragility of our meanings across time, and not being understood, or worst of all, being desecrated in memory. The translator in this context appears as either "keeper of the flame" or profaner of the dead.

On the face of it, translating the dead would seem to be a simple matter of writing by proxy with no resistance: the author is forever mute and cannot protest. There is a sense of communal ownership of their texts if they are now public domain authors. But one can say the same things about certain living writers who do not have a self-identity that includes an image of themselves as translated authors or the skills to collaborate or cotranslate, or who have jealous guardians and keepers, some in the symbolic order (critics, translators) and others in the legal domain (publishers, ex-spouses). But the literary output of a dead writer is not always fixed—new manuscripts may be found, new biographies written, and new criticism penned, producing disjunctures and dissonances. Approaches to translating the dead, therefore, may require a translator to adapt his or her identity. That decision may be irrational or intuitive, allowing for such paradoxes as *knowing the dead,* as we will see below. Translators of the living make far fewer claims of "empathic transcendence"—to use Sandra Gilbert's (1972:228) term for a Whitmanesque expansion of consciousness into the Self, which here stands for an embracing of the author-consciousness in one's own. Mystifications of living-dead communication, however, are commonplace, as the following passage suggests: "It is not fanciful . . . to see the translator as a shaman, in the sense that he or she opens a conduit between the present and the past that emphasizes the aliveness of both now and then. It is impossible, of course, to raise the dead, but translation offers us the possibility of reviving dead authors temporarily—always temporarily—through the rituals of performance and acts of radical recreation . . ." (Johnston 2008:70). Through metonymy we perform a simple transference of properties: *Writers are living and dead, so texts are living and dead.*[11] Far from the trope of translator as empty vessel, the translator in this passage is figured as a kind of zombie reanimator, the translation itself as mad science in a relativized time and space. Literary afterlife, according to this discourse, is sporadic, recursive, dependent upon the ritualistic, mythical time in which a work's performance is reenacted. But in this conception the dead come back as something else, their "aliveness" placed in the service of the living. In this light the elegiac undercurrent to Allen Tate's observation that "the literature of the past lives in the literature of the present and nowhere else; . . . it is all present literature" (2008:48) can be given a more sinister reading: The present can be seen as a death warrant for literature of the past as autonomous artifacts.

The mirror image of this conceit of translation as life-giving is also commonplace. In this view, translation is framed as a sapping of vital energy, a cannibalistic "feeding off the dead." The translator "dies" so the source author can "live": "[Translation is] a process whereby the original author or text is brought to life, resurrected, through a *depletion of the author's [i.e. translator's] vitality,* or more seriously, through a reification, a deadening, of his native language" (Tiffany 1995:191; qtd. in Katz 2007:125; emphasis added). Similarly, in the context of a discussion of Jack Spicer's Lorca poems, Daniel Katz notes, "If the 'original' text can be seen as a 'succubus' or 'parasite' feeding off the vitality of the living translator, the reverse is equally true, for the translator is a consummate 'grave-robber'" (Katz 2007:125). The translator's figuration as zombie master on the one hand, and as "host" to the dead "parasite" on the other, shows the ambivalence that exists about translating the dead. Ultimately, the act of translating dead writers has entered the imaginary as a transgressive act, a violation of an unwritten code, a boundary demarcating "natural" and "unnatural" translations.

How ironic, then, that trafficking with the dead has taken root simultaneously as a metanarrative, we might say, about all writing. Writing—translating—is writing *against death:* "all writing of the narrative kind, and perhaps all writing, is motivated, deep down, by a fear of and fascination with mortality, by a desire to make the risky trip to the underworld, and to bring something or someone back from the dead" (Atwood 2002:156). For Foucault the idea of writing as monument, as resurrection, has been replaced; writing, he notes, "has become linked to sacrifice" (1977:117); further, he observes, "where a work had the duty of creating immortality, it now attains the right to kill, to become the murderer of its author" (117). The writing subject effaces his or her particularities and is reduced to the discursive, the "author-function" (138), "a victim of his own writing" (117), or, as this Foucauldian phrase is better known proverbially, "the dead man in the game of writing."

Moreover, Foucault contends that when authors entered the system of property, discourses took on authors, and thus the authors could be transgressed, inasmuch as their creations began to be linked to their names. Could transgression of the dead author have arisen in part from anxieties over the instability inherent in the new poststructuralist idea of the author? Translation's subversive effects on authorial integrity perhaps reach their peak in Nabokov's well-known "still life" of the translator-ghoul's handiwork: "On a platter / A poet's pale and glaring head, / A parrot's screech, a monkey's chatter, / And profanation of the dead" (1955:34). Here it is the translator who *kills, zoomorphizes,* and *desacralizes,* a fuller series of crimes than mere desecration, as it adds murder and dehumanization. Or as another translator of the dead muses, "how does one distinguish between 'touching up' and vandalization?" (Halkin 1983:83). The burden of the diachronic translator is hindsight, the accursed sense that *we know more,* that we can see flaws made more evident by time, sometimes *from* time—that is, flaws shared by a whole era. Hillel Halkin sums this up in a devastating line about a beloved author whom he translated, warts and all: "He needed an editor fifty years ago, not a translator now" (1983:83). The sacred must give way to the profane because the translator deals close up where the aura—the "unique apparition of a distance," in Benjamin's (2003:255) phrase—cannot thrive.[12]

But the dead writer has an aura for the *reader* if not always for the translator.[13] David Morley writes, "if the host is dead, you can be sure that all the flaws of the work will be attributed to the living writer [i.e., the adapter or translator] and all its worth to the dead writer" (2007:73). Laskowski points to "new plays disguised as translations" emerging through the carte blanche known as the *version* (1996:188). This kind of aura-borrowing often obscures the humbler origins of a work, much in the pseudotranslation tradition—consider MacPherson's *Ossian*—though the motives may be different. The idea of the aura (Greek for "air, breath") brings us full circle to the human and to *voice*. And voice in turn brings us back around to the disputed text—for *whose* voice is it that we hear in translation? As Richard Pevear (2007:54) puts it, "A translation of mine, if it has any coherence or authenticity as an original text, will have *my* voice in it. There's no way I can get out of that, otherwise it won't have any voice at all."

The other side of this question is the dissolution of the writer's self into the common cultural stock. In this conception when an author dies, what follows is "a surrendering of the work to the flux and play of transformation . . . within a more generally held and plural sense of language and culture" (de Kock 2003:349). This idea of an ego-unbounded work accounts for some translators and stage directors adapting texts without compunction, perhaps in ways not available when working with living authors.[14] Another kind of communal ownership is displayed in Chaucer's *Troilus and Criseyde,* which came from a tradition in which no distinction was made between authorship and adaptation (Brown 2002:207). In death the common possession is more likely to be accompanied by collective agency. A multiply translated text is located in a diffused way *across* many texts rather than *in* one, and in a way that presents the author and authorship as constructs, potentialities variously activated but never exhausted. What James Brown writes of adaptation could easily be applied to translation proper: "one glimpses authorship as the realization of a kind of social and cultural potential—as never purely individual, and seldom purely dissolved in the play of impersonal forces" (2002:224).

The living and the dead authors both throw into question our ideas about authorship and identity, the relationships between texts and writers, translation ethics, and the ways that writing, meaning, and power intersect. At the heart of these problems lie the unanswered questions: Under what conditions do translators speak and under whose authority? The authority behind a translator's interventionism can take many permutations; it may be conferred (from a writer's heirs), negotiated (with a writer), or assumed de facto (of a work in the public domain or of an authorless text). It may come with an author's deterrence or acquiescence, contribution or hindrance. Translatorial authority contends with other authorities, both authorial and textual, particularly now that the role granted the reader has enlarged (as reading is no longer a search and recovery of an author's meaningful inscriptions), and now that the conception of the writer has expanded.[15]

The author or "author" in representation is the translator's first problem. The problem extends to the paratextual, the intertextual, and the intratextual, as the author or specter of the author looms in and around the text. The translator hence does not merely speak, but speaks relationally: *with, through, to, from,* and, historically, even *for* and *over* the author. Voicings that mark different sites of enunciation—most prominently, that of the implied translator—are crafted for different narrative purposes, complicating further any naive conceptions of an author and a translator simply and univocally meeting in discourse.

Collaborations sublime or disastrous take place between translators and their authors, or, from the authors' point of view, authors and their translators. Both phrasings are especially valid in view of the uncertainties about the translator's positionality. No fictional text in contemporary times expresses this anxiety, in my view, better than Barbara Wilson's "Mi Novelista."[16] The protagonist translator of the tale, Cassandra Reilly, laments not being a "real writer," and so invents a South American writer, Elvira Montalban, and a biography for the "author" that has more cachet than the translator's own. She then writes—"translates"—the writer's work, while slowly becoming Montalban, Spanish accent and all. The invented writer remains mysterious to the outside world, working reclusively in Iceland (where Reilly actually moves); the writer's book is released in English to great acclaim, while the pseudotranslator frets that the invented writer's fame "would plummet like a stone if it were revealed that she was really an Irish-Catholic girl from Kalamazoo, Michigan" (1998:205). Someone claiming to be Montalban, then, impossibly, surfaces in Madrid, and the Spanish "original," unusual in that it appears after the translation, takes Spain by storm. Reilly sets up a meeting, wondering who she could possibly be. The imposter writer turns out to be Maria Escobar, a former acquaintance. She confronts Reilly, claiming the translator had stolen her life story for the book. Hearing Escobar's voice was to the translator like "an inner voice of mine made visible" (213), though she, Reilly, had no stories of her own and had even been "inventing [herself] . . . as a translator" (214). Escobar reclaims her words and the authorial role of Elvira Montalban. When the pair's editor happens by their table, Escobar, now Elvira Montalban, introduces Reilly as her translator-collaborator and announces her new project, tentatively called *The Translator*. Wilson's parable, in sum, adds to the translational "I is an other," a subversive, "the other is an I." Whose "I" is whose? This can only be author trouble.

Notes

1. Ellmann writes, "We discriminate against the dead . . . because we—unlike the ancient Greeks—deny their existence" (1990:193; qtd. in Zilcosky 2002:633).

2. I realize the traps inherent in writing "for" a readership, though a translator working a full generation after *Skopostheorie* cannot well say "I translate for myself" in the way a writer probably still can say "I write for myself." A translation is *from* somewhere, *for* someone. Landow (1992:89) argues in his vision of collaborative writing that *documents* can collaborate; I define collaboration more traditionally to necessarily include subjects, document users.

3. The decentering technique was first theorized in Werner and Campbell (1970).

4. German author Uwe Timm explains with organic metaphors that texts are "living organisms. . . . As long as an author is still alive he can still make changes. And the great thing is that this organism lives on in the translation. . . . It's truly a reanimation, a further opportunity for change" (see Schulte 2003:7). Critics in textual criticism have questioned locating "final" intentionality in an author's most recent version of a text, citing outside forces that can motivate changes. Consistent with this orientation, Bornstein (1993:176) sees the text of a work in the sum of its iterations during its publication history.

5. A case study illustrating this point can be found in Cullhed (1998). The Swedish translator of Ernesto Sábato's *Sobre héroes y tumbas* [On heroes and tombs] added a postscript to the novel, indicating that Sábato "is anxious about being well translated, not betrayed. At his request I have cut out various passages from the original text: he found them too local, too exotic for a remote Swedish reader. Sábato does not want to write folklore; he wants to be universal, and so he is" (Cullhed 1998:67).

6. According to Machan, *authority* "can be used in reference to the individual or individuals who created (or 'authored') a literary work; to the legal or cultural entitlement certain individuals or institutions may have to a particular work or text (their 'authoritativeness'); to the claim imputed to certain texts to represent accurately the original texts from which they are judged to derive (their 'authenticity'); to the validity of what a work or text states about a certain topic and of its right to make such statements in the first place (its 'authorization')" (1994:93).

7. Flaws in literary works are discovered through the close reading translation provides, though the flaws are not apprised uniformly, and theoretically their impact on reception as a whole may be great enough, after other conditions and features of the literary system are factored in, to affect the success or failure of the translation and even serve as an edit to an original work in progress, as we saw in our discussion of decentering. Eliot Weinberger relates how "[a] few times, when I was translating poems that had not yet been published in book form, [poet Octavio] Paz changed a word or two of a line of the original after seeing the translation—*as another reading often points out or magnifies flaws in the original*" (1998:239; emphasis added). Similarly, Ezra Pound praises Lawrence Binyon's *Inferno* for revealing the source text's flaws with "honesty" and "transparency" rather than dressing Dante up in the ceremonial

garb often given him: "[Binyon] has carefully preserved all the faults of his original. This in the circumstances is the most useful thing he could have done. [The multiple Dantes existing in English preserve the] faults alien to the original, and therefore of no possible use to the serious reader who wants to understand Dante [. . .] Binyon has got rid of pseudo-magniloquence . . ." (1954:202–5). Logically we can proceed as follows. If the flaws exist in the source text and we accept that translation is a close reading, then these flaws cannot only be apparent in the Italian.

There are cases of translators who take the perceived flaws of the original to pursue unrealized potentialities or otherwise "redeem" the work: "the translation even seems to highlight the weaknesses of the original by proposing alterations; in this respect, it corresponds to Bloom's theory of the shaping of a poet's talent. Hughes counters García Lorca's dark sublime with sublimity of his own, creating a work that outdoes the original poem in its brooding ominousness" (Reddick 2013:692).

8. This idea recalls Georges Poulet, who wrote *criticism of consciousness*, which argued that a critic (translator?) must uncover an author's being or unitary selfhood, a presence available through a sympathetic, reconstructive reading of an author's whole oeuvre.

9. For more on this topic, see Berman (1990:1–7), who argues for retranslation for historical and reception-oriented reasons, but also because of the retranslator's necessary distance for overcoming deficient, "entropic" first translations. Isabel Alvarez-Borland (1998) uses a felicitous phrase for this trajectory from writer in history to a temporal distance through literature: *from person to persona*. Retranslation is one agency of an eternally renewed persona.

10. In Kurt Vonnegut's novel, *Galápagos*, a hand-held translation device can translate 1,000 languages, but "the only language it is ever called upon to translate is Kankabono, which is not in its memory banks. Although it is full of quotations, the only quotations it ever provides are grotesquely inappropriate to its circumstances . . ." (Boon 2001:131). The production of a repertoire of world knowledge breaks down into a context in which utterances once marked by genius subvert their own original meanings, are misappropriated by technology, and rendered banal. Plato's notion of the vulnerability of words extends to translations and to translators.

11. Genette's (1997) terms *transtextuality* and *textual transcendence*—the set of relationships of a text with other texts—include pastiche, parody, intertext, paratext, and translation. No distinction is made with respect to the text's authors. The idea of "textual transcendence," however, echoes a belief in the enduring author, in trans-subjectivity. Benjamin's image of an "afterlife" (*Überleben*), after all, is borrowed from religion and metaphysics. It has become a critical commonplace to describe a translation as "breathing new life" into a work. Note, finally, the title of a recent study, referencing Ezekial 37:3, which points to renewed life: *Can These Bones Live? Translation, Survival, and Cultural Memory* (Brodski 2007).

12. "The essentially distant is the inapproachable: inapproachability is in fact a primary quality of the cult image" (Benjamin 1997:148). Aura is tied to authority, existence in a place and time, and authenticity; we can argue that dead writers are more auratic in that their work, as McCaffey and Gregory phrase it, is "generated from a

distinct consciousness that exists but once, and briefly" (1987:5). This points to the fetishizing impulse of Benjamin and his followers.

13. See Adorno (1999) for his critique of Benjamin's conception of aura.

14. The caveat here, however, is that estates can control the way a play is produced, for example, even beyond the life of the author.

15. See, for example, Landow (1992:91) in which the author is reconfigured as a centerless or decentered network.

16. My thanks to Carol Maier for introducing me to this story.

Works Cited

Aaltonen, Sirkku. 2000. *Time-Sharing on Stage: Drama Translation in Theatre and Society.* Clevedon, UK: Multilingual Matters.

Adorno, Theodor W. 1999. *Aesthetic Theory.* London: Athlone.

Alvarez-Borland, Isabel. 1998. *Cuban-American Literature of Exile: From Person to Persona.* Charlottesville: University Press of Virginia.

Asimov, Isaac. 1954. "The Immortal Bard." *Universe Science Fiction* 5 (May): 97–99.

Atwood, Margaret. 2002. *Negotiating with the Dead.* Cambridge and New York: Cambridge University Press.

Benjamin, Walter. 1997. *Charles Baudelaire: A Lyric Poet in the Era of High Capitalism.* London: Verso.

Benjamin, Walter. 2003. "The Work of Art in the Age of Its Technological Reproducibility." In Walter Benjamin, *Selected Writings,* Vol. 4, edited by Howard Eiland and Michael W. Jennings, 251–83. Cambridge, Mass.: Harvard University Press.

Berman, Antoine. 1990. "La retraduction comme espace de la traduction." *Palimpsestes* 13(4): 1–7.

Berubé, Michael. 1998. *The Employment of English: Theory, Jobs, and the Future of Literary Studies.* New York: New York University Press.

Boon, Kevin A. 2001. *At Millennium's End: New Essays on the Work of Kurt Vonnegut.* Albany: State University of New York Press.

Borges, Jorge Luis. 1962. "Pierre Menard, Author of *Don Quijote.*" In *Ficciones,* translated by Anthony Kerrigan, 45–56. New York: Grove Press.

Borges, Jorge Luis. 1967. "Borges and I." In *A Personal Anthology,* translated by Anthony Kerrigan, 200–201. New York: Grove Press.

Bornstein, George. 1993. "What Is the Text of a Poem by Yeats?" In *Palimpsest: Editorial Theory in the Humanities,* edited by G. Bornstein and R. G. Williams, 167–94. Ann Arbor: University of Michigan Press.

Brodski, Bella. 2007. *Can These Bones Live? Translation, Survival, and Cultural Memory.* Stanford, Calif.: Stanford University Press.

Brown, James. 2002. "Adapting Authorship: Beyond Sovereignty and Death." *Cadernos de Tradução* 1(7): 203–27.

Bush, Peter. 1997. "Literary Critics' and Translators' Comments on the Translations:

The Translator as Arbiter." In *The Translator's Dialogue: Giovanni Pontiero*, edited by Pilar Orero and Juan C. Sager, 115–26. Amsterdam: John Benjamins.

Castellanos Moya, Carlos. 2009. "Sobre el mito bolaño." Available at: www.lanacion.com.ar/nota.asp?nota_id=1176451 (accessed 22 February 2011).

Cullhed, Anders. 1998. "Recognition or Estrangement: Discussion of Françcoise Wuilmart's Paper, 'Normalization and the Translation of Poetry.'" In *Translation of Poetry and Poetic Prose*, edited by S. Allén, 64–71. Stockholm: World Scientific Publishing.

de Kock, Leon. 2003. "Translating *Triomf*: The Shifting Limits of 'Ownership' in Literary Translation or: Never Translate Anyone But a Dead Author." *Journal of Literary Studies* 19(3/4): 345–59.

Dryden, John. 1821. "Dedication of the *Æneis* (1697)." In *Works*, Vol. 14, edited by Walter Scott, 223. Edinburgh: Constable.

Dydo, Ulla E., and William Rice. 2003. *Gertrude Stein: The Language That Rises: 1923–1934*. Evanston, Ill.: Northwestern University Press.

Eco, Umberto. 2004. *Mouse or Rat? Translation as Negotiation*. London: Phoenix.

Eliot, T. S. 1919. "Tradition and the Individual Talent." *Egoist* 6(4): 54–55.

Eliot, T. S. 1959a. "Note to the Revised Edition." In *Anabasis, a Poem by St.-John Perse*, 3rd ed., translated by T. S. Eliot, 13. London: Faber and Faber.

Eliot, T. S. 1959b. "Note to the Third Edition." In *Anabasis, a Poem by St.-John Perse*, 3rd ed., translated by T. S. Eliot, 15. London: Faber and Faber.

Eliot, T. S. 1959c. "Preface." In *Anabasis, a Poem by St.-John Perse*, 3rd ed., translated by T. S. Eliot, 9–12. London: Faber and Faber.

Ellmann, Maud. 1990. "The Ghosts of Ulysses." In *James Joyce: The Artist and the Labyrinth*, edited by Augustin Martin, 193–227. London: Ryan.

Filipova, Filipina. 2011. "The Death of the Translator." In *Translatum: The Greek Translation Vortal*. Available at: www.translatum.gr/journal/4/death-of-the-translator.htm (accessed 19 February 2011).

Folkart, Barbara. 2007. *Second Finding: A Poetics of Translation*. Ottawa: University of Ottawa Press.

Foucault, Michel. 1977. "What Is an Author?" In *Language, Counter-Memory, Practice: Selected Essays and Interviews*, edited by Donald F. Bouchard, 113–38. Ithaca, N.Y.: Cornell University Press.

Fresán, Rodrigo. 2006. *Kensington Gardens*. Translated by Natasha Wimmer. New York: Farrar, Straus and Giroux.

Genette, Gérard. 1997. *Palimpsests: Literature in the Second Degree*. Lincoln: University of Nebraska Press.

Gilbert, Sandra. 1972. *Acts of Attention: The Poems of D. H. Lawrence*. Ithaca, N.Y.: Cornell University Press.

Halkin, Hillel. 1983. "On Translating the Living and the Dead." *Prooftexts* 3(1): 73–90.

Heim, Michael Henry. 2007. "Translating Chekhov's Plays: A Collaboration between Translator, Director, and Actors." In *Chekhov the Immigrant: Translating a Cultural Icon*, edited by Michael C. Finke and Julie de Sherbinin, 83–88. Bloomington, Ind.: Slavica Publishers.

Howard, Matthew. 1997. "Stranger Than Fiction." In *Lingua Franca* (June/July): 41–49.

Johnston, David. 2008. "Lope de Vega in English: The Historicized Imagination." In *The Comedia in English: Translation and Performance*, edited by Susan Paun de García and Donald R. Larson, 66–82. Woodbridge, UK, and Rochester, N.Y.: Tamesis.

Katz, Daniel. 2007. *American Modernism's Expatriate Scene: The Labor of Translation.* Edinburgh: Edinburgh University Press.

Keeley, Edmund. 2000. *On Translation: Reflections and Conversations.* Amsterdam: Harwood Academic Publishers.

Kristal, Efraín. 2002. *Invisible Work: Borges and Translation.* Nashville: Vanderbilt University Press.

Kundera, Milan. 1985. *Jacques and His Master: An Homage to Diderot in Three Acts.* Translated by Michael Henry Heim. New York: Harper and Row.

Landow, George P. 1992. *Hypertext: The Convergence of Contemporary Critical Theory and Technology.* Baltimore: Johns Hopkins University Press.

Laskowski, Jacek. 1996. "Translating the Famous Dead, the Dead Obscure, and the Living." In *Stages of Translation,* edited by D. Johnston, 187–98. Bath, UK: Absolute Classics.

Levine, Suzanne Jill. 2009. *The Subversive Scribe.* Champaign, Ill.: Dalkey Archive Press.

Lewis, Philip E. 1985. "The Measure of Translation Effects." In *Difference in Translation,* edited by J. F. Graham, 31–62. Ithaca, N.Y.: Cornell University Press.

Loffrado, Eugenia, and Manuel Perteghella. 2006. *Translation and Creativity: Perspectives on Creative Writing and Translation Studies.* London and New York: Continuum.

Lunsford, Andrea A., and Lisa Ede. 1994. "Collaborative Authorship and the Teaching of Writing." In *The Construction of Authorship: Textual Appropriation in Law and Literature,* edited by Martha Woodmansee and Peter Jaszi, 417–38. Durham, N.C.: Duke University Press.

Machan, Tim William. 1994. *Textual Criticism and Middle English Texts.* Charlottesville: University Press of Virginia.

McCaffey, Larry, and Sinda Gregory. 1987. *Alive and Writing: Interviews with American Authors of the 1980s.* Urbana: University of Illinois Press.

Morley, David. 2007. *Cambridge Introduction to Creative Writing.* Cambridge and New York: Cambridge University Press.

Nabokov, Vladimir. 1955. "On Translating 'Eugene Onegin.'" *The New Yorker* (8 January): 34.

Ovidius Naso, Publius. 1717. *Ovid's Metamorphoses in Fifteen Books: Translated by the Most Eminent Hands.* London: Printed for Jacob Tonson at Shakespear's-Head over-against Katharine-Street in the Strand.

Pevear, Richard, et al. 2007. "Forum on Translation." In *Chekhov the Immigrant: Translating a Cultural Icon,* edited by Michael C. Finke and Julie de Sherbinin, 29–66. Bloomington, Ind.: Slavica Publishers.

Pellatt, Valerie, Liu Tin-Kun, and Eric Liu. 2010. *Thinking Chinese Translation: A Course in Translation Method: Chinese to English.* London and New York: Routledge.

Philcox, Richard. 2004. "On Retranslating Fanon, Retrieving a Lost Voice." In Frantz Fanon, *The Wretched of the Earth*, 241–51. Translated by Richard Philcox. New York: Grove Press.

Plato. 2012. *Phaedrus*. Translated by B. Jowett. Available at: http:ebooks.adelaide.edu.au/p/plato/p71phs/ (accessed 1 November 2011).

Pontiero, Giovanni. 1997. "The Task of the Literary Translator." In *The Translator's Dialogue: Giovanni Pontiero*, edited by Pilar Orero and Juan C. Sager, 55–66. Amsterdam and Philadelphia: John Benjamins.

Pound, Ezra. 1954. "Hell." In *Literary Essays of Ezra Pound*, 201–13. Norfolk, Conn.: New Directions.

Pym, Anthony. 1993. "Negotiation Theory as an Approach to Translation History. An Inductive Lesson from Fifteenth-Century Castile." In *Translation and Knowledge*, edited by Yves Gambier and Jorma Tommola, 27–39. Turku: University of Turku Centre for Translation and Interpreting.

Raffel, Burton. 1988. *The Art of Translating Poetry*. University Park: Pennsylvania State University Press.

Reddick, Yvonne. 2013. "'After Lorca': Ted Hughes and the Influence of Federico García Lorca." *The Modern Language Review* 108(3): 681–99.

Robinson, Douglas. 2001. *Who Translates? Translator Subjectivities Beyond Reason*. Albany: State University of New York Press.

Salama-Carr, Myriam. 2000. *On Translating French Literature and Film*. Vol. 2. Amsterdam and Atlanta, Ga.: Rodopi.

Schulte, Rainer. 2003. "Interview with Breon Mitchell and Ewe Timm: Collaboration Between Translator and Author." *Translation Review* 66(1): 1–7.

Tate, Allen. 2008. "Miss Emily and the Bibliographer." In *Praising It New: The Best of the New Criticism*, edited by Garrick Davis, 39–48. Athens, Ohio: Swallow Press/Ohio University Press.

Tiffany, Daniel. 1995. *Radio Corpse: Imagism and the Cryptaesthetic of Ezra Pound*. Cambridge, Mass.: Harvard University Press.

Venuti, Lawrence. 1995. *The Translator's Invisibility*. London and New York: Routledge.

Vonnegut, Kurt. 1985. *Galápagos*. New York: Delacorte Press/Seymour Lawrence.

Wall, Geoffrey. 1992. "A Note on the Translation." In Gustave Flaubert, *Madame Bovary*, xlii. Harmondsworth: Penguin.

Wechsler, Robert. 1998. *Performing without a Stage: The Art of Literary Translation*. North Haven, Conn.: Catbird Press.

Weinberger, Eliot. 1998. "The Role of the Author in Translation." In *Translation of Poetry and Poetic Prose*, edited by S. Allén, 233–48. Stockholm: World Scientific Publishing.

Weinberger, Eliot. 2002. "Anonymous Sources: A Talk on Translators and Translation." In *Voice-overs: Translation and Latin American Literature*, edited by D. Balderston and Marcy E. Schwartz, 104–18. Albany: State University of New York Press.

Werner, Oswald, and Donald T. Campbell. 1970. "Translating, Working through Interpreters, and the Problem of Decentering." In *A Handbook of Method in Cultural*

Anthropology, edited by R. Naroll and R. Cohen, 398–420. New York: The Natural History Press.

Wilson, Barbara. 1998. "Mi Novelista." In *The Death of a Much-Travelled Woman: And Other Adventures with Cassandra Reilly,* 195–215. Chicago: Third Side Press.

Zilcosky, John. 2002. "Kakfa's Remains." In *Lost in the Archives,* edited by Rebecca Comay, 630–42. Toronto: Alphabet City.

Victory by Verse

Maria Tymoczko

For Carol Maier,
who knows how to set her right foot
on firm ground after being at sea.

Lebor Gabála Érenn ("the book of the taking of Ireland," commonly referred to as *The Book of Invasions*) is a medieval pseudohistory, an invented history of Ireland purporting to explain the prehistory of the island antecedent to the historical conditions in the early Middle Ages. The Irish (and earlier the British Celts) were motivated to create such a history after conversion to Christianity when they inherited the historical time line of the Bible and the late Roman universal histories found in the works of such authors as Origen and Eusebius, only to discover that there was no column in the synchronisms for their own nations' histories.[1]

The general framework of *Lebor Gabála* probably goes back to a prototype composed in the seventh century and was probably originally restricted to the postdiluvian history of the Milesians, the accepted ancestors of the Goidelic stock (the Gaels) in Ireland. It was eventually expanded by the reformulation of pre-Christian mythic narratives into a narrative series of settlements or "takings" of Ireland by contending groups of claimants, many of whom are in fact refigurations of pre-Christian supernatural beings, including the old gods (Macalister 1938–56:1.xxix–xxxiv). As it has come down to us, this invented history takes the form of a series of migrations to Ireland by various peoples who arrive by sea in fleets of boats, as did all the historical settlers or invaders of the island, including the fully historical Vikings (who came in waves from the end of the eighth century through the tenth), the forces of the Anglo-Norman Conquest (in 1169), and Cromwell's armies (in the seventeenth century). In the final taking of Ireland narrated in *Lebor Gabála,* the seer-poet (Irish *fili,* plural *filid*) and judge (Irish *brithem*) Amairgen wins Ireland for his people by speaking a short poem as he steps right foot forward from his boat onto the land, thus initiating the taking of the island for the Gaels. Because the Gaels subsequently held the island for centuries (to the present in fact), clearly the land welcomed this group of settlers, a point made explicit later in the narrative by an encounter of the Gaels with the eponynmous Ériu herself.[2]

We might well ask why Amairgen's poem is so compelling that Ireland accepts this man and his people. To understand the situation and translate the text, we must use our imaginations and perhaps feel the situation in our bodies, as Carol Maier suggests that translation requires. The utterance must have been loud enough to have been heard over waves and wind, beautiful enough to have been enticing, and forceful enough to have been compelling. The early Irish word for *poem* is *laíd,* which means "song" as well, so perhaps the poem is to be understood as having been accompanied by instrumental music, sung to a melody, or at the very least chanted. This aspect of early Irish poetry probably explains why Ireland can hear Amairgen's words over the tumbling of the pebbles on the beach and the waves striking the shore, not to mention the creaking of the ships, the lowering of the sails, and the sound of the wind. In addition the beauty and the force of the poem must be compelling and present to us in a translation.

Amairgen is a fili, a poet and a seer: the word *fili* in Irish is cognate with roots meaning "see." It implies the ability to see, perceive, and understand worldly and otherworldly domains, and to be intervenient between those realms. Amairgen is also a brithem, a judge, namely one who has the knowledge and insight to deliver astute judgments, to make valid and just assessments, and to proclaim truth. The filid, the poets in early Irish culture, had inherited some of the functions and roles of the pre-Christian druids, described by Classical writers, Caesar in particular, as possessing knowledge of the stars, the earth, "natural philosophy," and the gods.[3] Thus the poem should be not only beautiful but also just, conveying the poet's integrity and truthfulness. It should communicate a strong sense of the special knowledge and supernatural insights about the natural, human, and supernatural worlds attributed to the native learned classes of the Celts and indicate Amairgen's ability to shape and direct those worlds and to mediate among them.

The poem itself is short and not immediately prepossessing to a modern eye or ear, particularly in the existing translations. How can a translator solve the dilemma of the poem's appeal to Ireland and then translate the poem in such a way as to communicate its compelling quality to readers? This is the central problem that must be faced by a translator and this is how I began in translation studies: as a translator. Supported by a grant from the National Endowment for the Humanities, I translated two challenging early Irish texts called "The Death of CuRoi" and "The Death of CuChulainn," neither of which had been translated in its entirety.[4] In my translations I wanted the beauty, irony, humor, and emotional force of the tales to be apparent to readers, but I felt constrained by the crippling dominant standards of scholarly philological literalism then reigning in Celtic studies.

I was liberated from those standards by publishing my translations with Liam Miller of Dolmen Press, who had earlier published *The Táin* (1969/1970), a wonderful set of translations of Ulster Cycle stories by Thomas Kinsella. Kinsella set a new standard for translations of early Irish literature, capturing its many moods from sarcasm and sexually charged humor to tragedy that pierces the heart. My encounter with the tension between dominant scholarly canons of translation and the desire to represent the literary texture of early medieval Irish literature occurred before any of my theoretical and descriptive inquiries into translation. The difficulties and paradoxes involved in translating early Irish texts explain why much of my work in translation studies has used specific early Irish texts as concrete reference points in problematizing translation processes, analyzing translation products, and articulating the significance of translation in cultural contexts. My own involvement with the concrete work of translation is one important reason that I have valued conversations with Carol Maier for many years and why I am gripped by reading her work. Beauty, representation, obligation, ethics, power, cultural interface, and social roles have been leitmotifs of our shared discourse on translation.

One of the earliest texts I grappled with on a theoretical level is the poem spoken by Amairgen, who interpellates Ireland on behalf of his people. The body of Amairgen's poem is a series of statements about his own identity with the natural world, constituting a claim "to subsume all being within himself" (Mac Cana 1970:64). Following is a sample of the lines with a gloss translation.

Am gaéth i mmuir
Am tond trethan

Am fúaim mara . . .

I am wind on sea
I am wave of stormy seas
I am noise of sea . . .

A gloss translation of this sort does not provide an answer to the question of why the poem induces Ireland to accept Amairgen and the Gaels as her chosen people nor does it help us feel or imagine a solution to the dilemma. A simple gloss translation enacts and represents neither the beauty nor the force of the poem, nor does such a translation impress modern readers or listeners with Amairgen's presence, weight, insight, and judgment. The semiotic, cultural, and functional aspects of the text exceed its semantic impact in English.

A significant difficulty in translating Amairgen's poem results from the linguistic asymmetries in the expression of definite and indefinite nouns and articles in English and Irish. Very briefly, they are examples of contradictory usages that involve not only linguistic differences but contradictory logic as well. There are a number of asymmetries, including the existence of both definite and indefinite articles in English (*the* versus *a, an*), whereas Irish has only definite articles, using a zero-grade article for an indefinite noun, in addition to the word *óen,* "one, a single" (conveying a somewhat emphatic tone), to indicate a specifically defined singular entity. Moreover, in English the existential quantifier is generally expressed by an indefinite article ("there was a man"), whereas in Old Irish the existential quantifier is often expressed by the definite article (*in fer,* "the man").[5] In addition, in Irish the universal quantifier ("all Xs are such that Y is the case") is expressed by indefinite singular nouns (that is, a noun with zero-grade article) where English uses a variety of constructions to express the universal quantifier including (1) a singular noun with no article, (2) a singular noun with either a definite or indefinite article, and (3) plural nouns either without an article or with a definite article.[6]

An approach to translating Amairgen's poem has eluded me for decades and I have found no fully satisfactory solution to the questions the text raises for a translator. The poem remains a live translation problem for me, and it also reminds me that I am neither an expert linguist (a textual scholar who can establish a definitive source text for the poem that might help a translator in this instance), nor am I the sort of translator whose work might satisfy other translators sufficiently so that they cease to be haunted by the need to retranslate the poem themselves. In short the poem defeats me existentially. I have returned to Amairgen's poem over and over, wondering what sort of translation might do the job.

At some point in my struggle with the text, I had the thought that perhaps one solution to representing the multiple ways of expressing the meanings of the Irish poem in English, each with its own nuance, might be *to refuse to choose* from among the various English possibilities and to refuse to relegate the alternate readings to footnotes or silence. Rather I could present all the English meanings in series, giving the alternate readings seriatim, and arranging the translations of the poem in rising and falling order of strength and power (to the English speaker's ear), paying attention to the nuances of assertion and defamiliarization in the grammatical constructions. Such a representation of the poem would increase its length, but this could be a plus, adding gravitas to the translated text for a modern reader or listener. Such a refusal to choose— that is, the refusal to eliminate some of the communicative and semantic values of the text—is, of course, heresy for a translator: decisions and choices are the stock in trade of translators and have been seen as key in theoretical discourses about translation since the time of Roman Jakobson (1959), Willard V. O. Quine (1959), and Jiří Levý (1967). A refusal would therefore be a creative transgression or intervention, but it might be just and perhaps truthful. It could be thought of as an intervenient move to say no to choice when choice requires killing your darlings and those darlings convey the force of a text.

Below is the translation that resulted, preceded by a minimalist edition of the Irish text, which serves as a reference point for the translation.[7]

Ic tabairt a choisse dessi i nHerind asbert Amairgen Glúngel mac Miled in laídseo sís.

Am gáeth i mmuir.
Am tond trethan.
Am fúaim mara.
Am dam secht ndírend   5
Am séig i n-aill
Am dér gréne
Am caín lubae
Am torc ar gail
Am hé i llind   10

Am loch i mmaig
Am brí a ndaí
Am brí dánae
Am gai i fodb feras feochtu
Am dé delbas do chind codnu.   15

Coich é nod-gléith clochur slébe?
Cía ón cota-gair aesa éscai?
Cía dú i llaig funiud gréne?
Cía beir búar o thig Tethrach?
Cía daín?   20
Cía dé delbas faebru a ndind ailsiu?
Caínte im gaí, cainte gáithe.

Item Amairgen cecinit.

Íascach muir!
Mothach tír!   25
Tomaidm n-eisc
Íasc fo tuind
Lethach míl!
Portach láid
Tomaidm n-éisc   30
Íascach muir!

I cind trí lá ocus trí n-aidchi iar sein ro brissiset meic Miled cath Slébi Mis for demno.[8]

Following is my refusal to adopt a narrowed representation in English of the rich, multiple, and weighty meanings in Amairgen's early Irish poetry. It is a small rebellion against the constraints of inadequate linguistic options in the target language for expressing the meaning of a very foreign text, a text reminding us that time as well as space can bring us to a farther shore. I have seized the power of translators to move beyond the literal meaning of the words of a source text in favor of representing meaning at a higher order of textual organization, here both logical and literary (cf. Catford 1965). My translation attempts to represent the multiple textured meanings in Amairgen's sung poem as he seeks to gain Ireland's favor and win her acceptance for his people.

Putting his right foot on Ireland, Amairgen Glúngel, son of Mil, uttered this poem:

I am a wind on a sea
I am a wave of a stormy sea
I am a sound of a sea
I am a stag of seven points   5
I am a hawk on a cliff
I am a flash of sunshine
I am a fair plant
I am a boar in fury
I am a salmon in a pool   10
I am a loch on a plain
I am a hill of a rampart
I am a hill of poetry
I am a spear in victory spoils
I am a god who shapes antlers for a head.   15

I am winds on seas
I am waves of stormy seas
I am sounds of seas
I am stags of seven points
I am hawks on cliffs   20
I am flashes of sunshine
I am fair plants
I am boars in fury
I am salmon in pools
I am lochs on plains   25
I am hills of ramparts
I am hills of poetry
I am spears in victory spoils
I am gods who shape antlers for heads.

I am the winds on the seas   30
I am the waves of the stormy seas
I am the sounds of the seas
I am the stags of seven points
I am the hawks on the cliffs
I am the flashes of sunshine   35
I am the fair plants
I am the boars in fiery fights
I am the salmon in the pools
I am the lochs on the plains
I am the hills of the ramparts   40
I am the peaks of poetry
I am the spears in the spoils rewarding war
I am the gods who shape the antlers for heads.

I am wind on sea
I am wave of stormy sea   45
I am sound of sea
I am stag of seven points
I am hawk on cliff
I am flash of sunshine
I am fair plant   50
I am boar in fury
I am salmon in pool
I am loch on plain
I am hill of rampart
I am hill of poetry   55
I am spear in war's booty
I am god who shapes antlers for head.

Who sanctifies the mountain's stones?
Who summons the phases of the moon?
Who knows where the setting sun sleeps?   60
Who raises the stars from Tethra's sea?
Does a mortal man do it?
Does a god edge blades in a mortal's fort?

Revile the spears, wail for spears
Sing of the sea, sing the wind!   65

Amairgen also sang the following:

Fishful seas!
Fertile land!
An eruption of fish
Fish under wave   70
Flounder, whales.
Song for a harbor:
An eruption of fish
Fishful seas!

Three days and three nights afterward, the sons of Mil fought the battle of
Slíab Mis, and they defeated the demons of Ireland.[9]

It should be clear from the discussion thus far (and the notes on the text and
translation) that the difficulties of translating early texts such as Amairgen's
poems go far beyond linguistic asymmetries, even the radical asymmetries of
contradictory usages. A significant factor is rooted in professional conventions.
My translation of Amairgen's poetry involves the sorts of shifts that translators of modern texts do all the time without apology, but that many philologists and linguists see as problematic. Although pragmatics, text types, and
literary forms are frequently guides to meaning in language in general and
translation in particular—guides as important as semantics and morphosyn-
tax—linguists and philologists often protest departures from literalism based
on such criteria.

Even without the constraints of literalism, however, many problems remain in the interpretation of the early Irish text. For example, symmetry in the
translated coda seemed to me not fully workable for lines 62–63, because the
meaning of the text itself is uncertain. A literal translation of line 62 (an emphatic line marked in Irish by its startling abbreviation and catalexis) would
be "Who is [the/a] man?" which is very general and makes little sense in context, forcing a translator to make a decision and interpret the meaning. Accordingly I have taken Amairgen's first four statements as existential questions

about the origins and workings of the cosmos. In my translation his answer to these questions is another question that represents a reductio ad absurdum: obviously no man can claim these powers. Amairgen then presents a further reductio: Are gods found acting as smiths in human forts?[10] As I understand it, the point of the coda seems to be that Amairgen affirms the proper cosmic order, indicating his assent to the view that gods and humans each have their own proper domains and that any inversion or transgression will result in disorder and chaos, notwithstanding his earlier claim to subsume and represent all being within himself.

Alternatively, perhaps there is an intended ambiguity.[11] It is possible that Amairgen intends to suggest or even assert that, like the druids of Gaul versed in the workings of the natural world and knowledge of the supernatural, *he does* in fact have the power to sanctify shrines to the gods, *he does* know what the phase of the moon will be, and *he does* know precisely where the sun will set on any day of the year and where the stars will rise, as druids were expected to do. Is there a strong claim here for druidical powers? Perhaps the line should be translated "Who is the man [who can do it]?". But then how is one to construe line 63 in a parallel manner? The choice would seem to be "Who is the god who edges blades in a mortal's fort?" Would that mean that there is no such god or that Amairgen knows the identity of a hidden god? Similarly if line 63 involves word play and double meanings, perhaps line 64 of the translation makes a veiled claim to Amairgen's ability to revile spears effectively (that is, deprecate and thwart them in a supernatural sense), even spears forged so to speak at the gods' commands. In this reading Amairgen would be making an oblique assertion about his ability to deploy *áer* (literally "cutting"), usually translated in English as "satire," which in early Irish culture was believed to have the power to inflict physical damage to or even kill an opponent. The threat of satire was one of the chief powers of a fili and an important means of maintaining the social order in premodern Ireland. These are some of the textual puzzles of the poem that linguists and textual scholars who are specialists in early Irish literature have yet to resolve.

Amairgen's poem is therefore difficult to translate in part because there is no accepted text and no consensus on the meaning of the text. Aside from the fact that the poem is not lineated in the manuscript and that there is minimal punctuation (no question marks, for example), in translating an early text, a translator often has to work word by word to establish the text before translating it as such.[12] A text such as Amairgen's longer poem is thus difficult to translate for reasons that are antecedent to translating.

Early texts are also difficult to translate because there is often no author *either living or dead* to whom the text can be attributed. Here the concept of the "author function" takes on new meaning—new immediacy and urgency. The anonymity of the actual author poses questions about the author function of most medieval texts and almost all ancient ones, including scriptural texts. Even when a name comes down in history associated with an early text, what does the name really mean? Who was Homer in fact and to what extent does knowing his name relate to translating "his" texts? Is there in fact always a single author of an ancient text or is the text a product of a group of authors and scribes? Is it the result of textual accretion over time, which may have differed by region as reflected in manuscript variants? At best in the case of an anonymous text or even a text with the name of an ascribed author, there is only a stand-in for an author: a person with the power to authorize and authenticate a text and hence give an acceptable basis for translation. Such a person can be a textual scholar or cultural power—religious or secular—who establishes, endorses, or authorizes a standard edition or "reading" of the text. The very word used to describe the action—*authorize*—suggests the surrogate relation to authorship and to the author held by such an authority.[13] This is obviously not the case for Amairgen's poetry.

In the absence of an author, a translator of early texts sometimes attempts to turn to interpretive frameworks in cultural memory for a reading of a text, but here too there are difficulties in many cases. Some cultures have a long history of interpreting important cultural texts—that is, their self-reflexive continuous interpretive view of texts is as much a part of the culture and cultural memory as the texts themselves.[14] Seldom, however, is this the case for ancient European documents in general and for medieval European vernacular literature in particular: often there is no fixed text, no continuous thread of cultural memory to explain what the text signified in its early cultural context, no hermeneutic with historical rootedness to bridge the gulf of time between the writing of the text and the modern translator. In fact many European medieval literary texts that are of greatest interest to current readers and translators have survived in single manuscripts; thus they were not necessarily part of medieval canons, a caveat underscored when there is an absence of allusions to the tales in other surviving texts (cf. Tymoczko 2014).

Absent a text, an author, and a hermeneutic, a translator sometimes looks to so-called tradition for the meaning of a text. Traditional oral literature inherited from the depths of time is seen as the source of many ancient and medieval written texts and takes diverse forms worldwide. Some oral literature has specific features that can guide a translator, such as locally distinctive narrative patterns (oicotypes), a predictable range of surface variation among versions, formal patterning, and performance constraints. In the case of early *written* texts based on tradition, however, there is rarely information about the way that tradition has been deployed in the generation of a specific text. Moreover it is well established that oral traditional literature is not fixed and that it evolves over time. Amairgen's poem is an example of these problems. When a later manuscript includes additional lines in the poem, does this mean that there were local variants that supplied the lines, that "tradition" expanded the poem, that a single fili or scribe indulged in a bit of literary creativity, or that the earlier manuscripts omitted the lines? As a result of such uncertainties, editorial and translational choices are usually intertwined and can be questioned by other scholars and translators. For example, am I right that the words I omitted in my minimalist edition are the result of incorporated glosses and dittography? There is seldom any way that a translator of an early text can answer such questions with certainty.

Not only do translators of early texts often work without a definitive text or author, frequently they are starved for cultural information as well. An early text often survives to the present with nothing known about the specific context in which it was composed, not even the century or location of its composition (which is the case for Amairgen's poems). Moreover, translators of modern languages can *go* places to learn a language and a culture. They can have an "immersion experience," an expression that suggests a sort of baptism into a language and culture. What are translators of medieval literature to do when there is no culture to visit, no place to go to learn the history and customs of the source culture or to learn the language in all its performative fullness? To learn the difference between ordinary language, high registers, and innovative defamiliarized literary language? To learn to recognize all the speech acts until they are so familiar that irony (the act of saying one thing and meaning the opposite) is apparent? To learn to recognize puns, allusions, and oblique partial references to a common cultural and textual stock of knowledge?

Erudition, scholarship, and study are poor substitutes for texts, authors, interpretive frameworks, and cultural immersion. To be sure research and scholarship help, as they do for translating living authors and contemporary texts. For example, it does help a reader to know that Amairgen's poems follow a recognized poetics: verse that is defined by stress, cola, and cadence, lacking rhyme but characterized by alliteration, and constituting a closed world where the first line is echoed in some form by the last line, a feature known as the *dúnad,* "closing, ending, shutting." Thus, the dúnad of Amairgen's first poem brings the text back to the poet's identity with the wind on the sea, and the translation should reflect that circularity. Similarly it is helpful to the translator and reader of the translation to know that *gáeth,* "wind," as an adjective also means "wise" and has associations with intelligence. In Irish culture, as in Indo-European cultures in general, wind and breath are also connected with spirit, inspiration, wisdom, and the abilities of a seer; thus, these meanings underlie Amairgen's implicit appeals and claims, and they should be stressed. The importance of Amairgen's stepping forward onto the land with his right foot rather than his left likewise has typical Indo-European connotations and is transparent in this context: it signals to Ireland that he and his people are not sinister or hostile arrivals. Amairgen's second poem also gains depth if the translator and reader/listener know that the poem is a blessing and a mantic invocation rather than a description. Amairgen is calling forth the fish in the sea and invoking the land to be fruitful and increase its fertility; he is demonstrating that his people will benefit the land of Ériu. His poem echoes the themes of sacral kingship and sovereignty in early Irish culture. Amairgen is obliquely telling Ireland that the Gaels will have good kings who will bring peace and plenty, fine weather, rich harvests, and fertility to the land, sea, animals, and humankind alike.[15]

In the context of translating texts such as Amairgen's poetry, translation itself becomes a mode of investigation and a mode of knowing. It involves intuition, feeling, life experience, the body, imagination, and connection, as well as linguistic skills and expertise related to culture, history, literature, and textual studies. This is true of translating modern texts as well, but the necessity of skills of this type is often highlighted in working with an early text. As a mode of knowing and discovering, translation of texts—early and late—is not unlike the processes of inquiry and the methods of discovery in fields such as mathematics, the natural sciences, archeology, anthropology, psychology, literary studies, history, and indeed linguistics.[16] In this sense translation is a disciplinary exercise dependent on a cognitive tool kit. In turn, understanding the products and processes of translation involves learning the tools of the field. The great achievement of translation scholars in the last half century has been to establish translation studies as a discipline and to define useful tools in its tool kit. Knowledge of this tool kit in turn benefits working translators.

The tools of translation studies are directed to understanding the nature of translation both as a system of processes and a system of products. In certain ways the tools are self-evident: recognition that translation involves negotiating anisomorphisms and asymmetries of languages and cultures and that such differences fall into categories and types. That there are always differences between a text and its translation: that a translation cannot be fully the same as the source text and that the process of translation cannot carry everything across from one language to another or one culture to another, nor can a translator avoid introducing associations from her own time (cf. Tymoczko 1999:41–61). There are tools related to the nature of texts and how they signify and change in cross-cultural contexts, as well as tools related to the analysis of the functions of texts and the position of texts in cultural systems. There are tools that are self-reflexive with respect to translators themselves: tools of analysis related to the operation of power internal to and across cultures that impinge on translators, but also tools related to the analysis of the power of translators in context, their modes of resistance and activism, their collusion with hegemony and dominance, and their relation to ethics and ideology. Tools of this order are at the foundation of any discipline, and this is another achievement of translation studies: as a discipline it creates new knowledge about translation and offers new tools to practitioners and scholars alike. The tools developed by translation studies help a working translator and give methods for evaluating existing translations, particularly in situations of difficulty such as the absence of a text, author, or context. As in any discipline the tools of translation studies are open-ended, evolving, developing, and changing. The tool kit provides a checklist of things to consider and methods to use when a translation becomes problematic.[17]

For example, it is instructive to note that my translation does not use a formal-equivalence strategy in any conventional sense because the fourfold repetition of the text of the main poem and the expansion of the text in the translation from 21 lines to 64 lines are in no way formally "accurate." Paradoxically, however, the translation does attempt to capture closely the specific formal *semantic meanings* of the poem with respect to expression of the universal quantifier: to indicate all the resonances suggested by the omission of definite articles in the Irish lines and a clear grammatical presentation of the universal applicability of Amairgen's words. By representing all possible expressions of the semantic meaning in English, the translation is an attempt to be grammatically scrupulous, hypercorrect, and informative in its representation of the significance of the linguistic substance of the Irish text in the service of specifying the semiotics of the poem in its cultural context. That attempt to be hypercorrect linguistically, however, distances the translation from other formal properties of the source text. Oddly enough, thus, my lengthy repetition of Amairgen's first poem is fully consonant with Jakobson's view that it is possible to say anything in any language: that "languages differ essentially in what they *must* convey and not in what they *may* convey" (1959:236; original emphasis).

Nevertheless this is not a dynamic-equivalence translation because there is no textual marker in the medieval manuscript that tells us to go back to the beginning and begin again with a reprise: no repeat to tell us to sing the text in multiple iterations and to listen to the music and the words again. Aside from the fact that a modern audience no longer believes what the original audience believed, it is impossible to produce a translation of Amairgen's poetry that is dynamically equivalent because we have very little idea of how the poem was performed and what musical setting the text was given.[18] Further, we are *readers* of the poem rather than listeners. The translation unites insistence on accurate semantic meaning with a literary representation of what the poetry apparently signifies culturally in the context of the literary narrative. Thus, to use the terminology of Dan Sperber and Deirdre Wilson (1995), all the semantic meanings of the English versions are relevant to understanding this early text and to conveying a literary representation of the semiotics of the Irish poems in an anglophone context in the twenty-first century.

None of the other categories or binaries in translation studies is able to provide a sufficient methodology for translating Amairgen's words: not the various distinctions of functionalism, not adequate versus acceptable, not foreignizing versus domesticating. We have no name for a translation such as the one I've offered. It's not even metonymic in any simple sense (cf. Tymoczko 1999) but rather hypertrophic, if there is such a way of speaking about a translation. One of the many difficulties in translating Amairgen's poem is that translation studies has not yet defined enough distinctions to guide the translation of a text of this antiquity, opaqueness, and defamiliarized context. The text strains the resources of the field and the profession; it illustrates that there are more tools to develop for the tool kit and more theoretical work to be done in and for the discipline of translation studies.

In exploring an early text such as Amairgen's poem, the translator's tools are not unlike the staff carried by a pilgrim, supporting the seeker along the way, helping the *theôros* find a firm path. Like translators of more modern literature, Carol Maier's (2006) metaphor indicates that translators of early literature must engage with their texts as whole persons, proceeding in exploratory and often tentative ways through a text and learning as they go. They must engage with the text using their minds and bodies, feeling their way through the text as well as thinking it through, calling on both explicit and implicit knowledge, understanding, and experience. The closest way to describe my approach to Amairgen's poem might be to call it performative: a rather personal attempt to perform for our time Amairgen's persuasive utterances to Ireland by spelling out my understanding of the multiple semantic and cultural meanings that convince the land to accept his presence and to value his authority, knowledge, power, and commitment to justice on behalf of his people. In my translation the rising and falling motion of Amairgen's first poem invests the final and most literal iteration of his claims with greater weight and substance than it can have alone as a single stanza. The increased length of the translation makes moderns listen longer and more carefully to the sound and sense: to think more deeply about the implications and to attend to the meaning as Ireland herself was intended to listen and consider the poems.

In translation studies there has been discussion of the necessity to have performative translations of genres recognized as such in contemporary Eurocentric cultures (songs and plays, for example) but too little discussion it would seem of the performative nature of texts in general and specifically the performative qualities of narratives and poetry, particularly those of oral literatures. Certainly my method of translating this poem is not an approved way to translate ancient texts of philological interest and importance to the history of literature. It is, however, no accident that other theorist/practitioners influenced by the work of Carol Maier, such as those whose essays are included in this volume, have also advocated similar approaches to translating contemporary narratives.

Despite the lack of theoretical and critical categories for such a translation, my approach is probably not too far-fetched or arbitrary a way to represent this specific early Irish poem that reads to us initially like a short lyric, a "nature poem," yet clearly has a different import. In performance a song (or sung poem, laíd), particularly a short song, often involves the repetition of stanzas or includes repeats, with minor changes of melody, wording, articulation, and so forth still today. Were poems such as Amairgen's texts well known, frequently sung, and traditional among the ordinary people of medieval Ireland, as well as remembered and conserved in writing by the native learned classes? Did such songs involve repetition of the stanzas? We don't actually know the answers to these questions, so my translation is a sort of pilgrim's offering, a result of wondering and witnessing. It is an example of how a translator/theorist "travels, observes, and contemplates, glimpses possibilities and learns about other people and their customs, but also risks becoming estranged, rejected, ridiculed" (Maier 2006:163).

The fact is that we know very little about the performative traditions of early medieval Ireland. We know that stories were told at feasts, that genealogies and lore were recited before kings. We know that the harpers had the greatest prestige among musicians, but we don't know much about how the vocal part of the music was delivered. There is some evidence that high-prestige poets had singers to perform their work, but did that mean that the poets themselves never sang? Specifically we don't know how poems in the middle of narratives were sung or performed in the context of storytelling. Following narratives in the manuscripts, there are frequently poems related to the same subjects. Were such poems also sung after the storyteller finished the performance of the narrative with its performed inset poems?

In part we don't know much about these things because Ireland was a colonized nation and many aspects of its learned legacy, including its medieval manuscripts, were deliberately destroyed by the English conquerors during the sixteenth and seventeenth centuries, especially during the Cromwellian period (see Ó Corráin 2011–12 and sources cited). Moreover, Ireland's most learned men and most valued literary practitioners were lost to the nation when the poets, storytellers, and musicians went in exile to the Continent following their patrons, the fighting aristocracy, who were driven out of Ireland after defeat in the seventeenth century. Donnchadh Ó Corráin (2011–12:223) observes that what distinguishes Ireland from the general European experience is "the ruthless and systematic assault on Irish society and its culture by the English government" during that period; he writes that "the government-sponsored Protestant Reformation, early-modern colonial practice and theory, and the geo-politics of European religious conflict were run together to form a potent and destructive ideology" (215). The result was "government terrorism, deliberately induced famine, and attempted genocide," as well as the murder of poets who were specifically targeted for elimination (214–15).

Notice that I have spoken of the poetry throughout as "Amairgen's poems," as if Amairgen were an actual person. For the Irish, *The Book of Invasions* (*Lebor Gabála Érenn*) was history: not pseudohistory or invented history or myth.

In popular culture the narrative was seen this way by many people in Ireland and the Irish diaspora right down to the twentieth century and perhaps is still viewed as history by some at present.[19] That view in part reflects the native concept of texts, particularly oral texts: *text* in the sense of words woven together so as to create a well-woven culture. The word for this collective heritage in Irish is *senchas,* meaning "old tales, ancient history, tradition" but extending also to genealogy and traditional law. It was literature in the broad sense that the English word *literature* conveyed in anglophone culture until the nineteenth century (cf. Eagleton 1983:17–22). Senchas includes not only narratives seen as historical, but king lists, proverbs, statements of right conduct, onomastic lore, proverbs, natural science, the law, genealogies, and poetry of all types, including mnemonic verse. Senchas includes all the various types of knowledge that the native learned classes were expected to master and to transmit, so long as the Gaelic order persisted in Ireland (cf. Poppe 2014). In the case of Amairgen's first poem, its utterance was seen as a foundational act of Irish culture, a culture that the English tried to obliterate and replace with their own language, literature, history, knowledge, valuations, and lineages. In a small way, therefore, allowing Amairgen's words to be spoken powerfully and to be heard reverberating their claims forcefully in English in our time is a pilgrim's small offering of reparation: a minor ethical act with ideological force.

Notes

1. I use *nation* here in its primary sense of "a people, united by language, history, customs, and origins, and usually the inhabitants of a specific territory."

2. Ireland is conceptualized as a personified female figure (and in fact a triad of such figures) in the full text. See Mac Cana (1970:64–65, 85–95) for a discussion of female representations of Ireland.

3. Cf. Dillon and Chadwick (1967:10). The first two chapters of this book continue to serve as a useful introduction to the early Celts.

4. The translations are published together in *Two Death Tales from the Ulster Cycle* (Tymoczko 1981).

5. The existential quantifier can be thought of as "there exists an X such that. . . ." The existential quantifier in Irish can also be expressed by the substantive verb (similar to Spanish *estar,* predicating existence) with an indefinite noun. For example, many early tales begin *boí ri amrae,* "there was a famous king," asserting the existence of such a king, a usage that continues in modern Irish folktales. Cf. Maier's second note to her translation of Octavio Armand's contribution to this volume on the benefits of having two verbs meaning "to be."

6. For a more detailed discussion of contradictory usages and the linguistic and logical problems involved in translating Amairgen's poem specifically, see Tymoczko (1985).

7. The Irish texts in this essay are based on the version in the twelfth-century manuscript known as the Book of Leinster and published under that name; this text is the earliest surviving manuscript of the first redaction of *The Book of Invasions* (Macalister 1938–56:1.xi–xii). It is supplemented by readings in the edition by Macalister (1938–56:5.110–11). For the full text in the manuscript, see *The Book of Leinster* (1954:1.49–52). The poem has been translated frequently; two translations are quoted in Tymoczko (1985) and a third is found in Kinsella (1986/1989:47–49).

8. *Notes on the text.* In the Book of Leinster, the poem is glossed throughout, but the glosses are not necessarily reliable indices to the semantic meaning and I have omitted them from the edited text here. In addition lines 2–3 seem to have incorporated glosses into the text, which I have also omitted here, and line 19 is followed by an obscure line that is omitted in my edition because it appears to be the result of dittography.

The word *ailsiu* in line 21 is obscure, with the *Dictionary of the Irish Language* listing it tentatively under *ailid,* "nurtures"; some translators, however, see it as a form of *aillsiu,* "sore tumor, abscess," presumably reading "fort of abscess" or "abscess of a fort," with an irregular inflexion or textual error in either case, or possibly as an appositive in the dative case. In line 22 I take the words *cainte* and *cainte* as second-person plural imperatives of the verbs *cainid,* "laments, bewails, keens, weeps" (with word play on cáinid, "reviles, reproaches, satirizes"), and *canaid,* "sings," respectively (cf. Thurneysen 1946/1961:88, 373). There may also be word play on *gáithe* (genitive of *gáeth,* "wind") and its homonym *gáeth,* "sea," with feminine declension. Thus the line seems literally to mean "weep/revile concerning spear, sing of wind/sea," leading to my decision to treat the line in translation as a couplet, each line of which expresses two meanings.

9. *Notes on the translation.* Line 7 and reprises, *dér gréne,* literally "tear of sun," represented by most translators as "dew drop," perhaps suggesting a belief that the dew was the result of the setting sun's tears; I've translated the line to focus on the sparkle of sun on dew in the morning, which is likened metaphorically to the sparkle of tears in the eye. Line 8 and reprises, literally "fairness of plant." Line 14 and reprises, taking *feras feochtu* as "which suffices warlike deeds"; cf. *fechtach.*

The meaning of the coda in lines 58–65 is difficult to decipher and translations of this section vary considerably. In line 58 the verb *nod-gleith* means "makes clear, purifies," and in some translations it has been taken in the literal sense of "clears (away), smooths." I have taken the verb in the sense of "purifies." *Clochur,* "heap of stones" (Thurneysen 1946/1961:170), may be an oblique reference to the numinous piles of stones sometimes built by generations of pilgrims or visitors and found at present at many ancient Irish sites. It is perhaps more likely that clochur alludes to the megalithic cairns and monuments that are often found on the tops of hills and elsewhere in Ireland, some of which were in a collapsed state until reerected in modern times. In some cases such megalithic sites were associated by the Celts with the pre-Christian gods (for example, the mounds along the Boyne). Hence my choice of "sancti-fies" rather than "clears (away)" for *nod-gleith*.

In part the coda is difficult to translate because it also turns on another linguistic asymmetry between Old Irish and English. In all but the last line, the coda is marked as a series of questions by an interrogative at the head of the clause. Aside from the initial line of the series, the lines are introduced by the interrogative *cía*. The initial interrogative *coich é* (literally "Whose is he?") marks a break in the flow of the poem for the audio-oral audience, but then the series of similar lines all beginning cía indi-cate a unified poetic sequence. The interrogative cía is difficult to translate in a sym-metrical way in English, however, because it functions in a variety of ways that are indicated by different words in English: *who?, what?, how?,* and even *where?* Thus, symmetry of form in an English translation is impossible to represent without shift-ing the grammar of the lines a bit, as I have done.

The phrase "the stars from Tethra's sea" is literally "the cattle from the house of Tethra"; the phrase is a metaphor (which I've eliminated in the translation in favor of the denotative meaning) in which the stars are figured as the (white) cows of the sea god dotting the dark blue meadow of the night sky, which seems to merge with or emerge from the sea as darkness takes hold. The line indicates that a sophisticated symbolic matrix rooted in native Irish religion and mythology continued to be vital in medieval Ireland centuries after conversion to Christianity.

If, as I suggest in the notes to the text, there is word play twice in line 22 of the text, then that line can be translated as a couplet, as I've done in lines 64–65 of the transla-tion. In oral literature double meanings signaled by homophony are common because the audience can hear and perceive the two meanings simultaneously (which is not fully possible in writing). Such effects are found frequently in oral texts, and there are many modern examples, including well-known instances in Shakespeare. See, for example, *Hamlet* (I.ii.129) in which there was simultaneous oral evocation of both *solid* and *sul-lied* in Elizabethan English (cf. notes to the passage in Shakespeare 1974:1145, 1187).

In the coda to the main poem and in the second poem, I am mixing English repre-sentations of the universal quantifier in English; one could, however, translate some of the lines in multiple representations as I did in the body of the first poem. The mul-tiplicity of possible meanings in the coda discussed below also suggests that iterated multiple representations of it in translation might not be amiss.

Finally, there is a cryptic ending to the episode in which the Gaels "defeated the demons"; the statement is provided with a gloss identifying the demons as the "Túatha Dé Danann," the name for the pre-Christian Irish gods. This manuscript version of the arrival of the Gaels seems to be given a Christianized interpretation, identifying the old gods as "demons," a common strategy in rivalry between two religions. The battle of Slíab Mis is thus also being presented as a version of the common Indo-Eu-ropean struggle between the gods of chaos and the gods of order; in Irish tradition it could figure therefore as a replay of *The Second Battle of Mag Tuired,* the story of the contention between the Túatha Dé Danann and the Fomoire, which begins by show-ing the chaos and disorder attendant upon the Fomoire having disrupted the natural and social order. The tale is a central text of early Irish literature. See Mac Cana (1970:59–64) and Gray (1982, esp. 28–35).

10. The word *dind* generally refers to a human hill-fort; in lines 62–63 I've supplied the word *mortal* to capture the sense of the queries, as I've interpreted them. Cf. the notes to the text.

11. There might also be a textual error. For example, perhaps line 20 of the poem is exceedingly short because the text of the manuscript is defective.

12. A medieval vernacular text can also vary from manuscript to manuscript and usually texts in the early manuscripts include obscurities and copying errors; thus even the choice of manuscript brings difficulty. The establishment of a text from a living oral culture is even more difficult in a translation project than a written text *from* an oral culture.

13. Hermans (2007:1–51) discusses the paradoxes of authorization in relationship to establishing the status of texts, including both originals and translations.

14. Jan Assmann (2011:175–233) argues that this is true of Jewish culture, for example, in which texts and their interpretive frameworks ultimately came to substitute for territory in defining Jewish culture and maintaining its cohesive identity. Similarly one can argue that Chinese culture established such frameworks of interpretation for written as well as oral texts. The inscription of the central Confucian texts in stone on stelae in Xian in 837 during the Tang Dynasty represents a clear (and successful) effort to fix the texts and prevent variation of these important documents; similarly the imperial examinations in China can be seen as another mechanism for controlling the interpretation of inherited texts (cf. Tymoczko 2014).

15. The Irish concept of sacral kingship is discussed in Mac Cana (1970:117–21).

16. The current world literature movement has turned to translation as a mode of understanding literature as a whole.

17. For a summary of my view of the theoretical achievements of translation studies and my assessment of the tools of the discipline at present, see Tymoczko (2013).

18. Using Amairgen's long poem as well as others, I argue in my 1985 article that the distinction between formal-equivalence and dynamic-equivalence translation does not in fact strictly exist: it collapses when the formal equivalence *is* the dynamic equivalence, notably so in the case of contradictory usages.

19. Paul Muldoon (2000) began his Clarendon Lectures at Oxford University with an account of Amairgen and Amairgen's first poem as an originary moment in Irish history. Muldoon's first words were "I begin at the beginning" (2000:3).

Works Cited

Assmann, Jan. 2011. *Cultural Memory and Early Civilization: Writing, Remembrance, and Political Imagination*. New York: Cambridge University Press.

The Book of Leinster, Formerly Lebar Na Núachongbála. 1954–83. Vol .1, edited by R. I. Best, Osborn Bergin, and M. A. O'Brien. Vols. 2–5, edited by R. I. Best and M. A.

O'Brien. Vol. 6, edited by Anne O'Sullivan. Dublin: Dublin Institute for Advanced Studies.

Catford, J. C. 1965. *A Linguistic Theory of Translation: An Essay in Applied Linguistics.* London: Oxford University Press.

Dictionary of the Irish Language, Based Mainly on Old and Middle Irish Materials. 1983. Compact ed. Dublin: Royal Irish Academy.

Dillon, Myles, and Nora K. Chadwick. 1967. *The Celtic Realms.* London: Weidenfeld and Nicolson.

Eagleton, Terry. 1983. *Literary Theory: An Introduction.* Oxford: Blackwell.

Gray, Elizabeth A., ed. and trans. 1982. *Cath Maige Tuired, The Second Battle of Mag Tuired.* Naas, Co. Kildare: Irish Texts Society.

Hermans, Theo. 2007. *The Conference of the Tongues.* Manchester: St. Jerome.

Jakobson, Roman. 1959. "On Linguistic Aspects of Translation." In *On Translation,* edited by Reuben A. Brower, 232–39. Cambridge, Mass.: Harvard University Press.

Kinsella, Thomas, trans. 1969/1970. *The Táin.* London: Oxford University Press.

Kinsella, Thomas, ed. and trans. 1986/1989. *The New Oxford Book of Irish Verse.* New York: Oxford University Press.

Levý, Jiří. 1967. "Translation as a Decision Process." In *To Honor Roman Jakobson: Essays on the Occasion of His Seventieth Birthday, 11 October 1966.* Vol. 2, 1071–1082. The Hague: Mouton.

Macalister, R.A.S., ed. and trans. 1938–56. *Lebor Gabála Érenn, The Book of the Taking of Ireland.* 5 vols. Dublin: Irish Texts Society.

Mac Cana, Proinsias. 1970. *Celtic Mythology.* London: Hamlyn.

Maier, Carol. 2006. "The Translator as *Theôros:* Thoughts on Cogitation, Figuration, and Current Creative Writing." In *Translating Others,* Vol. 1, edited by Theo Hermans, 163–80. Manchester: St. Jerome.

Muldoon, Paul. 2000. *To Ireland, I.* Oxford: Oxford University Press.

Ó Corráin, Donnchadh. 2011–12. "What Happened to Ireland's Medieval Manuscripts?" *Peritia* 22–23: 191–223.

Poppe, Erich. 2014. "The Culture of Memory in Medieval Ireland." In *Medieval Irish Perspectives on Cultural Memory,* edited by Jan Erik Rekdal and Erich Poppe, 135–76. Munich: Nodus Publikationen.

Quine, Willard V. O. 1959. "Meaning and Translation." In *On Translation,* edited by Reuben A. Brower, 148–72. Cambridge, Mass.: Harvard University Press.

Shakespeare, William. 1974. *The Riverside Shakespeare.* Boston: Houghton Mifflin.

Sperber, Dan, and Deirdre Wilson. 1995. *Relevance: Communication and Cognition.* 2nd. ed. Oxford: Blackwell.

Thurneysen, Rudolf. 1946/1961. *A Grammar of Old Irish.* Rev. ed. Translated by D. A. Binchy and Osborn Bergin. Dublin: Dublin Institute for Advanced Studies.

Tymoczko, Maria, trans. 1981. *Two Death Tales from the Ulster Cycle.* Dublin: Dolmen.

Tymoczko, Maria. 1985. "How Distinct Are Formal and Dynamic Equivalence?" In *The Manipulation of Literature: Studies in Literary Translation,* edited by Theo Hermans, 63–86. London: Croom Helm.

Tymoczko, Maria. 1999. *Translation in a Postcolonial Context: Early Irish Literature in English Translation.* Manchester: St. Jerome.

Tymoczko, Maria. 2013. "Translation Theory." In *The Encyclopedia of Applied Linguistics,* vol. 10, edited by Carol A. Chapelle, 5928–37. Chicester: Wiley-Blackwell.

Tymoczko, Maria. 2014. "The Nature of Tradition and Cultural Memory: Evidence from Two Millennia of Irish Culture." In *Medieval Irish Perspectives on Cultural Memory,* edited by Jan Erik Rekdal and Erich Poppe, 15–60. Munich: Nodus Publikationen.

Camp, Cubism, and the Translation and Editing of Style

Valle-Inclán's *Tyrant Banderas*

Peter Bush

How can one write about literary translation? More precisely, how can one write about one's own translations, or should one not write about them at all, allowing them to serve as grist to another theorist's mill or corpus data? What is the role, if any, of a translator's history, memory, and subjectivity? Or his or her scholarly erudition? Or his or her theoretical positions whether in the foreground or latent? Can translators recreate very distinct styles from different languages? Carol Maier and I have turned to these issues in many encounters over the last 25 years, and this chapter on my translation of Ramón del Valle-Inclán's *Tirano Banderas* continues these exchanges at a time when literary translators and translation are attracting more attention in the cultural sphere frequented by a public that still reads books, attends literary festivals—see the rise of the translation slam—and logs into literary blogs.

It is equally a time when translation studies is witnessing an increasing number of studies of literary style and an avowed turn to practice as a source of research. Tim Parks's *Translating Style* (1998) was one of the first such studies and it was deeply rooted in his university teaching of literary translation. His discussion of translation from English to Italian focuses on the modernist canon—Woolf, Beckett, Joyce—and develops a literary critique of the originals that pinpoints their experimental or innovative use of English before analyzing the translations that inevitably fall short in recreating these nuances of style, often because equivalent leaps aren't apparently available in Italian. Parks seems to be on the side of the translator—and comments on his own work as the leading translator from Italian that he is—in an art that is apparently doomed to heroic failure because of these inevitable losses. It is as if the translators and their critics are trapped by the inevitable linguistic difference between languages, compounded by the writers' subtleties of style, and thus can only be haunted by the utopian or benchmark translation that would be an accurate word-for-word effort in the best of all possible worlds.

Parks's close readings are framed by a desire to get closer to the realities of practice and avoid the mystification and abstruse language of "theory." His analyses undoubtedly get close to the styles of both the originals and the translations, though he hardly makes any mention of the commercial publishing context, the drafting process, and the overall interpretative moves of the translator, which are informed by everything from subjectivity, scholarship, and the historical moment to editorial interventions. Using the example of his own translation of a Roberto Calasso text before he really started writing his book and thinking about literary translation, he concludes, "while I was very much aware of the style of the original, I certainly had not consciously analyzed it, and the whole translation was done, as most translations are, intuitively" (Parks 1998:221).

A more recent approach to the translation of style is Clive Scott's *Translating Baudelaire* (2000). Unlike Parks, his focus is on poetry; like Parks, his authors—including Rimbaud and Apollinaire—are canonical in the extreme. Scott offers the reader multiple translations of poems, using methods such as tabulation that draw on the Brazilian concrete poets' tradition of translation. He is very translator-centered—that is, he prizes the interpretive agency of the translator and the subsequent life of the translation as recreated by the reader. His concern is translation as "self-expression" (2000:251) but one where "a foreignizing translation remains a fascinating proposition of much linguistic consequence, and a challenge and training for the reading mind" (2000:251). Scott's experimental translations assume a previous history of translation: there are many existing translations of these French poets and he assumes that his reader is familiar with some of them and can read the original. Though he is avowedly translator-focused, his translator—that is, himself—and his analyses are cerebral with little sense of a stirring of the personal in his interpretations or of any subjective emotional response: the body is completely absent in this sophisticated exercise in neutral reading and translation where the translations exist within the theorizing. Although it would be very hard to adapt a similar approach to long works of fiction, Scott's approach offers a way to loosen up translators as writers by letting them try their hand at different versions of the same poem. Although he prefers not to see his work as pedagogical in that sense and though his theorizing frameworks remove him from the Rainer Schulte tradition of translation workshops in terms of the practice of translation, this is perhaps where his work should be located insofar as he is a theoretical, experimental exponent of the workshop.

I offer the following as a complement, if not alternative, to these critical approaches to translating style, with a method that tries to find a way to encompass the act of literary translation as a crucible where history, subjectivity, scholarship, and critical consciousness—and the spontaneity of intuition, which is, in fact, enfolded within all the previous tangents—interact with the self-editing or editing by the publisher's editor and copy editor in the creation of the literary translation of *Tyrant Banderas*, a canonical work of Hispanic literature, but one translated into English only once before, in 1929.

At the time of the first round of uprisings in Egypt and Tunisia, the cultural supplement of the Barcelona daily *La Vanguardia* carried a review of Valle-Inclán's novel that proclaimed it a fiction for our times. The review didn't dwell on the levels of literary difficulty, on the text's impenetrability, on the need for glossaries or even introductions—the stock Hispanic critical reactions to *Tirano Banderas*. It was saying, read this book from 1926—it is still contemporary. By that time I had reached the final stages of revision of my translation, itself a reengagement with a book I'd not read for almost 50 years. Occasionally, a book, the actual physical copy, triggers a stream of memories that enter a translator's changing consciousness and critical relationship with the words on the old page and the new: an impulse that animates the imagination.

My first copy of *Tirano Banderas* evokes the scents of central Madrid, in August 1965, *calle* Arenal under a blistering sun, accompanied by the stench from sewers and the dry dusty smell of dingy shop fronts. On the corner of the street, a blind or war-wounded man bawls: "Veinte iguales para hoy" ("Twenty of the same for today"). In a bookshop sunk in shadows, I come across the novel in the wonderful 1954 Editorial Nova edition with its faux antique paper and pseudo-William Morris curlicues. I'm 19 and enjoying a long vacation after finishing my first year at the University of Cambridge. In Madrid I'm teaching English in a private school, owned by a refugee from democratic France, a pillar of the Vichy régime in flight from Madame Guillotine, or so the gossip went. Don Francisco likes to loom in the porch with his fat Havana and ask, "Who do you prefer, Plato or Aristotle?" As a teacher, I'm Mr. Addison, and my colleagues have other literary tags, such as Mr. Shakespeare, Miss Austen, or M. Molière: we come and go incognito; bodies change, names remain, to save on red tape. Twenty-six years have passed since the civil war and the defeat of the republicans, and in advanced conversation classes my students want to talk about Lorca and the welfare state, democracy, and a free press. I share a bedroom in a pension on calle Fernando el Católico with a Peruvian from Arequipa, who gets upset when I say he has Indian features, though he offers to explain the many words from Valle-Inclán that I don't understand. I gradually realize that Doña Carmen, my landlady, is running a clip-joint; most nights, she sets off at nine, in a low-cut, silvery lamé dress.

Newspapers are vapid and pompous and carry frequent large photos of Generalísimo Franco and short reports on trials of trade unionists or left-wing activists. Living in Francoist Spain helped me understand what I was reading. In 2010 and 2011 as I translate the grotesque deeds of dictator Tyrant Banderas in a country that could be Mexico or Peru or nowhere in particular, each day my mind becomes increasingly focused on Mugabe and Mubarak and Gaddafi, especially the latter in his green garb, ruined palace, then his grisly finale on a slab in a butcher's shop.

Whatever I made of *Tirano Banderas* in those first readings was never refined by study at university: though the novel was on reading lists, it was never a subject for tutorials and closer scrutiny, even though a tutor of mine, Theodore Boorman, was a specialist in Valle-Inclán. Perhaps it was the Latin American setting? After all, Latin American literature didn't enter the Cambridge syllabus proper until 1969! So what stuck was the bunch of memories prompted by the physical book and the eerie figure of the dictator. In that sense it wasn't similar to my revisiting *La Celestina* as a translator, a text I had read repeatedly at grammar school and Cambridge. As I began to reread the novel, I was surprised by features that were to become central to my translation inasmuch as this rereading was a critical reinterpretation, which is what all translations are to a greater or lesser degree.

Camp language and literary bawdiness are key elements in the humor of *Tirano Banderas* and immediately brought to my mind Juan Goytisolo, specifically *A Cock-Eyed Comedy* and *The Garden of Secrets,* which I have translated—not that Juan Goytisolo had ever written substantially about Valle-Inclán or mentioned the novel as part of his personal canon. The recognition of that affinity was liberating, helped reduce the trepidation I felt before the very idea of translating this classic, the inevitable deference a translator must shake off if the original is going to be emulated in any way. I could again take to heart Goytisolo's advice when translating the two above-mentioned works: "Don't be afraid to be inventive and bold when re-creating my parodies, satire, and wordplay."

Although I felt that English readers would feel the pomposity of the name of the Baron of Benicarlés, Spain's Minister to Tyrant's republic—Don Mariano Isabel Cristino Queralt y Roca de Togores—I did translate many of the other names. A name not translated would be a joke lost, innuendo out the window. The baron has a lover, a young bullfighter from Sevilla, Currito-Mi Alma, who becomes "Currito-My Cutie." An important part of the novel's universe is set in a brothel—El Congal de la Cucarachita. Though it would be obvious from the context that *Congal* is brothel and *cucaracha* is a familiar word, particularly in the United States, I felt its repetition as "Baby Roach's Cathouse" would be more amusing and would also ease the way in for the inevitable jokes about "psychic pussycats" that Tyrant makes in his interrogation of the medium/magician who performs in the brothel, namely Dr. Polaco, who becomes "Dr. Polish" after his possible country of origin but with the added layer in translation of reference to his glib talk and manners. Similarly with the brothel's blind pianist—Ciego Velones—"Blind Bright-Eyes," also frequently described as "el ciego lechuzo," which I translate variously as "owlish blind man" or "blind owl."

From the translator's perspective, what brings freedom of creativity to the art of translation is the knowledge that because one has no choice but to make decisions in respect to each word in the original in the process of rewriting, there is always the possibility that this recreation will evoke in the reader responses that go beyond the commonplaces of literary criticism that frame the spontaneous reactions of general readers in the country of origin or in the case of this Valle-Inclán novel, his reputation in the English-speaking world as a dramatist. In the Hispanic world it is well known that Valle-Inclán created the "esperpento," that his characters tend to be rather robotic and dehumanized, and that *Tirano Banderas* has a couple of hundred "strange" words that he has sometimes invented or harvested from various dialects and varieties of Spanish. These can be markers to warn readers off the book as "difficult and distant." As a translator returning to the book, I wanted to foreground aspects of style that are comic and original and don't create barriers, but rather draw in the reader. For example, Valle-Inclán's construction of the character of the Baron of Benicarlés relies on an innovative use of camp language and parody in dialogue and description and in various political and social contexts. These shades of meaning require distinct tones in English.

In the early chapter introducing Baron Benicarlés, the description of his physique and manner locates him simultaneously as a devotee of a certain kind of melancholy French Symbolist literature—though his darts may aim more widely at Verlaine (*Les Fêtes galantes*) and Proust (the Baron de Charlus)—and Spanish poets, such as Juan Ramón Jiménez, with a penchant for autumnal gloom in neglected grandiose gardens with dripping fountains, pergolas, and chipped statues. There is even an element of self-parody, as if Valle-Inclán were revisiting the Marqués de Bradomín, the decadent protagonist of his *Sonatas*. The baron looks at himself in the pond in what was the Vicereine's garden in past times of Spanish imperial glory. At the same time he is a bloated unprincipled diplomat and a homosexual whose written exchanges with his rent-boy lover have been snatched by the dictator's secret police and will be used to blackmail him into supporting Tyrant's political options. The baron's many facets, suggested in parody and satirical language, are not spelled out in precise references to authors: the novelist relies on his reader's imagination to make connections and, in any case, his wit and appeal reside in the language itself. Though the English translator can assume readers will have no problem relating the parody to their own Romantic or Symbolist traditions if they don't happen to be aware of the French and Hispanic varieties, his challenge is the creation of a language that is polysemic, dissimilar, and dissonant, advancing a narrative movement that is almost wholly in the language in these sequences with the baron and not in dramatic action as elsewhere. Take the stylistic choices in the translation of these sentences[1]:

> Le hacían rollas las manos y el papo: Hablaba con nasales francesas y mecía bajo sus carnosos párpados un frío ensueño de literatura perversa. (Valle-Inclán 1993:65)
>
> (Plain text: His hands and jowl made rolls of fat: He spoke with French nasals and rocked under his fleshy eyelids a cold fantasy of perverse literature.)
>
> His hands and throat dripped flab; he parleyed with a French nasal twang; and his fleshy eyelids harbored gelid fantasies from perverse literature.
> (Valle-Inclán 2012:20)

> El Barón de Benicarlés, con quimono de mandarín, en el fondo de otra cámara, sobre un canapé, espulgaba meticulosamente a su faldero. (Valle-Inclán 1993:67)

(Plain text: The Baron of Benicarlés, with a mandarin kimono, at the back of the other chamber, on a chaise longue was meticulously delousing his lapdog.) Sprawled on a chaise longue with a mandarin's kimono, the Baron of Benicarlés was meticulously delousing his lapdog. (Valle-Inclán 2012:21)

With the first sentence the translation radically changes the verbs. They become stronger than the Spanish and the source of parody and movement: "dripped" for "made," "parleyed" for "talked," and "harbored" for "swayed" in rhythm with combinations that suggested themselves in English—"dripped flab" for "rolls," "nasal twang" for "nasals," and "gelid fantasies" for "cold fantasy." These translations "suggested themselves," that is to say, in the process of drafting and redrafting, self-editing, and responding to my editor's edit, conscious decisions allied with "spontaneous" finds in a process of literary rewriting in the elaboration of the whole translation that is allied to a constant critical reinterpretation.

The second sentence that opens a scene where the baron meets a representative of the Spanish entrepreneurs—the "gachupines" or "whiteys—shows the baron in a different light in a way that debunks him: moody melancholy gives way to louse-spotting but also marks a shift in power relations. No longer under the shadow of the Vicereine's specter, the baron now confronts an underling; his activity is also a putdown to his visitor, who feels constantly imperiled by the yelping poodle. The translation reorders the sequence by bringing forward the description of the baron on the chaise-longue, introducing by "Sprawled," which is not in the Spanish but continues the feeling of a luxuriating decadence that is then punctured by the debunking sense of "delousing." The reference to his being in another room in the Spanish is carried over to the next sentence because in English it became an overload, sapping the energy of the sentence. This kind of posthoc commentary thus aims to provide some sense of the reasons behind thousands of microchoices made by a translator in the refashioning of a novel. These microchoices are made within a critical continuity of language and characterization across the whole work—as much as possible given the complexity of the process that is an amalgam of the conscious and the apparently spontaneous complemented by sympathetic editorial interventions, sympathetic, that is, to the sweep and detail of the original communicated through the final draft of the translation.

The baron's potential as a butt of parody is realized in two later scenes. The first, when he is visited by his rent-boy *torero*, when he again gives a horizontal welcome, this time suggestively posed with his dog in bed, rather than delousing, sporting his lace cap and pink nightdress:

> Tenía en el hocico el faldero arrumacos, melindres y mimos de maricuela. (Valle-Inclán 1993:259)
> (Plain text: the lapdog had on its snout little pansy petting, sweet touches and caresses.)
> The drooling doggy's snout kneaded, caressed and frotted his daddy. (Valle-Inclán 2012:157)

The translation demands rewriting and reshaping to reflect the alliterative camp resonances, again belying the idea that literary translation can ever be word-for-word and function as writing. In the English the alliteration is switched from "m" to "d" in the diminutives "daddy" and "doggy," and the sexual burden resides in the verbs and the gay inflection in "frotted." This is the prelude to the comic dialogue between the two in which the young bullfighter from Sevilla, unlike the earlier whitey, is nondeferential and ready to banter with the baron, though there is a serious issue at stake—the antigay blackmailing threats by the dictator's secret police: he plays with images from bullfighting and addresses the baron as "Isabelita."

Valle-Inclán's milking of the baron's lechery climaxes in the scenes of diplomatic negotiations toward the end of the novel when the various foreign diplomats are discussing what policy to adopt in relation to Tyrant and the liberal revolutionary opposition. These diplomatic encounters are led by the English representative, who is hopeful of a liberal outcome that will favor British imperial trade. While Valle-Inclán satirizes the self-interest behind the hypocritical humanitarianism of perfidious Albion, he continues to poke fun at the baron, who is much more interested in making eyes at the handsome Minister for Ecuador—Dr. Aníbal Roncali—than in focusing on the political principles at stake. In fact, this is so much so that Roncali feels the need to defend his heterosexuality to the Minister for Uruguay, Carlos Esparza, who has noted the flirtatious eye movements in the last diplomatic meeting, and Esparza suggests, via sexual innuendo, that that will be the reason for the Ecuadorian's possible refusal to back the baron.

> "Indudablemente."
> "¡Por una meticulosidad! ..."
> "¡No juegués vos con el vocablo!" (Valle-Inclán 1993:292)

"No doubt."

"Because of your jackassing it a round . . . !"

"Spare me wordplay, please!" (Valle-Inclán 2012:183)

Here Valle-Inclán draws his reader's attention to the innuendo that depends on the reference to anal intercourse in "meticulosidad," namely "meti—culo," "put in butt," and which is now highlighted in English by the use of "jackass" and which adds other resonances with donkeys (such as stupidity), with larking about, and with sex ("ass" and "it"). However, there is a further literary subtext embedded in these exchanges because Valle-Inclán's humor is aimed beyond the political context at the Nicaraguan poet Rubén Darío, the shadow looming behind the characterization of the Ecuadorian minister.

> "Lírico, sentimental, sensitivo, sensible", exclamaba el Cisne de Nicaragua! (Valle-Inclán 1993:292)
> "Lyrical, sentimental, sensitive, sensible," proclaimed Rubén Darío, the swan of Nicaragua! (Valle-Inclán 2012:183)

I decided to make the reference explicit, assuming it might bypass most English or American readers who wouldn't have had the same difficulty with earlier references to the Romantics and Symbolists.

In other words the translator must watch out for all kinds of references, subtexts, and jokes, particularly in such a loaded text, and sustain them in their development as reflected in style and characterization. The use of camp to construct the Baron of Benicarlés is only one stylistic strand in the novel that draws as much on early westerns and slapstick movies, political rhetoric and Cubism, and novels of the Mexican Revolution, as on varieties of Spanish, Galician, and neologisms.

To sum up thus far, a translator's critical consciousness must combine close reading with literary scholarship informed by a range of ideas and theories of which translation theory is only one relatively recent addition at that. Some translation theorists are wedded to elitist academic notions and maintain that translators must have a clear-cut theory. In fact, an artistic creative practice as complex as literary translation cannot be reduced to a single theory or driven straightforwardly by such a theory in practice.

My final example from this account of the translation of *Tyrant Banderas* centers on the Cubist facet of the style that Valle-Inclán uses at some moments of extreme violence as in the attack on a liberal democratic rally in a circus tent by the dictator's men and in the later scenes in the Santa Mónica prison, where Tyrant incarcerates and kills his opponents. The example and the various edits give a snapshot of the final process of the translation and the creative interaction between translator and editor, in this case Edwin Frank at the *New York Review of Books* (hereafter NYRB).

> The final paragraph of Book Two, which describes the political rally, ends as follows.
>
> Los gendarmes comenzaban a repartir sablazos. Cachizas de faroles, gritos, manos en alto, caras ensangrentadas. Convulsión de luces apagándose. Rotura de la pista en ángulos. Visión cubista del Circo Harris. (Valle-Inclán 1993:102)
>
> (Plain text: The gendarmes began to hand round sword cuts. Shards of lamps, shouts, hands up, bloodied faces. Convulsion of lights going out. Breaking of arena into shards. Cubist vision of the Harris Circus.)

I submitted my "final" draft to the NYRB, the product of seven previous edits from my first draft, which included this translation of the preceding paragraph. "The gendarmes began to slash with their sabers. Flashing blades, hands aloft, bloodied faces. Convulsed lighting blacked out. An arena split into shards. Cubist vision of the Harris Circus." After a few months I received the edit: "The police slashed with their sabers. Flashing blades, screams, lifted hands, bloodied faces. The light convulsed and blacked out. The stadium shattered. Cubist vision of the Harris Circus." (NYRB edit). My response was the following version, which became the final published text. "The gendarmes slashed with their sabers. Flashing blades, screams, hands held high, bloodied faces. The lights convulsed and blacked out. The big top collapsed. Sharp-angled canvas. Cubist vision of the Harris Circus" (Valle-Inclán 2012:46).

The edit by an editor who is reacting to the literary interpretative edge of the translation and my responses perhaps exemplify a positive editor-translator symbiosis, the antithesis of what I have analyzed in relation to my translation of Juan Goytisolo's *Juan the Landless*. The description of the police attack on the democratic rally is both highly cinematic, as in an action movie, and painterly, as if anticipating the combination of Cubism and antifascist politics in Picasso's *Guernica*. The Spanish is strong on violently alliterative nouns: sablazos . . . Cachizas . . . convulsión de luces . . . Rotura . . . ángulos . . . Visión. . . . My translation attempts to retain the violent alliteration and makes several shifts from noun to verb: "slashed . . . sabers . . . flashing blades . . . screams . . . bloodied . . . convulsed . . . blacked out . . . split into shards." Edwin Frank's edit goes further in the introduction of dramatic verbs. In the first sentence he dispenses with the "began to" of Valle-Inclán, thus condensing the action, heightening the drama: "slashed with their sabers"; in a similar vein, "lifted" hands rather than "aloft," "Light convulsed" rather than "convulsions," and "stadium shattered" rather than "arena split into shards," before leading into the "Cubist vision." The edits make the English much more direct, as if it encapsulated the "Cubist" sentence "Rotura en la pista en ángulos" in the final sentence, leaving the reader to imagine that Cubist panorama on the basis of the convulsed light. The use of the word "stadium" in such a context introduces an echo from Pinochet's coup, his use of a football stadium to corral opponents before execution. In my reaction to the edit I continue to strengthen the violence: "hands held high" (as in "put your hands up," there being a constant stream of Wild West reference in the novel) and "lights" rather than "light." I introduce a couple of radical changes that are prompted by the edit and by my wish to retain the short Cubist sentence: "Rotura de la pista en ángulos," "Break of the arena into angles." The "stadium shattered" leads me to reintroduce the circus in a more explicit image: "The big top collapsed," which is then undercut by the short Cubist phrase "Sharp-angled canvas" leading into the final sentence. I wanted to retain the Cubist wording and I felt this sequence of words served that function and "canvas" evokes both the canvas of the tent and the canvas of a painting. It also eases the end of the paragraph into an almost contemplative silence, as if the reader were looking at a painting. I should add that Valle-Inclán's prompting of the reader in terms of his artistic references is part of his constant puncturing of realism in fiction and exuberant tongue-in-cheek baroque as in Book Three, titled "A Touch of Guignol," which begins "It was like a movie chase!" (Valle-Inclán 2012:74).

My final changes were the result of an overall interpretive strategy in rewriting a difficult modernist text. The collaborative intervention of the editor enabled me to refine the expression of my interpretation because he grasped Valle-Inclán's controlled wildness of imagination in his great novel of dictatorship and revolution and loosened my occasional overcloseness to the original Spanish so that my English could leap back with the political violence and the Cubist vision reinforced. I also reversed the other lexical change from "gendarmes" to "police" because Valle-Inclán uses "gendarmes" throughout the novel for the dictator's police and the word *gendarmes* was the word used in various Latin American countries for particular police units.

My aim in this chapter has been to illustrate through a brief case study how a literary translator embeds his scholarship, literary criticism, subjective historical experience, and conceptual strategies within the process of drafting, redrafting, and responding to editors, which is the crucible of literary translation. Evidently these assumptions and explanations are highly personal. I am not saying that all literary translators work or reflect on their work in this way or that they should do. There are no categorical formulas or absolute theoretical parameters for the writing of literary translations.

Note

1. *Tirano Banderas* was first published in serial form in *El estudiante* in 1925–26, followed by publication in book form in 1926. When translating the text I used Zamora Vicente's first critical edition (1937) and his revised edition (1993). Quotations in this chapter are from the 1993 edition.

Works Cited

Bush, Peter. 2012. "Toil, Trouble, and *Jouissance:* A Case Study; The Editing of Juan the Landless." In *Creative Constraints Translation and Authorship,* edited by Rita Wilson and Leah Gerber, 119–31. Melbourne: Monash University Publishing.

Goytisolo, Juan. 2000. *The Garden of Secrets.* Translated by Peter Bush. London: Serpent's Tail.

Goytisolo, Juan. 2005. *A Cock-Eyed Comedy.* 2nd ed. Translated by Peter Bush. San Francisco: City Lights.

Parks, Tim. 1998. *Translating Style: The English Modernists and Their Italian Translations.* London: Cassell.

Scott, Clive. 2000. *Translating Baudelaire.* Exeter: University of Exeter Press.

Valle-Inclán, Ramón del. 1926. *Tirano Banderas: novella.* Madrid: Imprenta Rivadeneyra.

Valle-Inclán, Ramón del. 1937. *Tirano Banderas: novela de Tierra Caliente.* 1st critical ed. Edited by Alonso Zamora Vicente. Buenos Aires: Espasa-Calpa.

Valle-Inclán, Ramón del. 1954. *Tirano Banderas, novela de Tierra Caliente.* Madrid: Editorial Plenitud.

Valle-Inclán, Ramón del. 1993. *Tirano Banderas.* Rev. ed. Edited by Alonso Zamora Vicente. Madrid: Espasa Calpe.

Valle-Inclán, Ramón del. 2012. *Tyrant Banderas*. Translated by Peter Bush. New York: New York Review of Books.

"Antigone's Delirium"
by María Zambrano

Translated with commentary by **Roberta Johnson**

"Antigone's Delirium"

For my sister Araceli

Prologue

As we know, Antigone, who died for bestowing funerary honors on her brother, was condemned to be buried alive. She entered death alive and intact. As Sophocles tells us in *Oedipus at Colonus,* from childhood on she accompanied her blind father. Then for a very short time she lived with her brothers at the royal palace of Thebes until the fatal quarrel between the two brothers Eteocles and Polynices. Promised in marriage to her cousin Haemon, son of the tyrant who would condemn her to her cruel end, she scarcely had time to know that she existed, to see herself and be seen. Perfect symbol of virginity, she had not even noticed herself. Mystery of virginity in all its plenitude; and thus of consciousness in its virginal state.[1] The virgin consciousness illuminates and directs itself toward what is not itself, to what is not the subject to which it belongs. A rare moment of human perfection, the human being, emerges from his/her dream in order to enter into consciousness and conscience because of a misdeed, a crime. Consciousness is to awaken from life's dream; originally to live is to remain submerged in a dream without any knowledge of the difference between things, the difference that arises from the primary abysm between ourselves and the reality that surrounds us.[2]

Once human beings awake from their dream into consciousness, they immediately turn the light it sheds upon themselves; they become aware of themselves and what we call "I" takes on shape and what is worse, weight. And so, our own being comes to interject itself into the light, the glimmer of the original light that is consciousness. And we lose pure, original consciousness. Throughout its long history, philosophy has made a great effort to return us to the original light, deepening consciousness or rather returning it to, reintegrating it into, its point of origin—the divine.

But, here is Antigone, a girl who did not have time to contemplate herself. Awakened from her girlish dream by the horror of the paternal crime, she entered into full consciousness and conscience. But she never turned it upon herself. Thus the tragic conflict found her a virgin, and her womanly virginity perfectly suited her lucid consciousness. Innocent, intact life, and consciousness. And so, she had to descend among the dead while still alive. The terrible punishment was also appropriate for her; only an all-consuming fire would have been better, enveloping her as it did Joan of Arc, another perfect virgin. Human beings[3] only have a cell prepared for the perfect virginity of the soul and consciousness, a cell where they are slowly consumed. Or they have a bonfire, a fire that takes unto itself what in fact belongs to it.

As Sophocles tells it, Antigone hung herself in the death chamber. However much our respect for the author of Antigone's poetic existence may intimidate us, it seems impossible to accept such an end. No; merciful, pious[4] Antigone knew nothing about herself, not even that she could kill herself. This swift action was alien to her, and before she could come to it—supposing that it were her appropriate end—she had to enter into a long gallery of wailing and become captive to innumerable deliriums. Her soul had to reveal itself and even rebel. Her unlived life had to awaken. She had to live in delirium what she had not lived in the time that is conceded to mortals. Her time among the mortals was snatched from her, leaving it—irony of the condemnation—among the shades. From the moment she decided to pay due homage to her brother's corpse, her virgin being belonged to the shadowy kingdom. But there is more. Every perfect virgin must descend into hell, because hell, which seems to reside in the depths of the human soul and even beyond in the secret realm of the dead, reclaims them. It is as if the underworld, the depths of the earth and the souls, needed their purity and as if purity itself had to achieve its liberty only after suffering the consequences of the crime of which it is not a part.

And how could innocent Antigone, thrown alive to the dead, have killed herself without going through hell? By giving her a violent death, Sophocles wrested her from her destiny—immortality. Only purity that has passed through hell can be immortal. Demeter's daughter Persephone, image of spring, was kidnapped by the God of the viscera, by the God of fire, and from there she reemerges to bring happiness to the earth. One cannot imagine Antigone belonging to this line of spring-like heroines, kidnapped by the dead, by hell, from which they return time and again. Antigone is something more: she is the spring of human consciousness, purity of conscience, and for that reason she will return over and over from her grave to illuminate the world. It is the essence of the mystery of this perfect virginity—conscience and pity—which are one and the same thing in her;[5] since conscience does not discern unduly and only concerns itself with what is more than just, justice according to divine logic.

And how could Antigone, who did not have time to discover herself, or to be discovered, carry out the act of supreme violence, killing herself by hanging? She had to surrender to her delirium; she had to allow the expression of her unlived life—the cry of love asleep in the breast of a woman who bears latent life—to well up in her with the same purity as her cry against Creon. She could not strangle her latent life, which was clambering to be lived, since it would have betrayed her merciful, pious, virginal condition. And she would have avoided her punishment. Like Socrates, another victim of conscience and pity, her condemnation had to be hurriedly carried out—to expire while buried, handed over to the earth before death, because she had chosen it to be thus.

We do not know how long Antigone remained delirious between the four walls of her tomb. Nor do we need to know. Clepsydras do not measure delirium time. And each sacrifice alters time, an alteration that deepens and opens temporal abysses in which events that normally require decades are consummated.

In *La Femme pauvre*, León Bloy says his protagonist had the ability to accelerate time and make events that take an entire lifetime transpire in a few days. However, this girl protagonist of the poor woman (of the woman dispossessed of everything in order to be the human wife of the Holy Spirit) belonged to Antigone's species. One could recognize this by the sign of accelerating time. And thus it is perfectly plausible that in her death chamber Antigone reviewed her entire possible life in her delirium. But her life was not the question, as it never is with these virgins who come into the world to untie a terrible knot. Her potential life, her latent life, will occupy a small place in her delirium. The essential thing was the reconciliation of her tormented family, the final pacification and exhaustion of Oedipus's, Yocasta's, and their children's destiny. She had come to untie the knot of her parents' incest and therefore could not continue toward her future by marrying her fiancé Haemon, who shouldn't live either, since he was only Antigone's fiancé and nothing more. All individual personal life was stolen from Antigone because she did not have time to think about herself.

Antigone had not come to "live her life" but to offer it sealed in a vessel; her virgin body is the vessel that appears in all sacrifices. Only common mortals have come to live their respective individual lives and thus they carry out projects, draw their own profile, and cast it into the light of consciousness, into original life. And the projects and plans intercross one another, collide, and form what we call "reality," "things as they are," and even become tangled up with the laws. But those who, like the child Antigone, are chosen, do not live, do not have projects or plans. They do not decide about themselves, because their life is but essence enclosed in a vessel, which will be spilled intact so that others may feed on it and live. They are transformed into clarity and their voice is inextinguishable. They become confused with the elements, and their story forms part of the history of the formation of the world, of the history that remains of the drama for which nature and human beings continue to be born among anguish and horrors. No, child Antigone did not come "to live her life."

And there in the inferno of her enclosed soul, in the place where only the dead enter, in the sacred darkness of a sepulcher away from human eyes, hidden from light, she fulfilled her destiny for which life had no place. Nor did death, because such things, such sacred designs, must be carried out in a realm that is neither life nor death; that realm is a sacrificial place where mortals must cover their faces and not see. All sacrifices have a time of fulfillment, which demands that life stop and that eyes not look, that consciousness remain silent and that the heavens themselves be suspended!

If Antigone had lived "her life," how would she have been able to untie the terrible knot, verify the reconciliation? It was not a matter of expiating what Oedipus had already expiated, but of exhausting it. For that reason she was passive: her action was to harmonize, to equalize, to mediate between the brothers and beyond the familial circle, between life and death. Heroine, semi-goddess of virginal conscience, she had to hasten her learning of life's deepest secrets, suffer the weight of the laws, of justice, in order to offer us perennially the purity of an unsullied conscience, unstained by any shadow of individual "preoccupation" or "project." Clarity that illuminates the ultimate abyss, flame that never turned upon itself except to consume the slight body. For this reason it burned slowly without rapture. Winged light that peeks out from the shadows, clarity born of the abyss like a pale spring greening, and within the green fuzz a bluish flower, a red, purplish poppy that humans must not touch; uncontainable cries of delirium. Spring is a delirium of hope on Earth, and in the human world, conscience, upon being born in its inexorable clarity, is also a delirium of hopeful justice.

And thus, Antigone will continue to be transformed; she was like a bluish flower, that pure, sweet, violent blue of creative virginity. Enclosed, insane, she fades until she arrives at the last reaches of thirsty, unsatisfied being. She goes beyond rancor and becomes a gray, rough nettle; she only retains the thirst that can no longer be satisfied. But her life, now withdrawn from her body, will be concentrated in her spirit, and it burns. Antigone is not liberated from the torture of fire, which belongs to the spirit that, sunken in solitude and abandonment, feeds on itself. Then, transformed into a "burning bramble," symbol of the creative spirit, she will rebuke her gods. Before her gods, she burns and rebukes them, and she exposes them. She exposes their perfidy and also their terrible limitation of being forms. The Greek gods had all the beauty and the limitation of being a form: their beauty is deceptive. Or rather, they were shallow when mortals had to confront their profound destiny and suffer alone without their help or comprehension. They, glorious forms, transcended us. They were the opposite of humans; they were unenclosed, transcendent creatures, although they were imprisoned in their forms. The gods are fixed in their forms, and they cannot abandon them; in their essence Greek gods are the least able to transcend.

And thus, all poetic or real personages that transcend, like Antigone and Socrates, found themselves alone, and without premeditation they unmasked their gods.

Antigone, sacrificed, virginal conscience, becomes spirit in her solitude, separated from the dead and the living. What is the situation called spirit except to be detached from the gods, without a place and beyond life? Everything that allows the spirit to take it is freed, breaks away, and enters into the most complete solitude. Daringly, Antigone violated the limits of the laws, the mandates of the gods, and known justice and pity. She fell under the reign of an unknown god. She was the victim and servant of this god.

She transcended her gods; then she died in the abandonment of not having known God, the God she truly served. This is the ultimate essence of her tragedy. And for that reason she will found a species of saintly girls or adolescents that have traversed the world with their swords intact, full of pious mercy without commiseration. Not thinking of their fate, they rush forward lucidly; they accelerate time. Illiterate and without forethought, they assume a judge's role when they are submitted to the constant trial of interrogation, and the justness of their answers dazzles. Antigone constitutes a species whose forms and figures will always be recognizable for their gift of simplicity in which pity and justice, conscience and innocence are one and the same. Humanity always has a cell or a bonfire prepared for these girls, probably both because prison and fire go together.

And they will never emerge into full light. Even when, like Joan of Arc, they are commanding armies, something will keep them isolated, secret. And afterward they will weep because they are imprisoned spring, kidnapped purity, limited in their action, although not in their life.

And of them all, Antigone, who was buried alive, moans. We cannot fail to hear her through the cracks in her tomb. She, hopeful justice without vengeance, inexorable clarity, virgin conscience, always awake, continues to rave. We cannot fail to hear her, because Antigone's tomb is our own shadowy conscience. Antigone was buried alive in us, in each one of us.

First Delirium

Born for love, pious mercy has devoured me. What can I do with these entrails that moan? For the first time I have feelings when the time is no longer right. Why didn't you awaken these feelings? Now I see it—like all men you wait for the girl to die in order to possess her lifeless body. Why are you so afraid to awaken a mere chrysalis, enclosed in herself, asleep in the cocoon like a silkworm? Perhaps you tremble at the thought of her future wings? You are not made to possess a butterfly and pursue it. But I was, and I am now, the butterfly that does not want to tear itself free from its shroud and take flight toward liberty, because one who has not enjoyed love, who has not felt her body grow and fill out, like those few women molded by the Athenian sculptors, with their unconquered rounded bellies, their slight curves, their glorious bodies in the plenitude of love, cannot face liberty... I already feel my wings. They are so

weak, pale, and withered, even before they are born. How they beat upon being born of my body's paleness; like my body, they lack luster and glory. And
you, like a blond insect, were waiting for me in order to set fire to me with a
fair, golden light that I took to be its reflection. Why were you so blond? Why
did you surround yourself with your halo and not approach me? You always
passed by things without staining them. I remember it well. I see you barely
graze the sacred vessel during the sacrifices and spill the blood of the calf, tear-
ing his skin, grabbing him by the horns in the virility ritual, which you carried
out in spite of yourself. I felt your fingers on my skin when you cut the rose
and offered it to me. You never dared cut an oleander branch, because there
was a thick poison in its nectar and a secret in its calyx that you—blond male
bee—never dared to deflower. After all, it is the hard-working bee whose official occupation it is to enter the flower's chalice and snatch its syrup. And
you, who, as the blond queen's companion, had the passion, always avoided
all secret sweetness, and when you approached me, encircled by your golden
light, you preferred only to gaze at me and contemplate the trembling of my
breast from outside. Perhaps you wanted to be seen, pale reflection of a king,
pale prince of golden fog, always damp and cold, flame without fire, reflection, always reflection. I never knew the color of your eyes; I didn't dare look
at them; I was afraid they would decipher me, and I always lowered mine when
we walked together among the olive trees in the afternoon. I saw the red earth,
red and purplish, and in silence gathering up the respiration, the butterfly of
my breath, I waited, offering my neck, the only secret that a virgin can offer...
Only once did I feel your gaze on its center like a fine knife, like a little golden
knife slipping down the canal of my back. I remember that I went ahead two
steps, and the curve of my neck whitened and took on such form. Yes, I saw
it, like one of the women in the statues. My blood descended, and I was also
a flower and a lamb like those they give you crowned with roses, and a garland began to caress my neck falling on my breast like a water serpent. I bent
to the ground and pulled up some blue flowers, of that sweet, violent color,
and when I raised myself up, your eyes had ceased to plunge into the secret of
my neck. And it seemed as if I had no body, that I was sinking into a name-
less cold, and I shrank. How pale, gray, ugly, yes, ugly, I must have been at
that moment, because you were afraid. "Are you ill?" you asked, and I would
have fled if my feet had not been rooted in the earth!... But wait; now my hair
is nearly white. How long have I been enclosed here with myself? Not even
the dead receive me; I wanted to descend among the dead so that I would not

feel this cold... What will they say about me, Antigone, the good merciful sister? Now I realize that I only went to the tomb to embrace my brother's cadaver, my dead brother's body, in order to take vengeance on you, pale king of my dreams, on you, my fiancé brother, on you my only husband, my king for whom I was destined to enjoy my royalty at your side, my reality as a full woman, in fullness like a ship's hull when it runs on the open sea, pushed, caressed by the violence of the wind? What am I complaining about? You, you and no other were also my brother; like I, you were stained by the shadow of incest, tormented... like I. You must have been someone else, son of a different family, of another ancestral bird. What are men like? Fiancés, lovers who approach other women, those that embrace women violently and make them leave their damp wooden beds; those that make women dance. Violent to the point of spilling their blood like that of a sacrificial lamb, and the women die; yes, they die in order to leap when they have become others. Because the sacrifice kills us women, the victims, and turns us into others.

And I, unconsumed victim, flower without fruit, wanted to come among the dead so that they could be nourished by my sacred, untouched body. Only the little knife in the neck... Perhaps I did not come to them a complete virgin? Why do I continue alone, unaccepted, unconsumed victim, buried alive, with my hair now gray? Why has the death to which I delivered myself not come? My vestments are torn. Time. How long have I been here, neither alive nor dead? How, how long? Time and only time has destroyed my wedding dress, my dress for the bride of death, for the wife affianced to the dead. Time has hung spider webs in this tomb, this nuptial chamber; they get tangled up in my arms; they cling to my hair. Is my hair gray or is it time, only time and the spider web, my only companion, pale and bloodless like me? My blood is now pale blue; at first it was like those flowers that I pulled up along the roadside between the olive trees the afternoon you touched my neck with a little gold knife without plunging it in, when I was so cold, and now I moan here alone. Not even the dead receive me, because a man, no man raises his arm to defend me...

Man, male, unknown brother fiancé, why didn't you appear? Father... the only man I knew! But blind, you leaned on my shoulder; I was your staff; I served you as guide and support; I sang for you, lighting up your night; I was your lark. Perhaps your terrible destiny reached me? And have you called me through my brother's corpse? Father, brother, where are you? Why don't you come to rescue Antigone, of whom you always demanded pious mercy

without providing her the protection that all women enjoy? I am your victim.
Alone, your staff is here alone, your poor lost dove. What are you doing?

María Zambrano

Paris, July 1947

Havana, July 1948

Translation and María Zambrano's Antigone

In the mid-1990s I collaborated with Carol Maier on her translation of Spanish philosopher and Republican exile María Zambrano's *Delirio y destino* [Delirium and destiny]. *Delirio y destino* is a novelized autobiography or autobiographical novel that, while covering much of Zambrano's life from childhood to her exile after the Spanish Civil War in 1939, focuses on Zambrano's experiences in the late 1920s as a member of a student group militating for a republican form of government in Spain. At the end of *Delirium and Destiny*, Zambrano included eight *delirios* ("deliriums"), creative narrations that form a lyrical-allegorical counterpoint to the personal, social, historical, political, and philosophical account of the author's life. In honor of Carol and to commemorate the joy of working with her, I offer a translation of "El delirio de Antígone" (Antigone's Delirium), a *delirio* published in the Cuban journal *Orígenes* in 1948, six years before the composition of the novelized autobiography, and not included in *Delirio y destino*.

"Antigone's Delirium" captures some of the flavor of *Delirium and Destiny*, especially its political undercurrent, its philosophical lyricism, and its female perspective. In my translation, I have tried to emulate what I learned from Carol about translation as a scholarly and literary activity. Carol's method includes (1) knowing the author and subject well via substantial supplementary reading and (2) a fine literary sensitivity that balances faithfulness to the meaning and tone of the original Spanish with the demands of English cadence. The first I can do; the second requires talent and ear, and no one can match a master translator like Carol Maier in that realm. In keeping with Carol's custom, I place this commentary at the end of the translated text. Carol always wants the translated work to stand on its own, to "refuse any absolute definition" (Maier 1999:245).

The concept "to translate" also eludes "absolute definition." Although "rendering from one language into another of something written or spoken" is usually what comes to mind when we think of *translation*, this is not the first definition given in the dictionary. The dictionary's first definition of "to trans-late" invokes displacement: "to move from one place or condition to another; transfer; specif., a) *Theol.* To convey directly to heaven without death, b) *Ec-cles.* To transfer (a bishop) from one see to another; also, to move (a saint's body or remains) from one place of interment to another" (*Webster's New World College Dictionary* s.v.). Translation also connotes transformation: "to change into another medium or form/to *translate* ideas into action" and to transmit via automatic relay, and archaically "to enrapture; entrance." All of these meanings resonate in Zambrano's "translation" or "transformation" of Sophocles' story. In "Antigone's Delirium" and later in *La tumba de Antigone* [Antigone's tomb], Zambrano changes Antigone's fate. Zambrano's Antigone does not commit suicide in the tomb but lives to experience "deliriums." The Spanish philosopher endows the protagonist of Sophocles' *Antigone* with the subjectivity she lacks in the Greek play where her role is limited to the public sphere of Creon's law and condemnation. In the second part of "Antigone's Delirium," titled "First Delirium," we enter Antigone's consciousness and are privy to thoughts or, better, images that might have come to her while impris-oned in her tomb.[6] The voice that Zambrano creates for Antigone is lyrical, delirious, entranced (in the archaic sense of *translated*).

Along with transformation, the notion of transfer (inherent in some def-initions of *translation*) is central to "Antigone's Delirium" and contains its political message. When she began treating the Antigone theme, Zambrano had been exiled from Francisco Franco's Spain for some eight years, living in Mexico, Cuba, and Puerto Rico, teaching philosophy, delivering lectures, and writing articles and philosophical works.[7] Like many Spanish exiles, Zam-brano continued into the early 1950s to hope that the Western democracies, having vanquished two other fascist dictatorships in Europe, would finally oust Franco, allowing the exiles to return to Spain.

Surely Zambrano was drawn to the political aspect of Antigone's story in which the protagonist's burial of her brother countermanded the tyrant Cre-on's law. The Second Spanish Republic, so often depicted as a woman clothed in classical garb, can easily be read into "Antigone's Delirium."[8] The freedom of expression Zambrano allows Antigone recalls that of the quashed Republic, and Antigone's transcendence of her oppression signals Zambrano's hope for the Republic's restoration. In "First Delirium" Antigone conjures a scene in which she is walking with her fiancé Haemon through an olive orchard replete with Republican symbols. Olive branches, which represented peace or victory and were worn by brides in ancient Greece, often appear in Spanish Republican-era iconography. The earth on which the couple treads is red and purple (and the poppies—usually symbolizing sleep—are red and purplish) thus recalling the top and bottom stripes of the tricolor Republican flag (Haemon is golden, the color of the middle band of the flag). The traditional Spanish flag also had three bands, but both the top and bottom stripes were red. The Republic added the purple band to symbolize freedom. Importantly, the Spanish word *amoratado,* which I have translated as "purplish," also means "bruised."

Zambrano concludes her prologue by observing that Antigone "hopeful justice without vengeance . . . continues to rave" and that "we cannot fail to hear her, because Antigone's tomb is our own shadowy conscience. Antigone was buried alive in us, in each one of us." In this sense Zambrano's use of the Antigone figure echoes that of Hölderlin's Antigone play, which, according to George Steiner (1984:91), was "set in, and representative of, a moment of 'national reversal and revolution' (*vaterläudische Umkehr*). The hour is that of a dramatic revaluation of moral values and political power relations. From the fatal collision of tragic agents and worldviews, there will emerge a 'republickanishce Vernunftsform' ('a republican rationality,' 'a reasoned structure in the republican mode')" (91). Zambrano's Jungian-tinted idea of a shadow buried in the conscience "of all of us" unmistakably refers to the Spanish Republican exiles (transfers) and their hope for restoration and return.

"Antigone's Delirium," however, is much more than the "translation" of the classical story into a twentieth-century political allegory of Republican Spain. Zambrano was a master at blending political, philosophical, and literary themes and genres in her work. Antigone's situation as daughter of Oedipus's incestuous union with his mother, her defiance of tyrant Creon's law against bestowing funerary honors on the corpse of her brother Polynices, her condemnation to death by live burial, and her betrothal to Creon's son Haemon all conspire to make her an ideal subject for Zambrano's multilayered approach. As George Steiner writes, "in Antigone the dialectic of intimacy and of exposure, of the 'housed' and of the most public, is made explicit. The play turns on the enforced politics of the private spirit, on the necessary violence which political-social change visits on the unspeaking inwardness of being" (1984:11). Zambrano combines the philosophical and the public with the literary and the intimate by dividing "Antigone's Delirium" into two parts. The prologue is a philosophical meditation on consciousness and conscience, while the delirium is an experiment in representing consciousness, which, like Modernist stream of consciousness, employs a wide range of poetic techniques—metaphor, sensory references, synesthesia, ellipsis, alliteration, assonance, rhythm, and internal rhyme. These literary devices register the contents of Antigone's consciousness as they are transformed from her awakening sexuality to recognition of her advancing age in captivity.

The prologue on human consciousness contains a sophisticated response to phenomenologists such as Max Scheler, whom Zambrano read in the 1920s, and Zambrano's Spanish university professor, José Ortega y Gasset. If Scheler and Ortega believed that consciousness (self-reflectiveness) is what constitutes humanity and separates humans from the world around them, in the Antigone figure Zambrano posits a preconscious state. Antigone represents the preconscious in that "she scarcely had time to know that she existed, to see herself and be seen. . . . The virgin consciousness illuminates and directs itself to what is not itself; to what is not the subject to which it belongs. A rare moment of human perfection. . . ." For Zambrano, "consciousness is to awake from life's dream; at first to live is to remain submerged in dreams without any knowledge of the difference between things, the difference that arises from the primary abyss between ourselves and the reality that surrounds us." Zambrano interprets Antigone's eternal virginity as her having been denied the opportunity to reflect upon herself, to reflect upon her own existence.

In the "First Delirium" Zambrano attempts through the use of various literary strategies to reveal the consciousness, the inner self, that male writers—Sophocles, Hegel, Hölderlin, and Kierkegaard—deny Antigone. One of Zambrano's central philosophical concepts is poetic reason that finds in literature a means of considering the soul. She believed that the soul, abandoned in the rational age, should be restored to philosophical thinking, but she did not wish to completely relinquish the notion of reason (or standard philosophical concepts and methodology) in her literary approach, thus "poetic reason." The term *delirio,* which I have translated rather literally as "delirium," is both a literary and philosophical category. Philosophically it refers to a conscious state that is not the autonomous consciousness of modernist philosophy, especially the phenomenology within whose milieu Zambrano cut her philosophical teeth, nor is it a Jungian or Freudian subconscious, notions also contemporaneous with her philosophical formation. It is a personal consciousness (or conscience)—the moment when the individual awakes to reality.

Beatriz Caballero (2008:94) lists the contexts in which Zambrano employs the term *delirio* to describe a state of consciousness that results from "persecution," "creative intoxication," and "love." Delirio occurs when hopes and reality clash and the disparity between them becomes manifest; it is a coming into consciousness. Caballero defines delirium in Zambrano's work as "the mental state that arises as a result of a deep frustration and/or strong pressures placed on the individual. . . . Because the state borders on insanity, it confers a liberty on the individual, which he or she did not have before, and makes agency possible" (94; my translation). It is no coincidence that Zambrano began elaborating these ideas in Paris and Cuba in the late 1940s when she had seen the European horrors personally during her stay in France from 1946 to 1948 to attend to her sister after her mother's death.[9] In addition she was assimilating the fact that the Western democracies, having won the Second World War, were not going to turn their depleted energies toward Francisco Franco's Spain. Like Zambrano, Antigone descends to the depths, awakens to reality, falls into consciousness or conscience, and in the ensuing delirium (for Antigone the "First Delirium" and for Zambrano her lyrical philosophical writing) achieves liberty.

Like Kierkegaard in *Either/Or,* Zambrano appropriated the Antigone myth and gave it an inward focus, although unlike Kierkegaard she did not abandon the political aspect of the original. She also shared Kierkegaard's interest in the moral potential of the story. In the Antigone figure Kierkegaard relates tragic guilt to the transition from the aesthetic to the ethical. The philosopher positions himself as Antigone's father, and he sends her "out into the world" as though he were giving "the daughter of sorrow a dowry of pain as a wedding gift" (1971:151). Like the relationship of Antigone's father, Oedipus, to her mother, Kierkegaard's relationship to Antigone is incestuous. He is both father and lover: "She is my creation, her thoughts are my thoughts, and yet it is as if I had rested with her in a night of love, as if she had entrusted me with her deep secret, breathed it and her soul out in my embrace, and as if in the same moment she changed before me, vanished, so that her actuality could only be traced in the mood that remained, instead of the converse being true, that my mood brought her forth in a greater and greater actuality" (151). In Kierkegaard's "translation" of Antigone, she is his creation, but she eludes him: "she lies constantly before me, she constantly comes into existence only as I bring her forth" (151). Zambrano also brings forth Antigone, who moves from an awakening individual consciousness in the early part of the prologue to the moral conscience of us all by the end of the prologue. In this sense Zambrano seems to be following Kierkegaard's shift to the ethical in *Either/Or,* although her shift is from the phenomenological to the ethical, whereas Kierkegaard's is from the aesthetic to the ethical. Unlike Kierkegaard, however, Antigone does not elude Zambrano but becomes increasingly hers, as the girl grows into a withered womanhood, she could be Zambrano's own disappointed hopes.

Andrew Bush calls Zambrano's version of Antigone a "Christian translation" (2004:100, 102) in which "Antigone [is] the conductor, the translator" and also "the figure of love as 'mediator'" (105). Bush links the word *translation* to the survival of the sacred in Zambrano's thought. Quoting Walter Benjamin, he specifies that "translation [is] the language of a certain survival: the language that speaks after the life and death of the work of art; the language that speaks for the work of art in the time of its afterlife" (92–93). Bush reminds us that in Zambrano's prologue to *La tumba de Antigone,* she refers to her "translation" of Antigone as "tránsito," which Bush calls a "poetics or a theory of translation" (96). Although Bush does not note it, throughout "Delirio de Antigone," Zambrano employs the adjective *piedosa* ("pious," "merciful") for Antigone and often associates her with *piedad* ("piety," "mercy"), which has both religious and secular connotations, as I point out in endnote 4. Other religious dimensions with which Zambrano endows Antigone's story (not mentioned in Bush's analysis) include the girl's innocence and virginity ("innocent and intact life and consciousness"), her sacrifice ("Antigone, sacrificed virginal conscience"), and the chalice, which has both sexual and religious meanings in the "First Delirium."[10] In addition, in her prologue to the first delirium, Zambrano compares Antigone to some saintly women, including Joan of Arc, whose actions place them in a class of young girls chosen to be the conscience of us all.

Hegel also emphasizes action when employing the word *translation* to refer to Antigone in *Phenomenology of the Spirit* (Hegel was thinking particularly of Antigone's act of burying her brother): "Being is a 'pure translation' (*reines Uebersetzen*) of potential being into action, into 'the doing of the deed' (*das Tun der Tat*). No individual can attain an authentic knowledge of himself 'ehe es sich durch Tun zur Wirklichkeit gebracht hat' ('until it has brought itself into actuality through action')" (quoted in Steiner 1984:29). Zambrano emphasizes the fact that Antigone acted before she had the chance to reflect upon herself, an action that can be construed as Christian or saintly self-denial.

I have reserved for last the matter of Zambrano's translation of *Antigone* as a feminist interpretation of the classical figure, because this aspect of Antigone ties together the political, the philosophical, and the literary dimensions of "Antigone's Delirium." Hardly any of Zambrano's work is overtly feminist, and she did not consider herself a feminist. In her treatment of the Antigone theme, however, one cannot help but recall Luce Irigaray's feminist critique of Hegel's interpretation of Antigone as representing the traditional (and in his view, appropriate) role as defender of the family. Irigaray counters Hegel's interpretation of Antigone as fulfilling women's destiny to renounce their sensibility and their personal desires in favor of their family responsibilities. Elena Laurenzi believes that Zambrano definitely had Hegel's interpretation of Antigone in *Phenomenology of the Spirit* in mind when she "translated" or transformed Sophocles's defiant female character into a woman with an inner life. Laurenzi also argues that Zambrano's changing Antigone's fate from suicide to survival is a feminist move.[11]

Although Zambrano's "translation" of Antigone can certainly be considered feminist, the fact remains that Zambrano employs an existential/phenomenological vocabulary that gives her Antigone a universal dimension. Zambrano explicitly names all humankind in her identification of Antigone with "us" at the end of the prologue. Nonetheless, it is hard to ignore the fact that Antigone is a woman and that she interprets her own plight from a female (even feminist) perspective. In her delirium Antigone recognizes that she assumed the traditional passive female role in her relationship with Haemon. In a passage of the delirium where I have employed "men" (the male sex or gender) for *hombres,* rather than the philosophical "humanity," Antigone accuses Haemon of acting like many men in their relations with women—preferring not to become physically involved with the woman's body until after she is dead. In the end she pointedly remarks that she is left alone to suffer the consequences of her actions with no man to save or protect her. The latter of Zambrano's few works that focus on women (written in 1928 and in the early and mid-1940s) came at a crucial juncture in her life when she had separated from her husband and was fending for herself economically. At this point she was also developing her central ideas on the nature of the self. Paired with her "Eloísa, o la existencia de la mujer" [Heloise, or women's existence] (1946), "Antigone's Delirium" (written a year later) provides a more complete picture of how Zambrano transformed concepts such as *soul,* which she had first associated with literary and historical female figures, into universal notions in subsequent works, such as *El hombre y lo divino* [Man and the divine] (1955) and *Persona y democracia: La historia sacrificial* [Person and democracy: The sacrificial history] (1958).[12]

To conclude, I return to the present day's most common use of the term *to translate*—rendering a text into a language other than the one in which it was written. Zambrano's writing presents a number of difficulties to the translator. Her thoughts and meanings are subtle and oblique, and her language is dense and literary rather than expository and direct. Although her style could be called "luminous," it is elusive and must be read with some of the rational processes on hold. Zambrano tends to employ very long sentences, often with multiple punctuation marks that are not always helpful in elucidating the meaning. Carol Maier says in her afterward to *Delirium and Destiny* that she read Zambrano's texts out loud in order to hear where the natural breaks in meaning occur. I have tried this method to some extent, not always with Carol's success. As Carol also notes, many of Zambrano's texts are not stable. During her exile, she lived an itinerant life; she often wrote in haste, and there are multiple versions of some works. Carol traveled to the Fundación Maria Zambrano in Vélez-Málaga in southern Spain to see the original manuscript of "Delirio y destino" specifically to check on punctuation. She found that the typescript was often as confusing as the published copy. I have had to rely on the version of "Delirio de Antigone" published in Elena Laurenzi's *Maria Zambrano: Nacer por sí misma* [María Zambrano: Born of herself]. Laurenzi is a careful scholar, but even so, there are passages where the purpose of the punctuation is unclear.

By an uncanny coincidence, when I was finishing this project, Carol Maier contacted me for information on an entirely different matter. That contact, as with every communication I have had with Carol over the years, sparked new thinking, this time about *delirio* as a philosophical concept and as a literary genre. Perhaps these illuminations will lead to further collaboration. I certainly hope so.

Notes

1. *Conciencia* in Spanish means both ethical "conscience" and the philosophical concept "consciousness." Zambrano seems to be drawing on both these meanings in "Delirio de Antigone." Antigone's decision to honor her dead brother against Creon's edict has often been interpreted as a moral act of conscience. In the early part of the "Prologue" of "Antigone's Delirium," Zambrano appropriates the story for a consideration of phenomenological consciousness or existential self-consciousness, while later passages of the "Prologue" resonate with the moral dimension of conciencia. I have translated *conciencia* according to its apparent meaning in each individual context.

2. The Spanish word that appears in the published text is *abismal,* which means a certain kind of nail. However, the sentence makes more sense if the word is interpreted as *abismo* ("abysm" or "abyss").

3. I have translated *el hombre* and *los hombres* as "human being(s)" and "humanity" wherever Zambrano employs these masculine terms in the philosophical sense of "man" or "all people." In the "First Delirium," however, Antigone employs *los hombres* to refer to the male sex, and there I translate it as "men."

4. *Piedad* is another Spanish word with two meanings: "pious" in the religious sense and the more secular "merciful" (compassionate). I have consistently translated *piedad* with both English terms because Zambrano seems to mean both when describing Antigone.

5. Zambrano's punctuation is confusing here and I have made an interpretive translation. The original reads: "Y es la esencia del misterio de esta perfecta virginidad, que en ella son la misma e idéntica cosa; conciencia y piedad, pues la conciencia no discierne. . . ." I interpret "la misma e idéntica cosa" ("one and the same thing") as referring to "conciencia y piedad" ("conscience and pity") and not to any of the other possible pairs in the first part of the sentence—"misterio" ("mystery") and "virginidad" ("virginity"), for example.

6. The fact that the second part of the text is titled "First Delirium" suggests that this is an incomplete work and that Zambrano intended to write more deliriums for Antigone.

7. Zambrano addressed ("translated") the Antigone theme on at least four occasions. "El delirio de Antigone," written in 1947 and 1948 in Paris and Havana, Cuba, at a crucial juncture in Zambrano's thinking about the self and about women, is the first of Zambrano's retellings of Sophocles's version. The second comes toward the end of *Delirio y destino* (written in 1952 but not published until 1989) where Zambrano calls her sister Antigone. The third is found in a section of *El hombre y lo divino* (1955:211), and the fourth is a commentary and dialogued fiction or play titled *La tumba de Antigone* published in 1967.

8. See Cuesta and Johnson (2014) for a full accounting of these classically clothed female representations of the Second Spanish Republic.

9. Araceli, María Zambrano's sister, remained in Paris with her mother after the Spanish Civil War. In the French capital Araceli witnessed firsthand the horrors of the Nazi-dominated Vichy regime. See footnote 4 in my essay "María Zambrano as Antigone's Sister: Towards an Ethical Aesthetics of Possibility" (1997) for details of Araceli's life in Paris and for an analysis of *La tumba de Antigone*. There I only briefly mention the piece I have translated and am commenting upon here.

10. For this reason I have translated *cáliz* alternately as "chalice" and "calyx," the part of the flower bees penetrate to extract the nectar.

11. In addition Laurenzi (1995:57–59) believes that Zambrano avoids Luce Irigaray's interpretation of Antigone as trapped in a patriarchal system. Laurenzi may be right that Zambrano has avoided this view of Antigone, but, interestingly, Zambrano has been an important source of inspiration for Italian and Spanish difference feminists. See my "Hablar con el cuerpo" (2011) and "La filosofía de María Zambrano" (2009) for discussions of Zambrano's work in the context of European difference feminism.

12. See my essay "El concepto de 'persona' de María Zambrano y su pensamiento sobre la mujer" [María Zambrano's concept of "person" and her ideas on women] (2012).

Works Cited

Bush, Andrew. 2004. "María Zambrano and the Survival of Antigone." *Diacritics* 34(3): 90–111.

Caballero, Beatriz. 2008. "La centralidad del concepto de delirio en el pensamiento de María Zambrano." *Arizona Journal of Hispanic Cultural Studies* 12:93–110.

Cuesta, Luis F., and Roberta Johnson. 2014. "La niña bonita: Tradition and Change in Female Allegories of the Second Spanish Republic. *Journal of Spanish Cultural Studies* 14(4): 415–61.

Johnson, Roberta. 1997. "María Zambrano as Antigone's Sister: Towards an Ethical Aesthetics of Possibility." *Anales de la literatura española contemporánea* 22(1-2):181–94.

Johnson, Roberta. 2009. "La filosofía de María Zambrano y el pensamiento feminista europeo." *Antígona. Revista de la Fundación María Zambrano* 3:196–206.

Johnson, Roberta. 2011. "Hablar con el cuerpo: María Zambrano y el feminismo de la diferencia español." In *María Zambrano: Palabras para el mundo*, edited by Madeline Cámara and Luis Pablo Ortega, 171–90. Newark, Del.: Juan de la Cuesta.

Johnson, Roberta. 2012. "El concepto de persona en María Zambrano y su pensamiento sobre la mujer." *Aurora* 13:8–17.

Kierkegaard, Søren. 1971. *Either/Or*. Vol. 1. Translated by David. F. Swenson and Lillian Marvin Swenson. Princeton, N.J.: Princeton University Press.

Laurenzi, Elena. 1995. "Prólogo." In *María Zambrano. Nacer por sí misma*, edited by Elena Laurenzi, 55–65. Madrid: horas y Horas.

Maier, Carol. 1999. "From *Delirio y destino* to *Delirium and Destiny*." In *Delirium and Destiny. A Spaniard in Her Twenties*, edited by María Zambrano, 237–48. Translated by Carol Maier. Buffalo: SUNY Press.

Steiner, George. 1984. *Antigones*. New Haven, Conn.: Yale University Press.

Webster's New World College Dictionary. 1999. 4th ed. New York: Macmillan.

Zambrano, María. 1955. *El hombre y lo divino*. Mexico: Fondo de Cultura Económica.

Zambrano, María. 1967. *La tumba de Antígona*. Madrid: Siglio XXI.

Zambrano, María. 1989. *Delirio y destino. Los veinte años de una española*. Madrid: Mondadori.

Zambrano, María. 1995. "Delirio de Antígona." In *María Zambrano: Nacer por sí misma*, edited by Elena Laurenzi, 66–76. Madrid: horas y Horas.

Carolina Coronado and Martha Perry Lowe

Translating Sisterhood

Noël Valis

The literary fortunes of the Spanish romantic poet Carolina Coronado (1820–1911) have risen and sunk only to rise again in the past 25 years. Acclaimed, then forgotten, she has found a new place, in part as the central figure of a lyrical sisterhood of mid-nineteenth-century women poets.[1] This sense of female solidarity, however, actually extended beyond Spain's borders to include an American poet, Martha Perry Lowe (1829–1902), who became her sister-in-law in 1852, when Carolina married Horatio Justus Perry, the secretary of the American Legation in Madrid. Scholars have known for some time about this literary relationship, in particular the poem Martha wrote in praise of her Spanish sister, "Carolina Coronado, Poetess of Spain," which appeared in Lowe's first collection of poetry, *The Olive and the Pine,* in 1859.[2] But, to my knowledge, no one has pointed out that the New Englander dedicated at least one more poem to Carolina ("To Carolina Coronado," 1865) and, especially germane to my purposes here, also translated her "Oda a Lincoln" in 1864 as "Ode to Abraham Lincoln."

Taken together, the three texts suggest that one way to practice translation is through the literal and figurative bonds of sisterhood, in which individual and cultural differences are both heightened and smoothed out through the act of translating and in which sisterhood itself is lyrically translated into being. Fittingly, as both women were ardent abolitionists, the major theme of two of the poems issues out of the twin poles of slavery/freedom (while two stanzas of the first poem also dwell on the theme). In this way their sisterly bonds form the textual and affective basis for advocating the breaking of real bondage in historical time.

The two women were destined to meet only twice, first in 1853 when Martha (along with her sister Ellen) traveled to Spain to welcome her new sister-in-law and then in 1872 at which time Martha was married and had children. But they maintained a correspondence throughout their lives. Because of the difficulties and expense of transatlantic travel, along with the American Civil War and the fragile health of Martha's husband Charles, they were unable to see each other more than on these two occasions. It should also be pointed out that Carolina never traveled to the United States, and her husband never saw his homeland again, even though he was eager to join the Northern Army during the Civil War. In the obituary for her brother, Martha noted that "his wife's health was delicate." "His wife's death would be at his door," she wrote, were he to leave and take up arms (Lowe 1891:4). The truth is Carolina was enormously possessive of her husband, and her neurotic temperament, which only worsened over the years, led her to keep Horatio on a short leash (see Pérez González 1999:240–43, 265–66, 366). Martha, however, seems either not to have understood their relationship or to have forgiven Carolina's deficiencies of character, for she has nothing but praise for her sister-in-law, as we see in the first poem she published on the Extremaduran writer:

"Carolina Coronado, Poetess of Spain"

The walls of Badajoz looked down
Upon a gifted maid, who rose
Within that old, beleaguered town,
And startled Spain from her repose.

Her eyes were beaming with the fire
Of poet youth beneath her dark
And shining locks. She struck her lyre;
And, lo! the land of Spain did hark.

She calmed her deep, impassioned breast
With love to all the solitudes,
And hid beside the wild-bird's nest
Her verses in the rocks and woods.

She hung enraptured on the sweet
Young meadow rose, and lingered near
The turtle-dove, who did repeat
"Love, love," for ever in her ear.

Unto the Stars she told her tale,
Weeping her tears melodiously
At evening with the Nightingale,
Or with the Palm communing high.

Her genius moved not straight within
The prunèd walks of classic time,
But ran abroad, and revelled in
New laws that rose from out her rhyme.

She poured a tide of passion through
The sordid flats of Life's dull sea;
And, last, she dared to speak unto
Her nation that word—Liberty!

Yes, she—the fearless girl—did make
The slavish priesthood tremble at
The burning words of truth she spake,
And poets at her footstool sat.

At length the laurel wreath they set
Upon her in the royal dome;
But most she loves the coronet
Of wife and mother in her home!

The poem demonstrates that she knew Carolina's poetry well. There are, for example, references to specific poems such as "A la soledad" ("all the solitudes"), "La clavellina" ("meadow rose"), "A una tórtola" ("turtle-dove"), "A una estrella" ("Stars"), "A un ruiseñor" ("Nightingale"), and "A la palma" ("Palm"). Of greater interest is her characterization of the poet as full of fire and passion, as a fearless supporter of liberty. The first stanza sets up the leitmotif by contrasting Carolina with her home town, Badajoz, under siege during the War of

Independence, which pitted the Spanish and British against Napoleon's invading forces. The poet also walks freely as a romantic writer, "not straight within / The prunèd walks of classic time." Finally, Martha's reference to Liberty in the third to last stanza echoes Carolina's celebrated 1846 ballad, "Libertad," a rousing critique of the lack of freedom for women. Martha ends her poem on a triumphant note, recalling Carolina's lyrical coronation at the Madrid Lyceum in 1848 and her more recent domestic joy as wife and mother. This last image, a reassuring one for nearly all readers of the period, whether American or Spanish, reappears as an apostrophe ("O wife and mother") in Martha's 1865 poem.

The poem first stresses Carolina's foreignness, starting with the title words, "Poetess of Spain," and moving on to the "walls of Badajoz." The rest of the text, however, would have spoken directly to the American love of liberty and individualism, as Martha imagines her sister-in-law as a "genius" and a "fearless girl" who "dared to speak unto / Her nation that word—Liberty!" In the United States in the mid-nineteenth century, the emotional connection between poetry and nation was strong. Thus Carolina's stance in the poem assimilates her to an American ethos. Moreover, her poetic figure also makes "the slavish priesthood tremble." This unsympathetic comment on Spanish Catholicism resituates the Extremaduran writer within a particular national and cultural context, reminding us that Martha Perry was a Unitarian and had married a Unitarian minister, Charles Lowe. It is worth pointing out that Coronado's marriage to a Protestant in 1852 was cause for scandal in Spain.[3]

Martha, who married in 1857, finished the collection *The Olive and the Pine,* in which the poem appears, during this period. The collection is divided into two parts titled "Spain" and "New England" (with an additional section of miscellaneous poems). She marks the transition to the second half of the book with the penultimate poem of the first section, "The Steam-Engine in Madrid," when she is minded of her own country: "So young and strong, that stretches out its arms—/ Its interlacing arms—o'er all the earth; / And sweeter than its greatness is the thought, / That there I drew the breath of liberty" (1859:64–65). That same "breath of liberty" also infuses her second book, *Love in Spain, and Other Poems* (1867), which intertwines a love affair between a Protestant English gentlewoman and a Spanish Catholic aristocrat (shades of Carolina and Horatio) and a thwarted liberal revolution brewing in the background. The last section of the book, "The Shadow over the Land," consists of poems written during the American Civil War and includes moving passages on the death of Lincoln and the theme of emancipation.[4]

The interest in Spain and liberty is not surprising, given not only Martha's personal family history but also the political and cultural pedigree she shared with other enlightened New England women of the period. She was "an honorary member of the Castilian Club of Boston, a member of the Women's Education Association of Boston, of the Authors' Club, the Educational and Industrial Union, and the Unitarian Church Temperance Society," as well as a suffragist and a philanthropist, "advocating the cause of the Indian and the Negro," according to one contemporary account (Anon. 1903b:15–16). Another tribute stressed the importance of her Unitarian beliefs: "She was a typical Unitarian in that she exemplified [the] popular conception of good works. Her whole life and character was kindly, philanthropic, beneficent. She sought to be useful and to do good in the world" (Pierson 1903:39).

Like her husband and sister-in-law, Martha was a fervent abolitionist (see Lowe 1884:85–86). Slavery became a defining issue not only for Americans during the Civil War but for some Spaniards like Coronado, who deplored the existence of slavery in Cuba.[5] The theme of liberty, which was initially feminist in "Libertad," turns distinctly abolitionist in Carolina's "Oda a Lincoln":

¡Lincoln, salud! Tu nombre que ha vencido,
del pueblo el escogido,
atravesando por inmensas olas
el terrible océano,
del mundo americano
ha llegado a estas playas españolas.
Grandioso ejemplo de valor cristiano,
hoy ya tu acento humano
contra la injusta esclavitud levantas,
para que el genio altivo
del pueblo primitivo
rescate el libro de sus leyes santas.
El libro, admiración de las edades,
que en esas soledades
el genio de Washington ha inspirado,
y del cual torpemente
otra bastarda gente
las páginas sublimes ha rasgado.
Hijo fiel de Washington el glorioso,

el justo, el bondadoso,
el héroe sin rival de las naciones,
tú eres hoy elegido
para alzar del olvido
el escudo inmortal de sus blasones.
Yo te veo sereno en la pelea,
sin pavor a la tea
que en América enciende bando fiero,
hollar el pendón rojo,
que del honor sonrojo
tremola en el cañón filibustero.
Y oigo el "hurra" del Norte repetido,
al pueblo embravecido
luchando para darte la victoria,
y también sin sosiego,
alzo mi humilde ruego
por vuestro triunfo y libertad y gloria.
Porque también yo soy americana,
aunque el manso Guadiana
me vio nacer en su abrasada orilla;
como flor destinada
para ser trasplantada
y dar a otro hemisferio su semilla.
Y fueron de mi estirpe antecesores
como tú, exploradores
de América, valientes caballeros,
que dejaron memoria,
cual la tuya en la historia
dejarás a los siglos venideros.
Y siento que mi espíritu se agita
con zozobra infinita,
al ver que las conquistas de los bravos
hayan luego servido
para haber extendido
el odioso país de los esclavos.
¡Ay! ¿Qué será del pueblo americano
si el nubarrón insano,

que por su cielo amenazando vaga,
y el azul oscurece
con su sombra que crece,
nuestras estrellas vívidas apaga?
Yo, contemplando con los ojos fijos
la patria de mis hijos,
tiemblo también por la insegura estrella;
pues está ya mi vida
a su fulgor unida,
y he de extinguirme si se extingue ella.
Y al escuchar del Norte embravecido
el "hurra" repetido
que lanzan los que anhelan tu victoria,
yo también sin sosiego,
alzo mi humilde ruego
por vuestra paz y libertad y gloria.
Y a ti, señor, de América esperanza,
salud y venturanza
quiero enviar, por las inmensas olas
del terrible Oceáno;
¡que al mundo americano
lleven mi voz las brisas españolas!

The poem appeared originally in the daily *La Iberia* on 18 February 1861, and the journal *La América:Crónica Hispano-Americana* on 8 March 1861. On 12 April, the Civil War erupted, although the secession of several states even before Lincoln's first inauguration and the formation of the Confederacy in February made conflict inevitable, as the poem suggests through its imagery of turbulence and portent.[6] The tenth stanza, for example, speaks of a gathering cloud that threatens to extinguish "our bright stars" ("nuestras estrellas vívidas"), an image that Martha turns into a "vivid light," thus unfortunately losing the play of imagery between the heavenly stars and the stars of the American flag set within a blue rectangle ("el azul" / "the azure sky"). (But she compensates by bringing back the image in the eighth stanza with the line "I do tremble for those stars upon the blue.")

Coronado had already seen that flag under attack by "the fillibuster's gun" ("el cañón filibustero"), a reference to soldier-adventurers like Narciso López, who in the decade or so prior to the Civil War attempted on four different occasions to take over Cuba in order to annex it to the United States. The filibusters, also known as "freebooters," were popular in the South, although more recently historians have argued that the phenomenon, viewed as a form of nationalist expansionism, enjoyed widespread support in many parts of the country (see Chaffin 1995:87, 92). Abolitionists, however, saw the filibusters as pro-slavery. One prominent filibuster-backer from Louisiana, Pierre Soulé, as U.S. minister to Spain, quickly turned into a political headache for Horatio and Carolina (see Castilla 1987:117–38). For Carolina, too, the Southern cause was linked to the filibusters, and the image of the filibusters in the poem helped her to define her dual position. On the one hand she saw herself as an American, having married one ("yo soy americana"), which made her children U.S. citizens ("la patria de mis hijos"). On the other hand she was also, and primarily, Spanish. She could only have seen the filibusters' expeditions to Cuba, still a Spanish possession, as a threat to Spain's sovereignty.[7] Thus, the filibusters' cannon in her poem can be read simultaneously through both Northern U.S. and Spanish eyes.

The poem is also about liberty, which Lincoln and the North stood for in her view. Carolina deftly works in the abolitionist theme by establishing Lincoln's opposition to slavery through his Christian faith, using one of the main arguments of the day against bondage: namely, that it was not Christian to support "our peculiar institution," as it was euphemistically called. She writes in the second stanza: "Grandioso ejemplo de valor cristiano, / hoy ya tu acento humano / contra la injusta esclavitud levantas, / para que el genio altivo / del pueblo primitivo / rescate el libro de sus leyes santas." Martha Englishes the stanza in this manner: "Glorious exemplar of the Christian calling, / I have heard thy accents falling, / Heard thee raise thy voice against the tyrants' cause. / So the genius of the great, / Sovereign people of the State, / May preserve the volume of its sacred laws." The New England poet captures the epic roll of the first line but, perhaps for the sake of rhyme, abandons the phrase "injusta esclavitud" ("unjust slavery"), with its redundancy, for something less explicit, "the tyrants' cause." In the same stanza, she converts Carolina's "genio altivo / del pueblo primitivo" ("proud genius / of its original people") into "the genius of the great, / Sovereign people of the State," thus deemphasizing the historical origins of Lincoln's stance and strengthening the notion of national sovereignty, of union. But the association of Lincoln and his Christian faith with a nation founded constitutionally on laws that are also sacred remains strong in both texts.

In view of the fact that Martha's version of "Oda a Lincoln" was not published until 1864, it is possible that the circumstance of Civil War helped shape such phrases as "the great, / Sovereign people of the State." Martha's translation appeared in a miscellany, *Personal and Political Ballads*, edited by Frank Moore, a journalist and compiler of anthologies. The collection contains verse from both sides of the conflict and is presented without comment. Here is the complete text of "Ode to Abraham Lincoln":

Lincoln, I salute thee! conqueror thou art,
Chosen of the people's heart.
Traversing the mighty billows o'er
Of the wondrous, awful sea,
From America the free,
Thou hast reached unto this far-off Spanish shore.

Glorious exemplar of the Christian calling,
I have heard thy accents falling,
Heard thee raise thy voice against the tyrants' cause.
So the genius of the great,
Sovereign people of the State,
May preserve the volume of its sacred laws.

Wondrous book—the admiration of the ages!
In those solitudes, the pages
From the lofty soul of Washington were born—
Pages whose sublime commands,
Seizing with their reckless hands,
Bastard sons of liberty have rudely torn.

I behold thee calm, amid the tumult gazing,
Quailing not before the blazing
Of the traitors' fire within thy land begun.
They would in dishonor drag
At their feet the blushing flag,
Fluttering there before the fillibuster's gun.

My own ancestors, like thine of early story,

Saw of old thy country's glory.
Valiant men they were who sailed away from here,
Leaving traces all around,
Like thy names in history found;
Handing memories down to every coming year.

And I feel my longing spirit in me burning
With an infinite and tender yearning,
When I look upon the conquests of the brave—
Deeming they have served the end,
Only further to extend
The abhorred territory of the slave.

Ah! What will become of that great nation yonder,
If the maddening clouds that wander,
Threatening all the heaven, should gather in their sight?
Darkening in the azure sky,
With their shadows rising high—
What if they extinguish all the vivid light?

With a fixed and earnest eye that noble country seeing,
Whence my children drew their being
I do tremble for those stars upon the blue;
For my very life is blent
With the brightness they have lent,
And if they are waning, I am waning too.

But I listen to the Northern armies cheering,
Their huzzas and plaudits hearing,
Which they raise on high to herald thy increase;
And their ardor I do share,
Lifting up my humble prayer
For their liberty, their glory, and their peace.

And to thee, Señor, the hope of all the nation,
My good cheer and salutation
I would send amid the mighty billows' roar—

Send across the solemn sea,
To America the free,
Wafted by the breezes of the Spanish shore.

To my knowledge, there have been very few English translations of Carolina Coronado's work. In the obituary of her brother Horatio, Martha Perry Lowe writes that "some of [Carolina Coronado's] impassioned verses upon slavery and other American subjects have been translated and published here in the *New York Evening Post, Advertiser,* etc. etc" (1891:4).[8] William Cullen Bryant, who met Carolina in Madrid, published a version of her poem "El pájaro perdido" as "The Lost Bird," first in the *New York Ledger* in 1858 and later in his *Thirty Poems* (1864). He also translated her novel *Jarilla,* which ran in installments in the *Ledger* in 1869 (see Williams 1968:2.136–37). Thus, Lowe's translation is refound treasure for its rarity and for its intrinsic interest to translators, historians, and literary critics.

Martha Perry Lowe's version is prefaced with the header "A Voice from Spain." A notable feature of the translation is the omission of three stanzas (the fourth, sixth, and seventh) from Coronado's original Spanish. It is not clear why Lowe left out the fourth and seventh stanzas; the sixth, however, is very close in language and meaning to the penultimate stanza and hence repetitive. The fourth stanza continues Carolina's epic praise of Lincoln as another chosen one comparable to Washington. I can only speculate that Martha thought it expendable and perhaps even filler. But why omit the seventh stanza, in which Carolina declares she too is an American, a flower from the banks of the Guadiana destined to be transplanted and seed another hemisphere? It is possible that Martha thought these verses de-exoticized Coronado as a voice from Spain, though the contrary could also be argued: she remains a flower from the banks of the Guadiana. This stanza flows naturally into the next one, which centers on the poet's ancestors. Its omission makes the poem choppier in this section.

Overall the translation keeps faith with the tone, language, and purpose of the original, despite the missing stanzas and an occasional problematic word choice that I note here. The English version tends to be wordier in places, with additional phrases not found in the Spanish, though the desire to keep the syllable count of the translation as close to that of the original poem may explain her word choices. For example, where the original reads "el terrible océano" in line 4, Martha chooses "of the wondrous, awful sea." In the third stanza, she translates more verbosely the passage, "y del cual torpemente / otra bastarda gente / las páginas sublimes ha rasgado" as: "Pages whose sublime commands, / Seizing with their reckless hands, / Bastard sons of liberty have rudely torn."

In the ninth stanza of the original (the sixth in the English version), Carolina uses the word "zozobra" signifying worry and anxiety to express her agitated spirit ("mi espíritu se agita"). In my view Martha misinterprets the phrase "con zozobra infinita," which means "with infinite anxiety," as "with an infinite and tender yearning." "Anxiety" and "yearning" are not the same. She tries to offset the phrase by adding to the poet's "longing spirit" the word "burning," but "tender" in the second line represents a gratuitous addition by Martha and simply doesn't fit, especially in relation to what Carolina says after that, when she harshly criticizes the conquistadors for extending "the abhorred territory of the slave."

Finally, Martha ignores an ancillary meaning of "zozobra," which is "capsizing," thus furthering the nautical imagery of the source text.[9] She also chooses a weak substitute for the line "y he de extinguirme si se extingue ella" in the eleventh stanza (the eighth in the translation): "And if they [the stars of the flag] are waning, I am waning too." As Lisa Surwillo incisively observes, "playing on the meaning of the word 'extinguir' in Spanish, which means both to extinguish a flame and extinguish a species, Coronado recasts the Civil War as a battle over her own existence" (2007:412).

Martha's translation sometimes appears to reduce, either through omission or watered-down language, the presence of Carolina in the poem. She thereby ends up giving more weight to the American side of the text. This decision is reflected in the twice-repeated phrase "America the free" in the first and last stanzas, a phrase Carolina does not use. Similarly, the translator has gone from "otra bastarda gente" to "bastard sons of liberty." Such changes may be related to the reasons for writing the poem in the first place.

We know that Carolina wrote the ode not only to show her support of Lincoln and the North, but to curry favor from the new president. She would also write one more poem on Lincoln as the great liberator, "El águila redentora" (originally published 12 November 1868, in La Iberia) and an abolitionist-themed sonnet titled "A la abolición de la esclavitud en Cuba" (dated 14 October 1868).[10] Having clashed with Ambassador Soulé for his support of the filibusters who were attempting to wrest Cuba from Spain in 1853–54, Horatio lost his position as secretary of the American Legation (see Pérez González 1999:299–318). Carolina wrote Lincoln shortly after publishing her poem:

I suffered through the aggression of the enemies of the North who, in send-
ing the Frenchman Soulé to Spain to propose the purchase of Cuba or stir up
war, required of my husband to commit treason to the Republic. . . . Six years
have I [battled] for the triumph of the ideas of the North; six years have I suffered with my children looking forward [to] the day of reparation. This has
come with your triumph—and from you I seek in [the] name of my children
who are Anglo-Americans the restoration of their Father to the post of Secretary of Legation in Spain as an act of Justice (Coronado 1861; official English
translation in archives, slightly modified).

As Surwillo (2007:414) notes, the poem was "part of a personal campaign" to
have her husband reinstated as secretary. The campaign worked. Carolina, however, had an additional reason for getting Horatio his job back. She knew he
desperately wanted to fight alongside his fellow Northerners in the war and she
did not want him to go. Thus, by 1864 when the English translation appeared,
the poem's original purpose no longer served. Perhaps for this reason in her
translation Martha deemphasized some of the personal elements of Carolina's
presence, such as the phrase "I am an American," and heightened both the figure of Lincoln and that of the nation. They were, after all, in the midst of war.

Even with the changes, omissions, and altered circumstance, it seems to
me that Martha's version translates her sister-in-law as simultaneously Spanish and American, literally through the act of translation and figuratively
through ventriloquizing the voice of Carolina. The last stanza of the source
text expresses the desire for the winds of Spain to send the poet's voice ("mi
voz") to America. Although Martha omits the words "my voice" in the last
line, she acknowledges that voice not only in the phrase "A Voice From Spain"
placed above the title of the poem but also in the careful way she approaches
the tone and language of Coronado's text. Either the editor or Martha herself
also made clear the familial relationship between the two women by noting
below the title of the poem: "Translated from the Spanish of Carolina Coronado de Perry, by Martha Perry Lowe." The "I" of this poem belongs to both
women. The original impulse and emotion are Carolina's but the words are
now Martha's. Yet the reverse may also be said to be true. The emotions are
also Martha's and the words Carolina's, if dressed in a different linguistic
cloth. It is in this sense as well that Martha makes Carolina into an American
while Carolina makes Martha a Spaniard by lending the American writer her
words, feelings, and thoughts. An American reader of the period would have

been acutely aware of the presence of both women in this poem, indisputably written by a Spaniard but also written by an American whose evident sympathies have blended two cultures, two histories, two women.

Martha recreated the lyrical persona of her sister-in-law once more in her 1865 poem "To Carolina Coronado."

A lily anchored by the Spanish main,
Swaying and shining in the surge of youth,
Yet holding in thy breast the gold of truth,—

Such didst thou seem above the waves of pain,
And through the stormy turbulence of war,
Until we heard thy patriot voice afar!

Now, Sister, with the burning heart of Spain,
We speak to thee from this New England strand,
And grasp and hold thee with a firm right hand!

For thou hast touched our people with thy word,—
Only a gentle woman's word, but one
With the great work our Nation has begun.

By Liberty thy earnest soul was stirred,
And waked and urged Estremadura's men
To pour the heroic wind of life again.

As in the dawn of Summer flits a bird
From his low nest and springs into the air,
Hurrying a double concert and a prayer,—

So Liberty, with thy sweet voice allied,
Walks in thy footsteps, with her laurel strows
Thy footway, with thy trustful spirit glows.

Esteem her friendship with unwavering pride!
Teach thou thy children what the years have brought,
Wisdom and love superior to thy thought!

Once thou hast said, "All men may win her side,
But women never!" Sister, do not fear,
Recall thy words, since Love has made truth clear.

For love is master, and we know no other,
Save self-compelling service to the right,
Which is but Love in the seraphic sight.

Teach this thy sons and to each man thy brother,—
A secret learned in silent joys of home,
A secret whence the lights of being come.

So guided by this lamp, O wife and mother,
Turn thine eyes hither to the Western shore,
Where red streams run and iron thunders roar!

We watch the star of Freedom slowly rise
And glimmer through the changes of the time,
While errors beat their low retreating chime.

We ask for nought, we need not to be wise,
We find both men and women at their post,
Equal and different in one mighty host.

Divided suffering, unity of cries,—
Divided labor, unity of life,—
Divided struggle, one reward for strife.

As autumn winds sweep over tossing seas
And reach the happy shore, and fling the flowers
And lower each gorgeous head by their rude powers,—

So sweep the winds of war through quiet leas
And bend our budding treasures in the dust,
Yet Freedom's cause shall neither mar nor rust.

The seed shall spring where none can thirst or freeze,

Shall bear a floweret fairer than the old,
As lilies shine before all blossoms told:

A liberty for woman in her home,
Bound by the only chains which give her peace,—
Immortal chains which death may not release:

A liberty where Justice wide may roam,
And Reverence sit the chief at every feast,
With Love as master, and Contempt as least:

A liberty where the oppressed may come,
The black and white, the woman and the man,
And recognize themselves in Heaven's wide plan

Then while the morning odors of the sea
Blow from the westward and caress thy brow,
Remember where thy loving sisters bow:

Perchance beneath the hand of Victory,
Which leaves a tear and then a silentness,
While crowds move by forgetful of one less;

Or where a burst of gracious ecstasy
Rising shall fill the eastward flitting air,
And with thy spirit mount the hills of prayer.

The poem appeared anonymously in the *Atlantic Monthly* in June 1865, but the 1889 *Atlantic Index* lists M. P. Lowe as the author.

Martha addresses Carolina directly, saying: "Now, Sister, with the burning heart of Spain, / We speak to thee from this New England strand / And grasp and hold thee with a firm right hand!" As in the "Ode to Lincoln," this poem has two voices: Carolina's "patriot voice" alongside her sister-in-law's. The great theme is once again liberty. This time, however, Martha merges the political and the personal, the abolitionist and the feminist, into the single overarching theme. She also allies it to Carolina's "sweet voice," reminding us of the presence of her sister-in-law's voice in "Ode to Lincoln."

Martha sees Carolina as driven by the thought of liberty, urging "Estremadura's men / To pour the heroic wine of life again" and touching "our people with thy word." "Liberty," says Martha to her Spanish sister, "with thy sweet voice allied, / Walks in thy footsteps." In the eighth stanza, liberty is a kind of "friendship" ("esteem her friendship"). This notion leads to the next stanza: "Once thou hast said, 'All men may win her side [that of Liberty], / But women never!' Sister, do not fear, / Recall thy words, since Love has made truth clear." Here Martha once again echoes Carolina's poem "Libertad." More importantly, Martha conceives freedom in gendered and feminist terms, and freedom is a woman who "walks in thy footsteps." The friendship that is liberty is also the friendship between women, tied together by sisterly love. Liberty's personification is the personification of the loving bonds between Martha and Carolina.

"To Carolina Coronado" is infused with Martha Perry Lowe's profound Unitarian faith, in which "service to the right, / . . . is but Love in the seraphic sight."[11] The second half of the poem veers away from the relationship between the two women until nearly the end, framing the text within the larger theme of liberty, which issues from a lyrical philanthropic embrace of all creatures: "A liberty where the oppressed may come, / The black and white, the woman and the man, / And recognize themselves in Heaven's wide plan." It is not surprising that Martha links the freedom of women with that of the slave. By the late 1830s and especially after the 1848 Seneca Falls Convention on women's rights, abolitionists saw the two movements as one. The Cuban-Spanish author Gertrudis Gómez de Avellaneda made the same connection in her 1841 novel *Sab*. Moreover, Martha's poem appeared shortly before Northern women renewed their dedication to feminism right after the war.

Some of the more stirring lines in the poem appear here: "We find both men and women at their post, / Equal and different in one mighty host. / Divided suffering, unity of cries—/ Divided labor, unity of life,—/ Divided struggle, one reward for strife." This sense of unity within division, or difference, marks the entire poem. Just so the New Englander clasps the hand of her Spanish sister. Just so blacks and whites, men and women, "recognize themselves in Heaven's wide plan." In the last three stanzas, Martha returns explicitly to Carolina, asking her to "remember where thy loving sisters bow" (alluding to Ellen Perry here). Martha ends with the line "And with thy spirit mount the hills of prayer."

The loving spirit that encircles this poem, that blends different lives, is the same spirit of translation that creates sisterly solidarity between two cultures and two women. As with translation itself, Martha's poem recognizes differences, but embraces them within the larger scheme of a unifying spirit. Carolina's "patriot voice" comes from Spain but speaks to America. If a post-emancipation United States served as a model for Carolina, as Surwillo (2007:416) persuasively argues, it could also be said that "the burning heart of Spain" incarnated in Carolina Coronado spoke to Martha Perry Lowe.

It is worth noting that Carolina appears not to have reciprocated poetically to the same degree as Martha, although she did dedicate a poem to her, "Carta a Marta" (1993; dated 11 August 1898, and published in *La Epoca* on 30 August 1898), on the prickly subject of the Cuban war between Spain and the United States. It is not clear to me how much English Coronado really knew and whether she could fully appreciate the poems Martha wrote about her. In 1857, for example, after receiving William Cullen Bryant's translation of her poem, "The Lost Bird," she "promised him to learn English that she might understand his poetry," and this, despite being married to an American (Williams 1968:2.135). Her 1861 letter to Lincoln was written in Spanish. Fernández-Daza Álvarez, by contrast, suggests that Coronado knew enough English to read uncomplicated texts (2011:478).

Nonetheless, one is struck by the power and grace of these poetic exchanges and translating gestures in sustaining such a deeply felt relationship. We need to remind ourselves that a relationship of this kind, which was at once a real and lyrical sisterhood, did not have the ease of communications that we have today. When Martha translated Carolina, both literally and figuratively, for an American readership, she also saw herself and her country through Carolina's eyes. So too do we see their voices merge, separate, come together once more, and rising, "fill the eastward flitting air."

Epilogue

This essay on the sisterhood of translation is for Carol, dear friend and colleague, and our friendship of 50 years. We first worked together professionally with our coedited volume *In the Feminine Mode: Essays on Hispanic Women Writers* (1990). And in our latest collaboration Carol and I translated the essays of two other women, María Zambrano and Rosa Chacel, for *Two Confessions* (2015).

Notes

1. See Manzano Garías, "De una década extremeña" (1969), who first used the term *lyrical sisterhood* to speak of the mid-nineteenth-century flowering of Spanish women poets; Kirkpatrick's (1989) classic study; and Valis (1990, 1991).

2. Castilla (1987:141, 242n5) first made note of the 1859 poem; Pérez González, (1999:512–13) reproduces it.

3. See Pérez González (1999:239–66) and Gutiérrez Serrano (1994:197–245). In 1860 Horatio Perry converted to Catholicism (Pérez González 1999:344–45), despite apparent lingering doubts over both the doctrine and practices of the Church, doubts that Charles Lowe claimed, though without proof, Carolina also experienced: "'Carolina's belief is not far from ours. She distinctly repudiates the doctrine of transubstantiation. She is entirely free and broad'" (M. P. Lowe 1884:507). Fernández-Daza Álvarez (2011:469) discusses Horatio Perry's propensity to present his wife as critical of Catholicism to his Unitarian family.

4. Martha's husband Charles, who served as a chaplain during the war, also wrote on Lincoln's death, delivering a sermon at the Unitarian Church in Charleston, South Carolina, on 23 April 1865, in which he spoke of "the common sorrow which seems to prevail, South as well as North, over the grave of Abraham Lincoln" (C. Lowe 1865:16). Lowe was also active in the Freedman's Aid Society (Anon. 1903a:11).

5. For a fine exposition of Coronado's abolitionist politics and the diplomatic role she and her husband played in persuading Spain to support the North rather than the South, see Surwillo 2007; also Castilla (1987:155–69) and Pérez González (1999:348–56).

6. Both Pérez González (1999:349) and Torres Nebrera (Coronado 1993f:2.733) in his annotations mistakenly situate Carolina's "Oda a Lincoln" as having been written after the war began, but it predates the conflict.

7. As Chaffin (1995:104) points out, filibustering "violated laws—including the federal Neutrality Act of 1818 and the 1797 friendship pact between Spain and the United States." It is of interest to read in the 8 March 1861 issue of *La América*, in which Coronado's "Oda a Lincoln" appeared, this comment on filibustering and the Southern cause: "A este personaje [Jefferson Davis] le pintan como iniciador de la invasion en la república mejicana; como alma de la política representada por M. Soulé en esta córte respecto de la isla de Cuba; y como impulsador de Walker à las expediciones contra el territorio [de Nicaragua]" ("They say that [Jefferson Davis] is the initiator of the invasion into the Republic of Mexico; the heart of the politics represented by M. Soulé, of this Court, with respect to the island of Cuba; and the impulse behind Walker's expeditions against the territory [of Nicaragua]") (F. 1861:1).

8. This tantalizing clue of additional (and unknown) translations of Coronado's poems should prompt someone to do further research.

9. As Surwillo (2007:413) observes, "the entire poem is crafted in a nautical terminology that highlights the Atlantic connection between the two countries . . . Coronado allegorizes the United States' fate as a ship lost in the sea between America and Spain, with President Lincoln as a new captain."

10. See also Coronado's "Carta a los catalanes sobre la abolición de la esclavitud" (1999; originally published 27 February 1864, in *La Regeneración*), in response to a request from 54 Catalan abolitionists begging her to write a book on the American Civil War and the evils of slavery. They were unsuccessful.

11. For testimonies of Martha Perry Lowe's religious spirit, see Marsters (1903:29–30) and Pierson (1903:39, 42).

Works Cited

Anon. 1903a."A Memorial Sketch." In *In Memoriam: Martha Perry Lowe, 1829–1902*, 1–14. Cambridge, Mass.: Riverside Press.

Anon. 1903b. "Mrs. Martha Perry Lowe. Editorial from *Somerville Journal*." In *In Memoriam: Martha Perry Lowe, 1829–1902*, 15–20. Cambridge: Riverside Press.

The Atlantic Index. 1889. Boston and New York: Houghton, Mifflin.

Bryant, William Cullen. 1864. "The Lost Bird." In *Thirty Poems*, 40–42. New York: D. Appleton.

Castilla, Alberto. 1987. *Carolina Coronado de Perry*. Madrid: Beramar.

Chaffin, Tom. 1995. "'Sons of Washington': Narciso López, Filibustering, and U.S. Nationalism, 1848–1851." *Journal of the Early Republic* 15(1): 79–108.

Coronado, Carolina. 1861. "Letter to Abraham Lincoln." 25 March 1861. The Abraham Lincoln Papers at the Library of Congress. Available at: http://memory.loc.gov/ammem/alhtml/malhome.html (accessed 29 January 2011).

Coronado, Carolina. 1864. "Ode to Abraham Lincoln." In *Personal and Political Ballads,* edited by Frank Moore, 95–98. Translated by Martha Perry Lowe. New York: G. P. Putnam.

Coronado, Carolina. 1993a. *Obra poética*. Edited by Gregorio Torres Nebrera. 2 vols. Mérida: Editora Regional de Extremadura.

Coronado, Carolina. 1993b. "A la abolición de la esclavitud en Cuba." In *Obra poética,* Vol. 2, edited by Gregorio Torres Nebrera, 839–40. Mérida: Editora Regional de Extremadura.

Coronado, Carolina. 1993c. "Carta a Marta." In *Obra poética*, Vol. 2, edited by Gregorio Torres Nebrera, 850–52. Mérida: Editora Regional de Extremadura.

Coronado, Carolina. 1993d. "El águila redentora." In *Obra poética*, Vol. 2, edited by Gregorio Torres Nebrera, 835–38. Mérida: Editora Regional de Extremadura.

Coronado, Carolina. 1993e. "Libertad." In *Obra poética*, Vol. 1, edited by Gregorio Torres Nebrera, 389–90. Mérida: Editora Regional de Extremadura.

Coronado, Carolina. 1993f. "Oda a Lincoln." In *Obra poética,* Vol. 2, edited by Gregorio Torres Nebrera, 731–34. Mérida: Editora Regional de Extremadura.

Coronado, Carolina. 1999. "Carta a los catalanes sobre la abolición de la esclavitud." In *Obra en prosa*, Vol. 3, edited by Gregorio Torres Nebrera, 350–56. Mérida: Editora Regional de Extremadura.

F. 1861. "Revista extrangera." *La América. Crónica Hispano-Americana* (8 March): 1–3.

Fernández-Daza Álvarez, Carmen. 2011. *La familia de Carolina Coronado: Los primeros años en la vida de una escritora.* Almendralejo: Ayuntamiento de Almendralejo.

Gómez de Avellaneda, Gertrudis. 1993. *Sab.* Translated by Nina M. Scott. Austin: University of Texas Press.

Gómez de Avellaneda, Gertrudis. 1997. *Sab.* Edited by José Servera. Madrid: Cátedra.

Gutiérrez Serrano, Federico. 1994. "San Antonio María Claret y Carolina Coronado de Perry." In *San Antonio María Claret en Extremadura*, 197–245. Madrid: Editorial Alpuerto.

Kirkpatrick, Susan. 1989. *Las Románticas: Women Writers and Subjectivity in Spain, 1835–1850.* Berkeley: University of California Press.

Lowe, Charles.1865. *Death of President Lincoln: A Sermon.* Boston: American Unitarian Association.

Lowe, Martha Perry. 1859. "Carolina Coronado, Poetess of Spain." In *The Olive and the Pine*, 21–22. Boston: Crosby, Nichols.

Lowe, Martha Perry. 1865. "To Carolina Coronado." *Atlantic Monthly* 15(92) (June): 698–99.

Lowe, Martha Perry. 1867. *Love in Spain, and Other Poems.* Boston: William V. Spencer.

Lowe, Martha Perry. 1884. *Memoir of Charles Lowe.* Boston: Cupples, Upham.

Lowe, Martha Perry. 1891. "Horatio Justus Perry. A Noted Diplomat Native in New England." *Boston Daily Globe*, 2 March.

Manzano Garías, A[ntonio]. 1969. "De una década extremeña y romántica (1845–55)." *Revista de Estudios Extremeños* 25(2): 281–332.

Marsters, John M. 1903. ["Letter"]. In *Memoriam: Martha Perry Lowe, 1829–1902*, 25–30. Cambridge, Mass.: Riverside Press.

Pérez González, Isabel María.1999. *Carolina Coronado: Del romanticismo a la crisis fin de siglo.* Badajoz: Del Oeste.

Pierson, William H. 1903."Memorial Address. May 9, 1902." In *Memoriam: Martha Perry Lowe, 1829–1902*, 39–43. Cambridge, Mass.: Riverside Press.

Surwillo, Lisa. 2007. "Poetic Diplomacy: Carolina Coronado and the American Civil War." *Comparative American Studies* 5(4): 409–22.

Valis, Noël. 1990. "The Language of Treasure: Carolina Coronado, Casta Esteban, and Marina Romero." *In the Feminine Mode: Essays on Hispanic Women Writers,* edited by Noël Valis and Carol Maier, 246–72. Lewisburg, Pa.: Bucknell University Press.

Valis, Noël. 1991. "Introducción." In Carolina Coronado, *Poesías*, 7–41. Madrid: Castalia/Instituto de la Mujer.

Valis, Noël, and Carol Maier, trans. and eds. 2015. *Two Confessions.* Albany, N.Y.: SUNY Press.

Williams, Stanley T. (1955) 1968. *The Spanish Background of American Literature.* 2 vols. Hamden, Conn.: Archon Books.

Pro Pombo

From *Contra Natura* by Álvaro Pombo

Translated with commentary by Ronald Christ *with*
Héctor Magaña

Prelude

Álvaro Pombo García de los Ríos (b. 1939) is a great contemporary writer by any standard: his obra vast—six volumes of verse, 20 novels, two collections of short stories, as well as biographies, essays, journalism; his style copious, individuated, various—from colloquial narration to geometric and painterly lyric, in both prose and poetry, as well as formal, ceremonial discourse, and the homotextual, as established by Frederick Fajardo (2009); his themes psychologically, socially, historically, and philosophically momentous; his literary standing as the highest—member of the Royal Spanish Academy, winner of premium literary prizes, including the Premio El Bardo, Premio Herralde, Premio Nacional de la Crítica, Premio Fastenrath, Premio Fundación José Manuel Lara, Premio Fundación Germán Sánchez Ruipérez, Premio Nadal, Premio Planeta; his career in politics substantial, activist; his appearances on television authoritative, some popular, rounding out his status as a significant cultural figure. Yet Pombo is little known in the North American world of letters, despite Margaret Jull Costa's translations of two of his novels—*El Parecido* (1988; translated as *The Resemblance* [1989]) and *El Heroe de las mansardas* (1983, translated as *The Hero of the Big House* [1988])—and Chris Perriam's fine, favorable review of *Contra Natura* in the *Times Literary Supplement* (2006).

Pombo's distinguished literary personage of distinctly philosophical, psychological, and social bent, sounded but not sufficiently sounded out in English, well qualifies a translation of Álvaro Pombo's work for an anthology honoring Carol Maier. Besides, I found him by chance at Antinous, a Barcelona gay bookstore on Carrer Ample, one of the old city's narrower streets, and, after two pages, chose to interest myself in its translation, a choice comparable to Carol Maier's form of choosing and working from her own desire and her perception of want that distinguish her pioneering career as a translator, as does her persevering past obstacles. At that time in Barcelona I happened to be reading Carol's masterly draft of a masterpiece, Rosa Chacel's *Dream of Reason,* and my preemptive reliance on Carol as a critical reader of what I might attempt with Pombo's grandly talkative narrator—at once colloquial and classic, as well as classical—went without saying, for Carol, like Pombo himself, is scrupulously generous.

My demurrals, already arising from Pombo's current usage, ranging allusions, and acute specifics of places, products, verbal productions, once again meant that any translation possible for me would require a scale of collaborations. Translators are indeed generous—that I have found to be remarkably true, though generally ignored in most of what I've read or heard about translation—and Carol immediately came to my side by recommending a gifted Chilean translator, Héctor Magaña, whom she had taught at Kent. Translators, notorious as traitors, at least in Italian, are teachers too, through institutions and by intuitions. I've known that from my sophomore semester at Columbia College with Gregory Rabassa through my years of friendship with Helen Lane, Margaret Sayers Peden, Edith Grossman, and Peter Bush. So, with Carol and with federally certified court interpreter as well as brilliantly inventive literary translator Francisco Olivero, I engaged with an intricate verbal construction and felt aligned, even in confronting such European terms as *cutreluxe.* At least aligned.

Translators are explainers as well, not village explainers and not, one wishes, in their translations, sometimes putting on offer a sentence and even more in place of a word—prostheses Carol Maier does not resort to—but their motives for giving their verbal vehicle a fostering shove as well as the reader a spare tire, if not a life jacket, are legitimately powerful, while Carol Maier's exemplary afterwords to difficult texts distinguish her overall approach, confirming an evolving practice as opposed to previous translators' and/or publishers' erratic whims. Appreciating that approach, I am asking Pombo to move his present epilogue, with suitable revisions, to the position of foreword, for his inaugural publication in the United States so that we can follow up with a useful afterword and notes in abundance for any reader who wants them. Caring for the reader, taking care of the reader is more the concern of translators than of authors, though you might not think that; every translator does it, one way or in many others, and such care requires caution as well as tact, both developing from the translator's peculiar, possibly unique position, of serving simultaneously as writer and reader and, yes, critic.

Translators like Carol Maier are also brave. Cast your mind back over her prize-winning translation of Ana Chacel's *Memoirs of Leticia Valle* to see if a guy addressing Rosa as "Baby" fits your recall. It hadn't mine at first. In the paragraph where it appears, *Baby* is le mot juste, precisely. Such considered and encouraging courage does inspire, and provoke, in the dual etymological sense of that word; so, in *Contra Natura* I have often drawn my daring from Carol's example, facing down objections to carrying more of the Spanish over—*translating?*—as well as more of the English into that middle ground we may well call the modern world.

Translators may also be activists, not only accepting commissioned books but also, or principally, recruiting adventurous yet neglected writings chosen because the translator admires these works, approves and wishes to promote the author's style, thought, and values them as potential contributions to our culture, necessary as well as desirable. Carol Maier is such an activist, independently and in partnership recuperating for our well-being presently unattended writing, most especially writing that is difficult to translate. I pretty much follow the same path. Pombo's style seduced me first and pleasures me still, while his themes embodied by unnatural lovers, so called, merit our mindful attention, not least of all because they arise in a consciousness of freedom scarcely allied with some tenets of contemporary gay life, e.g., same-sex marriage. Just today, the *New York Times* reports the Supreme Court of India's reinstating an 1861 law that imposes a 10-year sentence for "carnal intercourse against the order of nature with man, woman, or animal" (Harris 2013).

Against the order of nature, *contra natura*. Such relationships, subjects of Pombo's narrative, "are unethical as well as unnatural," declared S. Q. R. Ilyas, a member of the All India Muslim Personal Law Board: "They create problems in society, both moral and social. This is a sin as far as Islam is concerned" (qtd. in Harris 2013:AG). As far as the prominently Christian, Roman Catholic society of Pombo's novel is concerned, they are *contra natura*.

With Carol Maier's encouragement, I translate Pombo's novel, considering this translation activism, at least in part. If you have not asked yourself

"What are the activisms in Carol Maier's many translations?", you have not asked yourself a major, basic question about her work.

You won't find much daring in the excerpt offered here, but with Carol's boost I present it as a virtual short story, a genre in which Pombo excels. Let the book's title stand here for the adventurous, tenacious excellence of her work: the title words *contra natura* obstruct few English-language readers. Pombo, however, introduces midway through *Contra Natura* another contra term: *contradiós,* against God. In Pombo's verbal scale, *contradiós* counterbalances the theological, philosophical title phrase, while simultaneously occupying a colloquial register and further obtruding an awkwardness for the translator since *contradiós* more frequently designates a mundane absurdity or annoyance, as the Real Academia *Española* now defines the word. Moreover, Álvaro Pombo himself commented on *contradiós* in *El País*'s *Un Atlas sonoro del español* [A sonorous atlas of Spanish] (Pombo 2013) in a survey of 21 Spanish-writing authors who were asked to choose their country's most autochthonous word in response to the VI International Congress on the Spanish Language, held in Panama City, Panama, in 2013. Pombo chose *contradiós:*

> *Contradiós* is a Spanish colloquialism used to designate nonsense (something absurd or contrary to reason). In the April 23, 1990, edition of *El Mundo,* Francisco Umbral wrote: "A capitalist democracy is a metaphysical impossibility, a *contradiós.*" Another example from my gleaning: "Coming into the house with muddied tennis shoes is a *contradiós!*" (uttered by a pissed-off mother). I find *contradiós* an essentially Spanish expression, a mix of the theological and the illogical; it proposes God (who is the absolute contradiction) as analogous to reason or common sense. God and things divine, things Catholic, are hot branded on our lexicon and on our linguistic usages. (Pombo 2013)

So while the linguistic trinity encapsulated in Pombo's opposing title may represent here the adventurous, tenacious, successful excellence of Carol Maier's work, English has not yet supplied a term that preserves the linguistic, aesthetic equilibrium created with the use of *contradiós*—English is not so searingly branded as Pombo says Spanish is, so let *contradiós* represent the ongoing agon in translation—Carol's as well as the rest of ours. (If you discover such a term, please submit it: www.propombo.blogspot.com). The closest I've come so far, and it's a far miss, are nominal, adjectival, adverbial forms of *god-*

damn, including *goddamned* and *goddamnest,* or *godforsaken.* These words don't have the contra element, but they do preserve *Diós* ("God"), yet their connotation and implication can be more severe than *contradíos* and would scarcely figure in translations, say, of Aquinas or Augustine. Moreover, they are imprecatory, dismissive, and scarcely connote the illogical. I have witnessed Carol Maier in such agon again and again, and I esteem her more, I do really, for her struggle—without agony it would seem, and totally veiled from the reader—than for her evident triumphs, which I merely envy. What she put into understanding *La Sinrazón* as *Dream of Reason* itself comprises a novel of artistic endeavor, one we shall never read but can and now do honor.

Contra Natura

1.

Javier Salazar came to the clear realization on that late November afternoon that, for the first time in his life, he felt really at ease and comfortable in the living room of his own apartment. And this made him smile, because that feeling—for a man who, like him, saw himself as a homebody (his friends, in addition to Salazar himself, had always taken him for an interior man and a man of interiors, almost agoraphobic)—produced an incomprehensible paradox. Until then, during most of his adult life, this man of interiors had lived in offices, meeting rooms, and clubs, including exclusive literary gatherings in the deluxe hotels of Barcelona and Madrid or New York, but had rarely stopped to spend afternoons at home, not even on the weekends. Nevertheless, he had the reputation of being an introverted man. And he was. This paradox—one Salazar recognized but whose examination he was not accustomed to dwell on—left, on occasion, a bad taste in his mouth.

He had already spent the entire afternoon installed in his wing chair drawn up to the glass doors that opened out onto his terrace. The room was illuminated by two lamps, the larger of which, brass and crystal, illuminated a novel by A. S. Byatt and a red vase filled with red tulips still in full bloom, despite their having lasted one whole week, still glowing among their undulating fleshy green stems and their apparently still fresh, broad leaves. Salazar had interrupted his reading only once, for an hour, at six-thirty, with the idea of taking a quick walk along Rosales. The afternoon was quickly growing cold. Night temperatures these days went down to freezing. Comfortable with himself and sitting in his own home at age sixty-four made Salazar not only feel but also look younger, 10 years younger. In cooler weather, Salazar drew his usual chair up to the wide-open glass doors in order to breathe in the first scents of early autumn in mid-November, then winter's frosty, misty scent, winter's bonfire scent, during all of December and January and February right up to the end of March. Everything tended toward making Salazar a prince in this world. His principality was not splendid but had the stability and flexibility of lifelong economic well-being that, added to his labors as a researcher and, for some years, editor of a series of books on philosophy and history, maintained him well above the average, in that agreeable stratum of the learned who have always lived as they liked to live and who, with retirement looming, are professionally satisfied. In fact, retirement was merely a nominal point of reference for Salazar, who continued working, in his own way, on various subjects that interested him. (What was Salazar doing during the day once he retired? Not one of his friends is close, so no one, really, unless out of passing curiosity, would ask that question. But it's a fitting question, it's a question, at this point, left hanging; and in his barrio not a single newspaper dealer or proprietor of a grocery store or a hardware or a fish store who had Salazar among his most distinguished clients has dared to ask him: What do you do the whole blessed day, aside from reading the Spanish and foreign newspapers you usually carry under your arm while you do your mid-morning shopping?) He liked sitting in the warmth of the *mesa camilla,* its heater concealed under the small round table by the heavy cloth's folds, and contemplating his drenched terrace and his new, dripping jasmine tree, the rain falling noisily on the terrace's pinkish tiles, the water's origami-like drumming when it stopped raining, making an airy pause and then starting up again.

In Madrid, during autumn, six is the hour for a light meal before a late dinner or, of course, for drinking tea, or a French-style unsweetened hot cocoa, or a perfect, rather sweet gin fizz: at that hour chicos seem much taller, less ashen, and much more guapo, Salazar thought. And at that hour the fog is soft, not gravid; rather, it's light, a misty assonance among the golden elms and dead leaves on the paths in the Parque del Oeste, on Rosales, and all along the Viaducto and the Jardines del Moro and the Palacio Real, unoccupied, fortunately, except sometimes by the God of discoveries and encounters: it was at such an hour around this time of year when Salazar encountered Ramón Durán in a dry streambed inside the Parque del Oeste: the two of them there, just them, at times it was drizzling, at times it cleared up, and Salazar said:

"We're going to get wet."

And Ramón Durán said:

"I'd fix that with a good cocktail."

"And which cocktail would you have right now?"

"A real Bloody Mary, neat, no garbage."

"So, a Bloody Mary, eh?"

"And why not? Petiot and I were the first to serve them at the bar in the New York Sheraton, as you surely know."

"A little young, aren't you, for Bloody Marys at the Sheraton?"

"Maybe I look young and maybe I don't. I'm able to look however I want," Ramón Durán declared assuredly.

They had been advancing toward the Paseo de Camoens. And Salazar, after thinking for a couple of minutes, remarked, in a very subdued voice, nearly neutral, reflecting a degree of indecision on his part as well as an effort to conquer indecision and detain the boy:

"We could have a cocktail, if you like, right now."

"I'm canine."

"What's that mean? That you're hungry? Ravenously hungry?"

"It's jail talk, means no *chapas:* no brass."

"Surely you learned that in Alcatraz."

"Yes. I've been in several prisons."

"Well, you look more like a computer student now."

"I'm not a student, I'm not, and I don't want to be. I'm a bartender, believe it or not."

"You mean, between the Sheraton Hotel and Alcalá Meco prison, you've been working a lot of bars."

"Yes, both sides of the bars: drinks behind, tricks out front."

They had been going uphill at a fast pace because the drizzle was soaking them, and they were walking without any protection from the rain.

"We could go round to the Charing Cross, if you like, if you have the time," said Salazar. "They'll make us some Bloody Marys, and they have very good potato tortillas."

There was almost nothing, in Salazar's memory, to this initial scene. In any case, a certain old-fashioned air, a *démodé* seduction, more characteristic of the dark years of Salazar's youth than of the years of this new century's liberated, postmodern homosexualities. Naturally, in recalling it, Salazar had modified this scene: there, in that first scene, Durán appears out of the blue, in an autumnal park, the Parque del Oeste. Durán immediately talks about himself, not like someone giving out information, but like someone depending on his physical attractiveness, who omits all positive information in order to suggest, as though joking, one after the other, various interpretations of himself, some anachronistic, like that business about being a bartender at the Sheraton, others aggressive or cocky, like that business about being a chapero, others, ultimately, almost metaphysical, as when he said: "I can look like anything I want." That a handsome young man, a guapo, who couldn't have been thirty at the time, should assert that he can look like whatever he wants seemed fascinating to Salazar: a declaration from a twin soul.

That first scene, whether or not so complete as Salazar recalled it, led to a highly precise sequel that not only Salazar but also Durán recalled and was fond of retelling frequently: after the Bloody Marys and a walk toward the Palacio Real and another couple of whiskeys in the Parque de las Vistillas area, Salazar and Durán went to bed together that night. And at this point, the communicative structure of that first night became notable, though confusing as well. Durán, naked, standing before him, appeared very beautiful to Salazar. And the boy's beauty, his erection, his at least momentary tenderness, inhibited Salazar, who dared only to caress the boy's penis with his cheek and bring its tip to his lips without deciding between making him come or coming himself.

"What's the matter?" Durán asked. "Don't you like me?"

Salazar swallowed saliva: "I like you a lot," he answered. "I don't know what's come over me."

And that was true, at that moment, which was luscious and perplexing at the same time, he did not know what had come over him. Salazar sat on the sofa next to the fireplace where they had lit a fire, and Durán knelt down before him, caressing his legs and penis. Salazar still had his shirt on. He felt sweaty, he felt incompetent, he felt inhibited. He thought, in a flash of shame, that he was not even capable of letting his own desire flood through him—that desire he, of course, felt. Deep down he thought of himself as a pitiful, vulgar man, half impotent. All these negative, obstructive thoughts increased his perplexity. This perplexity would have to congeal later and, once congealed, be thrust dangerously deep into Javier Salazar's abstract heart, but that would come quite a while later.

"Better stop," Salazar said finally.

"Want me to fuck you?" Durán asked.

"Better not. I'm not used to it."

"I'll fuck you good," Durán declared, in a tone of voice not inherently erotic but, rather, informative, like someone mentioning that he's capable of cleaning your distributor or attaching a shelf to a wall without causing any damage.

"Excuse me. I'm not in the habit."

"Doesn't matter if you're not gay," the boy remarked. "Doesn't matter to me whatever you are. Don't worry."

"But, I am. Obviously, I'm gay. Except I'm old, and you're really guapo, and I want you so much I don't dare touch you."

These phrases suddenly seemed fluid to Javier Salazar, not his own, contrary to his character, slipped in and spewed out of his mouth like a Vaseline suppository from his rectum: they had his repugnant lusciousness, his own intestinal sentimentality, drool or sweet saliva, inauthentic, circumstantial, which he repented of as soon as he sensed it, pronounced it, relished it. Especially seeing that, from a strictly strategic point of view, there had been adequate results to move or to mellow the good chico, who at times seemed lewd, at others infantile, at times profound and at others banal. Aside from that, the encounter ended like every erotic situation—every intense erotic situation—between adults. And Javier Salazar, who all his life had hated feeling ridiculous, felt for an instant the bitter jab of the ridiculous: which never perishes, which men like Salazar never pardon.

They ended up sitting together, alongside each other, in front of the fire. Finally Durán masturbated, and came copiously, because Salazar had said he would like to see him come. But the scene ended abruptly, and Durán left around one in the morning. Then Salazar masturbated, thinking about the boy, and later he felt ridiculous. He wished that what had happened had never happened. It took a long time for him to fall asleep. The next day his downstairs buzzer woke him at noon. It was Ramón Durán.

Translators' Notes

You don't need notes to appreciate Álvaro Pombo's *Contra Natura*. Until now, its readers didn't have notes; yet the author's critically acknowledged allusiveness, especially in the categories of philosophy, theology, literature, and the fine arts, invite a broadening of the novel's impact and the reader's experience. By its very nature as an urban novel with a rural background, *Contra Natura* tours Madrid with a knowing eye and also travels north and westward as well as eastward, precisely to the coastal city of Marbella, presenting a fully Spanish rather than a local novel. Then, too, beginning with its title, the novel tempts the reader into historical as well as international territories, so this translation purposefully propels its verbal vehicle into increasingly fluent drifts between idioms, as already known to you in bilingual expressions such as *barrio, café con leche.* We also introduce some new candidates for absorption, such as *chico* ("boy," "young man"), particularly in a gay sense. Some questions of translation provided their own answers; for example, each native English reader we have asked about the title phrase "contra natura" has forthrightly asserted its comprehensibility, often following up with something like, "It's Latin for a sin against nature, I learned it at church." Immediately, then, the novel situates itself among an ancient language, falsified—*contra naturam* is Augustine's, Aquinas's phrase; a contemporary Romance language, undetected; and the English-American language, osmotic.

Perhaps by having begun to read in three languages simultaneously, you will be emboldened to continue on your own. You should; but, if along the way an unfamiliar name or place or person or phrase piques your reading comfort, look for its page number among the notes. We have tried to scout the territory for you in advance, and if you don't find the trail blazed or, worse, marked inadequately or incorrectly, then write ronaldchrist.com/lumen. A website for these notes, with illustrations and URLs, will appear shortly.

Glossary

Barrio: Neighborhood, district, suburb, from Arabic *barriya* (fem.), open country, from *barr* ("outside"). The first use of *barrio* in the United States referred to East Harlem or Spanish Harlem, New York, in 1939. The word is now widely used throughout the United States.

Bloody Mary: A cocktail, originally half vodka and half tomato juice, without spices, celery, etc., that is, "without the [bartender's] garbage." Common versions of its history run like this: (1) Fernand "Pete" Petiot, an ex-patriot, invented this "restorative cocktail" in 1920 at Harry's New York Bar in Paris. (A patron suggested that Petiot name the drink for the Bucket of Blood Club in Chicago, but Petiot chose the name of his favorite actress: Mary Pickford. (2) Georgie Jessel independently created the drink in 1939, naming it after Bloody Mary, Henry VIII's daughter, who slaughtered Protestants. When Petiot came to work at New York's St. Regis Hotel—not the New York Sheraton—he added spices, but his employers rejected the name as gross, and it was served as a Red Snapper. The cocktail is not named for Bloody Mary in *South Pacific*.

Chapas: In the singular a *chapa* may signify a thin leaf, sheet, or foil, one layer of plywood, a metal tag or ornament, such as the decorations worn by charros and mariachis on their hats and clothes; hence coins as well, because of their thinness and metallic substance. *Chaperos* derive their name from tags attached to hotel keys: youths who formerly dangled from their pants pocket an identifying brass tag with the hotel's incised room number, while the attached key hung inside the pocket, thus signaling the boy's availability and room number. Today, *chapero* still names the professional youth, but he no longer dangles his hotel key tag, though Spanish men do frequently dangle their key-chain fobs in that way. Often translated as "hustler" or "rent boy," *chapero* retains a nearly invisible period air.

The Charing Cross: The Charing Cross Bar-Pub at 32 Paseo del Pintor Rosales skirts the Parque del Oeste ("West Park") across the street; a sole suggestion for the pub, Marianna C.'s, at foursquare.com: "try the tortillas."

Javier Salazar: The character's last name evokes Antonio de Oliveira Salazar (1889–1970), Portugal's prime minister and virtual dictator from 1932 to 1968. He had wanted to be a priest but left the seminary; he never married; he founded the Catholic Center Party in 1921. His right-wing, authoritarian Estado Novo ("New State") government controlled the country's political, social, economic, and cultural life starting in 1933, when he wrote a new constitution, subsequently validated by plebiscite and continuing to 1974. With a motto of "Control by Stability" and modeling his regime on Mussolini's while later recognizing Franco's, Salazar suppressed opposition and subsequently isolated Portugal from international concerns under a more infamous motto: *Orgulhosamente Só* ("Proudly Alone"). The military eventually overthrew his government in response to having to fight independence movements in the Portuguese empire. Like Franco, Salazar appeared as the enemy of Communism and Socialism while upholding traditional family values and aggressively repressing gay people, partly by force of the PIDE, a secret police he established and controlled.

A counterpoised, symmetrically named principal character, Paco Allende, will appear shortly.

Mesa camilla (table + diminutive of *cama* ["bed," "stretcher," "litter"]): Sometimes simply *camilla,* a small table equipped with a frame between the legs near the bottom for holding a brazier or electric heater; a heavy cloth covers the table and almost touches the floor. See http://puebloman.com/2012/02/03/history-of-cutar-in-objects-6-and-7-the-brasero-and-the-mesa-camilla/.

Neighboring parks: In a city of parks, Salazar mostly chooses traditional landscape and garden parks, avoiding the newer, outlying, and more urban. They are Campo del Moro ("Moors' Field"), a vast eighteenth-century park behind the Palacio Real; Parque del Oeste; Casa de Campo ("Country House"), dating from the sixteenth century, the former royal hunting grounds, which is one of Europe's largest public parks, containing a zoo, an amusement park, trade fair grounds, a cable car, and the Madrid Arena; Parque del Buen Retiro ("Pleasant Retreat Park"), Madrid's best-known park; royal land until the nineteenth century, its palace now houses museums; Jardín de la Quinta de la Fuente del Berro ("Garden of the Villa of the Watercress Fountain"), a seventeenth-century estate that contains a botanical garden and the famous source of fresh water; Parque Juan Carlos I, a twentieth-century project, not far from the airport, which is named for the current monarch and which opened in 1992 when Madrid was the cultural capital of Europe; Enrique Tierno Galván Park, begun in 1986 and named for the then mayor, which is the site of the planetarium, an auditorium/amphitheater, and an Imax cinema.

Parque de las Vistillas: Also known as the Jardín ("garden") de las Vistillas ("prospects," "views"), a quiet district, somewhat set apart, and accurately described by *Lonely Planet Spain:* "the leafy area around and beneath the southern end of the viaduct that crosses Calle de Segovia, . . . an ideal spot to pause and ponder the curious history of one of Madrid's oldest barrios. . . . the best place to do this is just across Calle de Bailén where the *terrazas* (open-air cafés) of Las Vistillas offer one of the best vantage points in Madrid for a drink, with views towards the Sierra de Guadarrama" ("La Vistillas").

Parque del Oeste ("West Park"): Acclaimed for its British, naturalistic land-scaping and containing the ancient Egyptian Temple of Debod.

Paseo de Camoens: Road inside the Parque del Oeste, running parallel to and connecting with Paseo del Pintor Rosales; named for Portugal's greatest poet, Luís Vaz de Camões (c. 1524–80).

Potato tortillas: In Spain, a tortilla is a large omelet, relatively thin or quite thick, made with eggs, potatoes, and onions, sometimes with spinach or another veg-etable added or replacing the potatoes; eaten with bread, hot or cold, as a tapa or used as a filling for sandwiches and other combinations.

On Rosales: Paseo del Pintor Rosales ("Painter Rosales Avenue"), named for Eduardo Rosales Gallina (1836–73), who painted chiefly portraits and historical works, two of which hang in the Casón del Buen Retiro ("Pleasant Retreat Man-sion"; see parks below). Rosales was much influenced by the work of Velazquez and, later, by Manet. He became director of El Prado and of the Spanish Acad-emy in Rome. The street is pleasant, peaceful, as the guidebooks say: "elegant, distinguished, and attractive . . . perfect location for a leisurely stroll" along the edge of the Parque del Oeste, according to travel.yahoo.com, in what is called the "privileged" Argüeles quarter of Madrid, where Álvaro Pombo lives.

The Viaducto and the Jardines del Moro and the Palacio Real: The iron Via-ducto de Segovia ("Segovia Viaduct"), constructed in 1930s to replace an ear-lier one, is a present-day Madrid landmark; the Jardines del Campo del Moro ("Moors Encampment Gardens") lie behind the Palacio Real ("Royal Palace"), where an early Arab fortress and a settlement named Mayrit once stood. The name Madrid derives from Mayrit. Conquered in the eleventh century, the site was unsuccessfully besieged by a Berber chieftain in the twelfth century but has retained the name of his encampment.

Works Cited

Chacel, Ana. 1981. *La sinrazón.* Barcelona: La Bruguera.
Chacel, Rosa. 1994. *Memoirs of Leticia Valle.* Translated by Carol Maier. Lincoln: University of Nebraska Press.

Chacel, Rosa. 2009. *Dream of Reason*. Translated by Carol Maier. Lincoln: University of Nebraska Press.

Fajardo, Frederick John-Maria. 2009. "Homotextuality in the Writing of Álvaro Pombo: A Phenomenological Perspective on Existential Dissonance and Authentic Being." PhD diss., University of British Columbia.

Harris, Gardiner. 2013. "India's Supreme Court Restores an 1861 Law Banning Gay Sex." *The New York Times*, 12 December, AG.

Perriam, Chris. 2006. "A Strange Unnatural History." *Times Literary Supplement*, 14 April, 21–22.

Pombo, Álvaro. 1979. *El Parecido*. Barcelona: La Gaya Ciencia.

Pombo, Álvaro. 1983. *El Héroe de las mansardas de Mansard*. Barcelona: Anagrama.

Pombo, Álvaro. 1988. *The Hero of the Big House*. Translated by Margaret Jull Costa. London: Chatto and Windus.

Pombo, Álvaro. 1989. *The Resemblance*. Translated by Margaret Jull Costa. London: Chatto and Windus.

Pombo, Álvaro. 2006. *Contra natura*. Barcelona: Editorial Anagrama.

Pombo, Álvaro. 2013. *Atlas sonoro / 4: Elige las palabras de España, Bolivia y Honduras* (21 October). Available at: http://blogs.elpais.com/papeles-perdidos/2013/10/atlas-sonoro-4-elige-las-palabras-de-espana-bolivia-y-honduras.html (accessed 20 October 2014).

"La Vistillas, Viaduct & Calle de Segovia." Available at: www.lonelyplanet.com/spain/madrid/sights/parks-gardens/las-vistillas-viaduct-calle-de-segovia (accessed 20 October 2014).

Real Academia Española. 2014. *Diccionario de la lengua española*. 23 ed., Edición del Tricentenario. Madrid, Spain.

"Dimitra" by Octavio Armand

Translated with commentary by Carol Maier

"Dimitra" by Octavio Armand

Siempre atento a la corrección política de sus sílabas, Borges dijo en alguna entrevista que no discutía con niños, con mujeres ni con negros. Yo, sí. Y también con locos, vagos, dioses, ancianos, gatos, perros, cubanos, muertos, plomeros, maracuchos, traumatólogos, octosexuales y electricistas. Hasta he discutido con teóricos y gente de peor calaña aún. A diario mi viuda y mi hija me arrastran irresistiblemente a una agradable discusión. Conmigo mismo discuto para poner de acuerdo a mi cuerpo y mi sombra, que no siempre se llevan bien.

Mimetizo el lenguaje de los niños, por ejemplo. Eso, para comunicarme con ellos. Por mimarlos. A veces, para lograr que me entiendan, extremo el mimetismo hasta enmudecer. Me convierto entonces en un mimo. Hablo sin palabras. Soy el gesto, el payaso cuya lengua es la rojísima nariz, el rostro como un cascarón de huevo pintorreteado, la caída estrepitosa, el lagrimón negro fijo bajo la mirada enorme.

Digamos, pues, que soy un Mimotauro. Oyeron bien: *Mimo*tauro. Digamos además que quizá sea poeta. Que escribo mal para que me entiendan bien ustedes, niños de mi exagerada edad. Supongamos que todo esto es cierto y digamos ya y sin mayores preámbulos quiénes están aquí conmigo.

Dimitra es una joven griega, cretense si preciso el gentilicio, que recientemente pasó unos meses en Venezuela. La trajo Leonardo, de gentilicio cumanés. En realidad, la atrajo, pues él vino primero y en singular, solo y desolado. Yo reía para este venerable profeta del dimitraísmo la epifanía de su simpatiquísima diosa y las agradecidas resonancias homéricas de su importante importada conquista. Costas lejanas arracimaban de nuevo a las islas, y se juntaban, se volvían a juntar, pero esta vez sin sobresaltos troyanos, gracias al Paris casero y la Helena afortunadamente soltera, que casada a alguna Casandra hubiera alborotado. Melao sin Menelao, la aventura no obligaba a ruinosas guerras y funestas piñatas de madera sino a los gratos rituales de la amistad.

Como el griego de Dimitra era literalmente griego para mí, tuve que estrenarme en varios nuevos idiomas, de esos inventados por sus aprendices con milagrosas conjugaciones y pronunciación de canto gregoriano venido a menos. Esto, por supuesto, como colofón o cloroformo del lenguaje corporal, del cual también abusé, como si bailara a solas sones de Ñico Saquito. A los gestos, las miradas, las torsiones y hasta contorsiones de las cejas, los codos, la nariz y los labios, sumé bífidas entonaciones, pasando del tentativo babelspañol inicial al inglespañol de unisex gramatical para iniciados, hasta recalar por fin en el inglés a secas como lengua franca por lo afrancesada y tranca por lo demorada.

Para que Dimitra no se perdiera de mi sabiduría hablé *jáguar ínglich*—nuestro inglés exclusivo—muy lentamente y con acento grave pero cubano; y para entender a Dimitra la escuché con atento oído sajónico y retorcido laberinto. Aquello era como un retrato del verbo isabelino en negativo y cámara lenta. Menú de lengua al ralentí y sonrisa al dente para decisivas ayunas.

¿Hablar mal para que se nos entienda? Como ustedes, que por cortesía tratan de disimular la perplejidad, yo también me lo he preguntado. Y muchas veces. La comunicación en lengua ajena, o en alcances muy dispares de la propia, por ejemplo, al hablar con niños, ancianos, locos o dioses, suele obligar a torpezas elementales, a trámites de elocución o dicción capaces de superar la perfecta mudez de quien no entiende o no logra hacerse entender. Somos entonces como el grito de Munch o estamos frente a ese grito, inaudible por inoído pero perfectamente comprensible; extrañísimo pero comunicante a todo dar por la tremenda retórica del rostro y la ciceroniana oratoria del gesto que pone a la cabeza de cabeza, entre el paréntesis de las manos que parecen querer destornillarla, como si fuera un bombillo fundido.

Ante el páramo de la incomunicación, ante un lenguaje sin éxtasis, sin silencio fecundante, la poesía es la voz que le falta y le sobra al grito de Munch: un empecinado esfuerzo por comunicar lo incomunicable, haciendo inteligible lo ininteligible, como si por instantes la confusión babélica se rindiera al milagro de Pentecostés.

2 Y de repente vino un estruendo del cielo como de un viento recio que corría, el cual hinchió toda la casa donde estaban sentados;

3 Y se les aparecieron lenguas repartidas, como de fuego, que se asentó sobre cada uno de ellos.

4 Y fueron todos llenos del Espíritu Santo, y comenzaron a hablar en otras lenguas, como el espíritu les daba que hablasen.

5 Moraban entonces en Jerusalén judíos, varones religiosos de todas las naciones debajo del cielo.

6 Y hecho este estruendo, juntóse la multitud; y estaban confusos, porque cada uno les oía hablar su propia lengua.

Pésima elocuencia, retórica retrógrada, retorcida, arcaizante, glosolalia, un hablar mal que revela lo incomprensible, la poesía se semeja al estruendoso viento recio que reparte lenguas de fuego. Embriaga al que la escribe y a quien la lee con su alcohol de 10000 grados, prendiendo bajo el cielo de la boca una llama que es la lengua. Embriaga también como el alcohol del beso. Lengua ardiente en el secuestro mutuo y recíproco de los amantes, la poesía hace del silencio y su sombra, que es el lenguaje, un asombroso beso de lenguas.

"¡Y si después de tantas palabras," advierte Vallejo, "no sobrevive la palabra!" Si la poesía, o el beso, o estar juntos y ser uno; si la palabra en comunión singular que nos une no sobrevive a las palabras plurales que nos separan, entonces ¿qué hacer? "Entonces . . .", dice el peruanísimo peruano del Perú, "¡Claro! . . . Entonces . . . ¡ni palabra!"

Otro *poema humano*, demasiado humano, pero de *Trilce*, recoge este espléndido grito. En el XIII, número de mal agüero, leemos: "Oh estruendo mudo." Y de inmediato se repite la exclamación, pero al revés, callando en su expresiva imagen reflejada: "¡Odumodneurtse!" El aullido hacia dentro de Vallejo le da a Plauto un giro estremecedor: "lovo de mí," dice en *Sermón sobre la muerte*. El hombre que es lobo para el hombre es también lobo de sí mismo.

La ortografía le falla al poeta. Escribe mal para que lo comprendan bien. Maravillosa pésima ortografía que le da voz a la escritura y que nos permite oír su personalísimo grito de Munch. El *lovo* de Vallejo es el propio Vallejo. Se autorretrata en la vigesimotercera letra del alfabeto español, que no la segunda.

Abierta hacia arriba, aullándole a la noche y a la luna, y a los demás lobos con su pobre b tan bien escrita, la V de Vallejo se aúlla a sí misma. Voz de la desesperación, de la culpa, acaso del genético pecado: voz del *ovo,* hurga en lo oscuro, en el abismo, en eso que suele llamarse el alma.

Caracas

January 31, 2011

"Dimitra"

Always afraid that he might let slip some politically incorrect syllable, Borges once told an interviewer that he never argued with children, women, or blacks. I do. Also with mad men, vagrants, gods, old people, cats, dogs, Cubans, dead men, plumbers, Ohioans, orthopedic surgeons, octosexuals and electricians. I've argued with theorists too, and people of even worse ilk. There's never a day goes by when my widow and daughter don't drag me into some enjoyable argument. I often argue with myself in order to broker an agreement between my body and soul, which don't always get along.

For example, I mimic the language of children. To communicate with them. Kid them into understanding me. Sometimes, to make myself clear, I mimic them 'til I'm mute. At that point I turn into a mime. Speak without words. I'm the gesture, the clown whose tongue is a shiny red nose, an Easter egg face, a resounding fall, a large tear stilled beneath his far-reaching gaze.

So let's say I'm a mimotaur. You heard right. *Mimo*taur. Let's double the bet and say I'm a poet. Say I write bad verse so that you, children of my adulterated age, understand me better. Let's assume that all this is squeaky true and without further ado introduce the people here with me.

Dimitra is a young woman from Greece, from Crete, to be specific, who recently spent a few months in Venezuela. She came with Leonardo, who's from Cumaná. In truth, she came because of Leonardo, since he arrived first, in the singular, alone and unhappy. I was amused by the epiphany his highly appealing goddess afforded this prophet of Dimithraism and by the grateful Homeric resonances of his important imported conquest. Threads from distant coasts knit the islands together, and they joined, joined again, but this time without threats from Troy, thanks to the local Paris and the fortunately unmarried Helen, who would have raised quite a ruckus with some Cassandra or other had she not been single. A sweet melee without Menelaus, the adventure brought pleasant rituals of friendship rather than ruinous wars and deadly wooden piñatas.

Since Dimitra's Greek was literally Greek to me, I was forced to debut in several new languages, the sort invented by their apprentices, who grace them with marvelous conjugations, uttered like Gregorian chant fallen on hard times. This was of course by way of a colophon or chloroform for corporeal language, which I abused as if I were dancing solo to Ñico Saquito's *sones*. To his gestures, gazes, convolutions, even the contortions of eyebrows, elbows, nose, lips, I added bifid intonations, moving from my initial tentative Babel-spanish to Spanglish with its unisex grammar for initiates, until we would up with straight English as our lingua franca, its cant continually prompting can't.

So that Dimitra would not lose one bit of my wisdom, I spoke *jaguar inglich*—our exclusive English—very slowly, my accent grave but Cuban; and in order to understand Dimitra I listened with attentive Saxonian ear and coiled labyrinth. The whole thing was like the negative portrait of Elizabethan grammar made in slow motion. A plate of slow-simmered tongue and smiles al dente for toothless diners.

Speaking poorly in order to be understood? Like you people, courteously trying to hide your perplexity, I've asked myself the same thing. Many times. Communication in another's language or in milieus very different from one's own, talking with children, for example, or old people, madmen, or gods usually requires simple trip ups, complicated elocution or forms of address capable of overcoming the perfect muteness of someone who doesn't understand or can't manage to make himself understood. We're like Munch's scream then, or we're in front of that scream, which is inaudible because it's unheard although perfectly comprehensible; very foreign but communicating at top speed with the tremendous rhetoric of that visage and the Ciceronian heads up that sets the head on its head, between a parenthesis of hands that look like they're trying to unscrew a burned-out light bulb.

Given the wasteland of incommunication, facing a language that lacks ecstasy, a fertile silence, poetry is the voice of which Munch's scream has both too much and none at all: a paltry effort to communicate the incommunicable, making the unintelligible intelligible, as if, in some instants Babelian confusion surrendered to the miracle of Pentecost.

2 *And suddenly the heavens roared as with a rushing mighty wind, which filled the entire house where they were sitting;*

3 And there appeared unto them tongues like as of fire, and it settled over each one of them;

4 And they were all filled with the Holy Spirit, and they began to speak in other tongues, as if the Spirit enabled them to speak;

5 At that time there dwelling in Jerusalem Jews, devout men from all the nations under heaven;

6 And hearing that roaring, the multitude came together; and they were confused, because each one of them heard his own language being spoken.

Dreadful eloquence, archaic, writhing, retrograde, rhetoric, glossolalia, poorly spoken speech that reveals the incomprehensible, poetry resembles the rushing mighty wind that distributes tongues of fire. With its 10,000-proof alcohol, poetry intoxicates everyone who writes or reads it, igniting a tongue of fire beneath the roofs of their mouths. Intoxicating too like the alcohol in a kiss. A burning tongue in lovers' mutual and reciprocal kidnapping, poetry turns silence and its shadow—language—into a stunning French kiss.

"And if after so many words," César Vallejo warns, "the word does not survive!" If poetry, or the kiss, or being together and being one; if the word in the singular communion that unites us does not survive the plural words that separate us, then what will we do? "Then," says the poet, Peruvian to the hilt, "That's simple! . . . Then . . . not a word!"

Another of Vallejo's *human poems,* one too human, but from *Trilce,* takes up that splendid cry. "Oh mute crescendo," we read in number XIII, number of ill omen. And immediately the exclamation is repeated, but reversed, now silent in its expressive reflected image: "Odnecsercetum!" The howl within Vallejo gives Plautus' wolf a shocking turn: "woelf is me!" he says in "Sermon on Death." The man who is wolf to man is also wolf to himself.

Spelling fails the poet. He writes things wrong to make himself better understood. Wonderful woeful spelling that gives voice to writing and allows us to hear his very personal Munch scream. Vallejo's *woelf* is Vallejo himself, his self-portrait drawn in the alphabet's fifteenth letter. Opening up, howling to the night and the moon, and to the other wolves with their poor perfectly written o's, Vallejo's vowel howls to itself. Voice of despair, guilt, perhaps genetic sin: voice of the *oeuf,* it digs deep in the darkness, in the abyss, in what we usually call the soul.

Caracas

January 31, 2011

"Dimitra" in English: Three Notes by Carol Maier

(1) Introducing "Dimitra," which he wrote to preface a reading from *Clinamen,* his most recent collection of poems, Octavio Armand told the audience that before taking a photograph he likes to develop it. His readings, he said by way of explanation, always begin with an incident that will provide a context for the poems to follow. The incident that afternoon concerned Armand's deliberately slow and erroneous usage of language to make possible the development of a friendship. Poetry is precisely that, Armand said, referring to the deformation of English that allowed him to converse with Dimitra.

(2) From a family twice exiled, Armand traveled to the United States in early adolescence and lived here for some three decades, as a student, writer, and university professor; he considers himself so bilingual that he told the audience in Caracas he knows English intimately enough to be a spy. Nevertheless, over the years he has said consistently that he could never write in English. Spanish is the language of his exile and, consequently, the site of *his* deformation. Exile deforms things, forcing one to be and not be at the same time, Armand has explained. He finds that English, in which one either is or is not, cannot offer him that disconcerting, often demoralizing simultaneity; Spanish, however, offers *ser* for being as existence and *estar* for being as location and transitory state, making it all too easy to be and not be at one and the same time. Within and against that paradox Armand has worked since his first book, *Horizonte no es siempre lejanía* [Horizon not always means distance], writing in a mother tongue he calls moribund, for a fatherland effectively dead to him. It's painful business, but Cuban literary tradition is known for its transformative verbal pyrotechnics: one starts writhing, but writing prompts pleasure.

(3a) Armand wrote "Dimitra" as a text to be spoken, so his translator best hear him read it. Although I was not able to be in the audience in Caracas, thanks to Johan Gotera, who videotaped the reading and posted it on YouTube, I could hear Armand read "Dimitra" as many times as I wanted. I could even read *with* him, in his language or in mine, as I wrote the translation (www.youtube.com/watch?v=NhWt_7MzX9g).

(3b) In addition to the video of the book launch for *Clinamen,* Johan Gotera has posted several others, from earlier readings and interviews, thus enabling

me to see Armand as he is today—an internationally known poet and essay-
ist, his work the subject of various monographs, theses, and dissertations—
and, simultaneously, as he was years ago when we met as graduate students
and I began to translate his work. I found the experience quite moving, reminded by both images and words of bilingual readings we gave together
and of long conversations about translation. Our talk then often centered on
the limitations that language places on all forms of communication. Some of
the most memorable conversations concerned the effectiveness of carefully
crafted playfulness at once silly and serious as a strategy for circumventing
those limitations.[1]

(3c) One of the best known poems in contemporary Latin American poetry,
Vallejo's "Sermón sobre la muerte" [Sermon on death] has been translated
into English several times. Each time, Vallejo the man becomes Vallejo the
wolf in different words, a verbal magic he worked in Spanish by replacing
the *b* in *lobo* ("wolf") with a *v,* a substitution that deformed the word without
altering its pronunciation. I knew that following Vallejo's alteration to the
letter would work no magic in English, so my thought was to come up with
something appropriately wrong—what in our correspondence Armand referred to as a "nutritious well-done misteak." Being a vegetarian, I preferred
to meet that requirement with an egg.

Note

1. "The (L)imitation of Language in Two Tongues" (1977), the first essay I published about translation, arose from those conversations and my work with Armand's
poetry.

Work Cited

Maier, Carol. 1977. "The (L)imitation of Language in Two Tongues." *Escolios* 2(1/2): 7–61.

Bibliography of Carol Maier

Edited Books and Guest-Edited Journals

Between Languages and Cultures: Translation and Cross-Cultural Texts. 1995. Edited with Anuradha Dingwaney. Pittsburgh and Delhi: University of Pittsburgh Press and Oxford India.

Ethics and the Curriculum. 2011. Special issue. Guest-edited with Mona Baker. *The Interpreter and Translator Trainer* 5(1).

Evaluation. 2000. Special issue. *The Translator* 6(2).

In the Feminine Mode: Essays on Hispanic Women Writers. 1990. Edited with Noël Valis. Lewisburg, Pa.: Bucknell University Press.

Literature in Translation: Teaching Issues and Reading Practices. 2010. Coedited volume with Françoise Massardier-Kenney. Kent, Ohio: Kent State University Press.

Ramón María del Valle-Inclán: Questions of Gender. 1994. Edited with Roberta L. Salper. Lewisburg, Pa.: Bucknell University Press.

Translation/Interpreting and Social Activism—Traducción/Interpretación y Compromiso Social. 2010. Coedited volume with Julie Boéri. Universidad de Granada and ECOS (Spain). Selected proceedings of a conference on Translation and Social Activism held at the University of Granada, Spain.

Book Chapters

"A afirmación coma un seguido contradicir: Cinco claves adicionais para aproximarse ós grabados de Conde Corbal." 1989. Translated from the Spanish, Anxos Sumai. In *Conde Corbal*, 13–21. La Coruña, Spain: Fundación Caixa Galicia.

"Acercando la conciencia a la muerte: Hacia una definición ampliada de Ia estética de Valle- Inclán." 1988. In *Valle-Inclán: Nueva valoración de su obra*, edited by Clara L. Barbeito, 125–36. Barcelona: PPU.

"Between Languages and Cultures: Translation as a Method for Cross-Cultural Teaching." 1992. With Anuradha Dingwaney. In *Understanding Others: Cultural and Cross Cultural Studies and the Teaching of Literature*, edited by Joseph Trimmer and Tilly Warnock, 47–62. Urbana, Ill.: NCTE.

"Bilingualism" and "Translation." 1997. In *Feminist Literary Theory: A Dictionary*, edited by Beth Kowaleski-Wallace, 43–44 and 401–402. New York: Garland Publishing Company.

"Carol Maier" (An interview by Ronald Christ). 1996. *On Translation: The Transla-tors,* edited by Ronald Christ, 56–67. Atlanta, Ga.: Atlantic College of Art Gallery.

"Choosing and Introducing a Translation." 2010. In *Literature in Translation: Teach-ing Issues and Reading Practices,* edited by Carol Maier and Françoise Massardier-Kenney, 11–21. Kent, Ohio: Kent State University Press.

"Conversation with Cola Franzen." 2008. In *Borinsky: Tatuajes, tango y la escritura holográmatica de Buenos Aires,* edited by Miriam Balboa Echeverría, 133–42. Bue-nos Aires: Nueva Generación.

"De cifras, desciframiento, y una lectura literal de *La lámpara maravillosa.*" 1992. In *Suma valleinclaniana,* edited by John P. Gabriele, 223–50. Barcelona: Anthropos.

"*El embrujado* as a Spiritual Exercise." 1990. In *Selected Proceedings of the "Singu-laridad y Trascendencia" Conference held at Hofstra University, November 6, 7, 8, 1986,* edited by Nora Marval-McNair, 149–60. Boulder, Colo.: Society of Spanish and Spanish American Studies, University of Colorado at Boulder.

"Exégesis trina: Enigma, engaño y el principio estetico de *La lámpara maravillosa.*" 1987. In *Genio y virtuosismo de Valle-Inclán,* edited by John P. Gabriele, 125–38. Madrid: Orígenes.

"Figurations of a Finale Less Than Grand: Fiction by Nivaria Tejera, Rosa Chacel, and María Zambrano." 2014. In *María Zambrano: Between the Caribbean and the Med-iterranean,* edited by Madeline Cámara, 227–36. Newark, Del.: Juan de la Cuesta Hispanic Monographs.

"From Words to Divinity: Questions of Language and Gender in *Divinas palabras.*" 1994. In *Ramón Maria del Valle-Inclán: Questions of Gender,* edited by Carol Maier and Roberta L. Salper, 199–221. Lewisburg, Pa.: Bucknell University Press.

"Gender, Pedagogy, and Literary Translation: Three Workshops and a suggestion." 2003. In *Beyond the Ivory Tower,* edited by Brian James Baer and Geoffrey Koby, 157–72. Amsterdam: John Benjamins.

"How to Ask the Right Questions or, the Pedagogy of Specialized Translation on the Graduate Level." 1990. With Françoise Masssardier-Kenney. In *Looking Ahead. Proceedings of the 30th Annual Conference of the American Translators Associa-tion,* edited by A. Leslie Willson, 371–79. Medford, N.J.: Learned Information, Inc.

"*La lámpara maravillosa* de Valle-Inclán y la invención continua como una constante estética." 1986. *Actas del VIII Congreso de la Asociación Internacional de Hispanis-tas. Brown University, 22–27 August 1983,* edited by A. David Kossoff et al., 2:237–45. Madrid: Ediciones Istmo.

"Literary Translation for Specialized Translators?" 1991. With Françoise Massardier-Kenney. In *Horizons. Proceedings of the 32nd Annual Conference of the Ameri-can Translators Association,* edited by A. Leslie Willson, 249–53. Medford, N.J.: Learned Information, Inc.

"Lugares maravillosos: La creación de un espacio estético en la ficción de Ramón del Valle- Inclán." 1985. In *La Chispa 85. Selected Proceedings,* edited by Gilbert Paolini, 219–30. New Orleans: Tulane University.

"Notes After Words: Looking Forward Retrospectively at Translation and (Hispanic and Luso- Brazilian) Feminist Criticism." 1989. In *Cultural and Historical Grounding for Hispanic and Luso-Brazilian Feminist Literary Criticism,* edited by Hernán Vidal, 625–53. Minneapolis, Minn.: Institute for the Study of Ideologies and Literature.

"Octavio Armand Santana." 1990. In *Dictionary of Twentieth-Centurv Cuban Literature,* edited by Julio Martinez, 27–32. New York: Greenwood Press.

"¿Palabras de armonía?: reflexiones sobre la lectura, los límites y la estética de Valle-Inclán." 1988. In *Estelas, laberintos, nuevas sendas: Unamuno, Valle-Inclán, Garcia Lorca, la Guerra Civil,* edited by Angel G. Loureiro, 151–70. Barcelona: Anthropos.

"Prólogo/Prologue." 2003. Essay and self-translation. In Noël Valis, *Mi casa me recuerda (My House Remembers Me),* 9–24. Ferrol, Coruña, Spain: Esquío.

"Questions of Review" and "Gender in/and Literary Translation." With Françoise Massardier- Kenney. 1996. In *Translation Horizons. Beyond the Boundaries of "Translation Spectrum,"* Translation Perspectives IX, edited by Marilyn Gaddis Rose, 225–42 and 243–68. Binghamton, N.Y.: SUNY Binghamton Press.

"Ramón María del Valle-Inclán." 1985. In *Critical Survey of Long Fiction: Foreign Language Series,* edited by Frank Magill, 1830–43. Englewood Cliffs, N.J.: Salem Press.

"Recovering, Re-Covering, and the Translation of Work by Rosa Chacel and María Zambrano." 1996. In *Feminism: Multi-Cultural Literature,* edited by Antonio Sobejano-Morán, 202–22. Lewiston, N.Y.: Edwin Mellen.

"Reviewing and Criticism." 1998. In *Routledge Encyclopedia of Translation Studies,* edited by Mona Baker, 205–10. London and New York: Routledge.

"Reviewing and Criticism." 2008. In *Routledge Encyclopedia of Translation Studies,* rev. ed., edited by Mona Baker, 236–40. London and New York: Routledge.

"Sor Juana in English." 2007. In *Approaches to Teaching Sor Juana,* edited by Emilie Bergman and Stacey Schlau, 9–14. New York: MLA.

"Symbolist Studies in Spanish: The Concept of Language in Valle-Inclán's *La lámpara maravillosa.*" 1979. In *Waiting for Pegasus. Studies of the Presence of Symbolism and Decadence in Hispanic Letters,* edited by Roland Grass and William R. Risley, 77–87. Macomb: *Essays in Literature.*

"Teaching the Literature of the Spanish Civil War in Translation." 2007. In *Teaching Representations of the Spanish Civil War,* edited by Noël Valis, 248–57. New York: MLA.

"Toward a Methodology of Specialized Translation." 1993. With Françoise Massardier-Kenney. In *Scientific and Technical Translation,* Vol. VI of the American Translators Association Scholarly Monograph Series, edited by Sue Ellen Wright and Leland D. Wright Jr., 151–60. Philadelphia: John Benjamins.

"Toward a Theoretical Practice for Cross-Cultural Translation." 1995. In *Between Languages and Cultures: Translation and Cross-Cultural Texts,* edited by Anuradha Dingwaney and Carol Maier, 21–38. Pittsburgh: University of Pittsburgh Press.

"Translating as a Body." 2006. *The Translator as Writer,* edited by Susan Bassnett and Peter Bush, 137–48. London: Continuum.

"Translation, *Dépaysement,* and Their Figuration." 2002. In *Translation and Power,* edited by Maria Tymoczko and Edwin Gentzler, 184–94. Amherst and Boston: University of Massachusetts Press.

"Translation into English from the Spanish." 1993. Review essay and reviews. With Kathleen Ross. In *Handbook of Latin American Studies* 52, edited by Dolores Moyano Martin, 684–710. Austin: University of Texas Press.

"Translations into English from the Spanish." 1995. Review essay and reviews. With Kathleen Ross. In *Handbook of Latin American Studies* 54, edited by Dolores Moyano Martin, 675–99. Austin: University of Texas Press.

"Translation into English from the Spanish." 1999. Review essay and reviews. With Maureen Ahern and Kathkeen Ross. In *Handbook of Latin American Studies* 56, edited by Dolores Moyano Martin, 657–77. Austin: University of Texas Press.

"Translation into English from the Spanish." 2002. Review essay and reviews. With Maureen Ahern and Kathleen Ross. In *Handbook of Latin American Studies* 58, edited by Lawrence Boudon, 675–703. Austin: University of Texas Press.

"Translation into English from the Spanish." 2005. Review essay and reviews. With Maureen Ahern, Kathleen Ross, and Steven White. In *Handbook of Latin American Studies* 60, edited by Lawrence Boudon, 653–80. Austin: University of Texas Press.

"Translations into English from the Spanish." 2007. Review essay and reviews. With Maureen Ahern, Kathleen Ross, and Steven White. In *Handbook of Latin American Studies* 62, edited by Katherine D. McCann and Tracy North, 525–58. Austin: University of Texas Press.

"Translations into English from the Spanish." 2009. Review essay and reviews. With Maureen Ahern, Kathleen Ross, and Steven White. In *Handbook of Latin American Studies* 64, edited by Katherine D. McCann and Tracy North, 459–503. Austin: University of Texas Press.

"Translations into English from the Spanish." 2011. Review essay and reviews. With Maureen Ahern and Steven White. In *Handbook of Latin American Studies: 66*, edited by Katherine D. McCann and Tracy North, 600–638. Austin: University of Texas Press.

"Translations into English from the Spanish and Portuguese." 1990. In *Handbook of Latin American Studies* 50, edited by Dolores Moyano Martin, 590–607. Austin: University of Texas Press.

"The Translator as Intervenient Being." 2007. In *Translation and Intervention*, edited by Jeremy Munday, 1–17. London: Continuum.

"The Translator as *Theôros*: Thoughts on Cogitation, Figuration, and Current Creative Writing." 2006. In *Translating Others*, edited by Theo Hermans, 163–80. Manchester, UK: St. Jerome.

"Translators." 1995. In *Oxford Companion to Women's Writing in the United States*, edited by Cathy N. Davidson and Linda Wagner-Martin, 883–85. New York: Oxford University Press.

"The Translator's Visibility: The Rights and Responsibilities Thereof." 2007. In *Translating and Interpreting Conflict*, edited by Myriam Salama-Carr, 254–66. Amsterdam: Rodopi.

"A Working Model for the Pedagogy of Specialized Translation." With Françoise Massardier- Kenney. 1997. In *Actes. I Congrés International Sobre Traducció. Abril 1992*, edited by Miguel Edo Julià, 2:429–38. Barcelona: Departament de Readucció i d'Interpretació, Universitat Autònoma de Barcelona.

Articles

"The Construction of 'Further, Alternative Signs': Notes from a Workshop in Translating Women Writers." 1994. With Ana Fuentes and Lynda Privitera. *Letras Femeninas* Número Extraordinario Commemorativo 1974–1994 20(1-2): 167–75.

"Eggshells, Self-Translation, and the Encouragement of Student Translators." 2003. *In Other Words* 21(Summer): 53–61.

"Fitting It All in One Semester: An Intensive Introductory Spanish Course for Health Care Personnel." 1986. *Hispania* 69(3): 714–19.

"Gaining Multiple Competences through Translation." 1998. *ADFL Bulletin* 30(1): 30–33.

"The Image at the Empty Center: Toward a Re-evaluation of Ramón del Valle-Inclán's *Claves líricas.*" 1987. *Symposium* 41(2): 110–26.

"An Interview with Marilyn Gaddis Rose." 1999. *Translation Review* 57(1): 3–14.

"An Interview with Peter Bush." 1997. *Translation Review* 53(1): 5–9.

"An Interview with Ronald Christ." 1996. *Translation Review* 50(1): 4–11.

"La aportación cervantina a 'Yo soy aquel que ayer no más decía.'" 1977. *Mester* 6(2): 93–96.

"*La lámpara maravillosa* y la reforma drámatica de la ficción española." 1983. *Faro de Vigo* (23 September): 222, 228.

"La voz, lo que se quiere decir: Notas sobre la poesía de Octavio Armand." 1983. *Revista Nacional de Cultura* 251(August-December): 110–24.

"The (L)imitations of Language in Two Tongues." 1977. *Escolios* 2(1-2): 57–61.

"Literary Re-creation, the Creation of Readership and Valle-Inclán's *La lámpara maravillosa.*" 1988. *Hispania* 71(2): 217–27.

"Love Unfaithful but True: Reflections on *Amor infiel.Emily Dickinson por Nuria Amat.* 2009. *Emily Dickinson Journal* 18(2): 77–93.

"Notas hacia una definición del concepto de historia en *La lámpara maravillosa.*" 1981. *Explicación de Textos Literarios* 9(2): 153–58.

"Notas sobre melancolía y creación en dos narradores valleinclanescos: el Marqués de Bradomín y el poeta de *La lámpara maravillosa.*" 1981. *Revista de Estudios Hispánicos* 15(1): 99– 108.

"Perspectives on Translation Studies in the U.S.: A Conversation with Marilyn Gaddis Rose." 2007. *Translation and Interpreting Studies* 2(2): 147–52.

"The Poetry of Ana Castillo: A Dialogue Between Poet and Critic." 1980. *Letras Femeninas* 6(1) (Spring): 51–62.

"*Por tierras de Portugal y de España,* e de Galicia: Unha rectificación galega da perspectiva castiza, planteada por Valle-Inclán." 1982. *Grial* 75(January-March): 45–62.

"Reviewing Latin American Literature in Translation: Time to Proceed to the 'Larger Question.'" 1990–1991. *Translation Review* 34 and 35(1): 18–24.

"Rosario Refracted: Three Notes on Mutation and Translation." *Letras Femeninas* 18(1-2): 127– 37.

"Seis grabados de José Conde Corbal: Notas para una exposición valleinclanesca." 1978. *The American Hispanist* 8(24): 10–12.

"Siete claves de la obra de Conde Corbal." 1983. *Faro de Vigo,* 17 June, 112.

"Siting *Leticia Valle:* Questions of Gender and Generation." 1992. *Monographic Review/Revista Monográfica* 8: 79–98.

"Teaching Literature in Translation." 2005. With Rosemary Arrojo and Marlyn Gaddis Rose. *ATA Chronicle* (February): 19–20, 35.

"Teaching Literature through Translation: A Proposal and Three Examples." 1994. *Translation Review* 46(1): 10–13.

"Teaching Monolingual Students to read in Translation (As Translators)." 2001. *ADFL* 33(1): 44–46.

"Toward a Definition of Woman as Reader in Valle-Inclán's Aesthetics." 1986. *Boletín del Museo de Pontevedra* 40: 121–30.

"Traducción corpórea: meditaciones sobre la meditación." 2008. Translated by Estefanía Herschel- Junyent. Special Issue: *Traducción/Género/Poscolonialismo,* edited by Patrizia Calefato and Pilar Godayol. *DeSignis* 12: 41–48.

"Translating Women's Fiction." 1998. *Bulletin of Hispanic Studies* 75(1): 95–108.

"Translation as Performance: Three Notes." 1984. *Translation Review* 15(1): 5–8.

"Translation, Imagination and (Un)academic Activity." 1980. *Translation Review* 6(1): 25–29.

"Untwisting the Castilian Tongue: Some Suggestions from Valle-Inclán's *La lámpara maravillosa.*" 1985. *Hispanic Journal* 6(2): 59–67.

"A Woman in Translation, Reflecting." 1985. *Translation Review* 17(1): 4–8.

"Women in Translation: Current Intersections, Theory, and Practice." 1992. *Delos* 5(2): 29–39.

"Xosé Conde Corbal e a estética do grabado: Unha reforma do ollo por medio da deformación da liña." 1980. *Grial* 70(October-December): 400–414.

Reviews and Review Essays

"Assimilationist Pressures in Puerto Rico." Review of *Mi mamá me ama* by Emilio Díaz Valcárcel. 1984. *American Book Review* 7(1): 17.

"Putting the US Stamp on the Puerto Rican Psyche." Review of *Mi mamá me ama* by Emilio Díaz Valcárcel. 1984. *The San Juan Star,* 14 March, 17.

Review of *A Forbidden Passion* by Cristina Peri Rossi. Translated by Mary Jane Treacy. 1994. *Letras Femeninas* 20(1–2): 191–92.

Review of *The Answer / La Respuesta* by Sor Juana Inés de La Cruz and Electa Arenal. Translated by Amanda Powell. 1995. *Comparative Literature* 47(1): 79–82.

Review of *Aproximaciones al estudio de la literatura hispánica* by Carmelo Virgiilo, L. Teresa Valdivieso, and Edward H. Friedman. 1985. *Hispania* 68(4): 803–4.

Review of *¿Cómo se dice . . . ?* by Ana C. Jarvis, Raquel Lebredo, and Francisco Mena. 1987. *Hispania* 70(1): 193–94.

Review of *La ruta de Severo Sarduy* by Roberto González Echevarría. 1990–91. *Siglo XX / 20th Century: Culture and Critical Discourse* 8(1–2): 129–35.

Review of *Looking Within: Selected Poems 1954–2000 / Mirar Adentro: Poemas Escogi-dos 1954–2000* by Nancy Morejón. Edited by Juanamaría Cordones-Cook. 2005. *African American Review* 39(1–2): 252–54.

Review of *The Oxford Guide to Literature in English Translation*, edited by Peter France, and *The Encyclopedia of Literary Translation*, edited by Olive Classe. 2002. *The Comparatist* 26: 148–49.

Review of *Palimpsesto y subversión: El estudio intertextual de "El ruedo ibérico"* by Mercedes Tasende Grabowski. 1996. *ALEC* 21(1/2): 219–22.

Review of *Pleasure in the Word: Erotic Writing by Latin American Women*, edited by Margarite Fernández Olmos and Lizabeth Paravisini-Gebert. 1995. *The Women's Review of Books* 12(8) (May): 19.

Review of *The Subversive Scribe: Translating Latin American Fiction* by Suzanne Jill Levine. 1992. *Sulfur* 31(Fall): 260–65.

Review of *Talking Back: Toward a Latin American Feminist Criticism* by Debra A. Castillo. 1992. *Journal of Hispanic Philology* 17(1): 71–74.

Review of *Translating Literatures, Translating Cultures: New Vistas and Approaches in Literary Studies*, edited by Kurt Mueller-Vollmer and Michael Irmscher, and *Hölderlin and the Dynamics of Translation* by Charlie Louth. 2001. *The Comparatist* 25: 166–69.

Review of *Women Are Not Roses* by Ana Castillo. 1986. *Third Woman* 3(1–2): 140–43.

Review of *Women Writers of Spain: An Annotated Bio-Bibliographical Guide* by Carolyn L. Galerstein. 1988. *Hispania* 71(1): 85–86.

"Taking Stock: Observations on Recent Materials for Teaching and Research." 2011. *Translating and Interpreting Studies* 6(1): 103–9.

"Translation and Interpreting Studies in Review." 2010. *Translation and Interpreting Studies* 5(2): 243–44.

Translations

Books

Angel Dust / Polvo de ángel/ Polvere d'Angelo. 1990. Chapbook of poems by Carlota Caulfield. Madrid: Editorial Betania.

Beach Birds. 2007. Posthumous novel by Severo Sarduy. Translated with Suzanne Jill Levine. Los Angeles: Otis/ Seisimicity.

Christ on the Rue Jacob. 1995. Essays by Severo Sarduy. Translated with Susanne Jill Levine. San Francisco: Mercury House.

Delirium and Destiny. 1999. Novelized autobiography by María Zambrano. Albany, N.Y.: SUNY Press.

Dream of Reason. 2009. Novel by Rosa Chacel. Lincoln: University of Nebraska Press.

Memoirs of Leticia Valle. 1994. Novel by Rosa Chacel. Lincoln: University of Nebraska Press.

"Poetry As *Eruv*." 1997. In *The Voice of the Turtle: An Anthology of Cuban Stories*, edited by Peter Bush, 1–8. London: Quartet Books.

The Ravine. 2008. Novel by Nivaria Tejera. Albany, N.Y.: SUNY Press.

Refractions. 1994. Essays and poems by Octavio Armand. New York: Lumen Books.

Two Confessions. 2015. Translation of essays by Rosa Chacel and María Zambrano, with introduction and afterword (with Noël Valis). Albany, N.Y.: SUNY Press.

Written on a Body. 1989. Translation of *Escrito sobre un cuerpo* and part of *La simulación,* by Severo Sarduy. New York: Lumen Books.

With Dusk. 1984. Poems by Octavio Armand. Durango, Colo.: Logbridge-Rhodes. Four poems reprinted in *Twentieth-Century Latin American Poetry: A Bilingual Anthology,* edited by Stephen Tapscott, 365–69. Austin: University of Texas Press, 1996.

Poems and Prose

"Anais Nin." 1977. Essay by Julieta Campos. *Under the Sign of Pisces* 8(4): 1–5.

"The Anthology as Systematic Ruin." 1977. Essay by Octavio Armand. *Review* 21/22(Fall–Winter): 9–11. Reprinted in *Toward an Image of Latin American Poetry,* edited by Octavio Armand, 9–13. Durango, Colo.: Logbridge-Rhodes, 1982.

"Birth Certificates as Fiction." 1986. Essay by Octavio Armand. *Fiction International* 16(2): 78– 98.

"Blind Man's Dream." 1982. Poem by Octavio Armand. *New Orleans Review* 9(2): 56–57.

"Braille for Left Hand." 1982. Poem by Octavio Armand. *New Orleans Review* 9(1): 77. Reprinted in *Anthology of Magazine Verse and Yearbook of American Poetry,* edited by Alan F. Pater, 19–20. Beverly Hills, Calif.: Monitor Book Co., 1984.

Chapbook of poems by Octavio Armand. 1995. *The Ohio Review* 54: 9–21.

"Children Can Wait." 2003. Excerpt from *The Ravine* by Nivaria Tejera." In *Spain: A Traveler's Literary Companion,* edited by Peter Bush and Lisa Dillman, 219–35. San Francisco: Whereabouts Press.

"Conversation with a Flame." 2002. Poem by Octavio Armand. *Hotel Amerika* 1(1): 71.

"Corporeal Writing: A Conversation with Margo Glantz Conducted by Noé Jitrick." 2007. *Mexican Writers on Writing,* edited by Margaret Sayers Peden, 86–95. Austin, Tex.: Trinity University Press.

"Cuba Is Not, But She Calls." 1984. Essay by Octavio Armand and Translator's Note. *Spectacular Diseases* 7: 49–50, 73–74.

"Doorknob." 1987. Poem by Octavio Armand. *New Orleans Review* 14(1): 55.

"For a Small Tribute to Guillaume Apollinaire." 1980. Essay by Octavio Armand. *Review* 80(25/26): 72–80.

Four poems by Octavio Armand. 1982. *boundary 2* 10(2): 271–81.

"Getting It Down: A Get-Up." 1990. Essay by Octavio Armand. *Fiction International* 18(2): 22– 31.

"Indifference as Therapy." 1976. Prose poem by Octavio Armand. *Review* 10(19): 73–74.

"Kafka's Living Room." 1986. Essay by Octavio Armand. *Tyuonyi* 2: 141–46.

"A Mini-Course for Erasing the Cuban Writer from Exile." 1980. Essay by Octavio Armand. *PEN Freedom to Write Report* 2 (December): 6–9.

"Parable with Bison and Pits, or the Poem as Image." 1984. Poem by Octavio Armand and Translator's Note. *Sites* 12: 40–42.

"Penitence (Posters)." 1989. Prose poem by Octavio Armand. Special Issue. *Voicing,* edited by Don Wellman, *O.ARS* 6: 99–105.

"The Photo That Watches." 1990. Poem by Carlota Caulfield. In *Looking for Home: Women Writing about Exile,* edited by Deborah Keenan and Roseann Lloyd, 117. Minneapolis, Minn.: Milkweed Editions. Reprinted, with *Interior with Figures,* in *Luz en Arte y Literatura* 2(1992): 20–23.

Poems by Ana Castillo. 1987. In *The Renewal of the Vision: Voices of Latin American Women Poets 1940-1980,* edited by Marjorie Agosin and Cola Franzen, 21–25. Cambridge, UK: Spectacular Diseases. "One Fifteen" reprinted in *The Virago Book of Wicked Verse,* edited by Jill Dawson, 37. London: Virago Press, 1992.

Poems by Octavio Armand. 1983. *Maryland Poetry Review* 3(2): 1–11, 29, 48.

"Poetry as *Eruv.*" 1989. Essay by Octavio Armand. In *Index on Censorship* 18(3): 19–21.

"Possible Love Poem to the Usurer." 1980. Poem by Octavio Armand. *New Orleans Review* 7(2): 101. Reprinted in *Anthology of Magazine Verse* and *Yearbook of American Poetry,* edited by Alan F. Pater, 12. Beverly Hills, Calif.: Monitor Book Co., 1981.

"Reading of Light." 1983. Essay by Octavio Armand. *Translations: Experiments in Reading. O.ARS* 4: 149–59.

"Robert Morris: Mirage, Reflection (A Small Tribute to Vision)." 1978. Essay by Octavio Armand. *October* 6(Fall): 75–80.

"Second Cemetery." 1980. *Sites* 2: 2.

Selection from *Beach Birds* by Severo Sarduy. 2005. With Suzanne Jill Levine. *Fiction* 19(2): 46–58.

"Selections from *Desvelos en el alba.* 1995. Essay by Amanda Labarca. In *Rereading the Spanish American Essay: Translation of 19th and 20th Century Women's Essays,* edited by Doris Meyer, 135–48. Austin: University of Texas Press.

"A Stop on the Way." 1898. Short Story by Carmen Martín Gaite. In *Longman International Anthology of Women Writers,* edited by Marian Arkin and Barbara Shollar, 719–25. New York: Longman.

Three poems by Ana Castillo. 1979. In *The Invitation,* 14, 17, 27–28. Chicago: Privately published.

Three poems by Octavio Armand. 1980. *International Poetry Review* 6(2): 46–55.

Three poems by Octavio Armand. 1983. *Nimrod* 26(2): 56–58.

Three poems by Octavio Armand. 1985. *Review* 34(January-June): 48–51.

Three poems by Octavio Armand and translator's note. 2010. *Zoland* 4(Spring): 14–20.

"Touch." 1983. Poem by Octavio Armand. *New Orleans Review* 10: 4. Reprinted in *Anthology of Magazine Verse and Yearbook of American Poetry,* edited by Alan F. Pater, 17. Beverly Hills, Calif.: Monitor Book Co., 1985–86.

"Toward an Urban Art." 1988. Essays by Severo Sarduy. *Sites* 20: 4–7.

Two poems by Octavio Armand. 1982. *Perception. O.ARS* 2: 17–19, 92–93.

Two poems by Octavio Armand. 1985. *Tyuonyi* 1: 4–7.

Two poems by Octavio Armand. 2010. *VLAK* 1(1) (September): 28–29.

"A Wart on My Foot." 1994. Essay by Severo Sarduy. In *Life Sentences: Writers, Artists, and AIDS,* edited by Thomas Avena, 208–9. San Francisco: Mercury House.

"Water Color." 1979. Poem by Octavio Armand. *New Orleans Review* 6(3): 197.

"Writing as Erasure, the Poetry of Mark Strand." 1979. Essay by Octavio Armand. In *Strand: A Profile,* 49–63. Iowa City, Iowa: Grilled Flowers Press.

Published Fiction and Poetry

"Exercise in the Translation of Desire: Three Versions of Octavio Armand's 'Viento.'" 1995. *The Ohio Review* 54: 23–24.

"Four." 1991. From *Writing Pictures,* a novella. *Caprice* (October): 24–29.

Contributors

Maggie Anderson is professor emerita at Kent State University, where she was the founder and director of the Wick Poetry Center and editor of the Wick Poetry Series of the Kent State University Press from 1992 to 2010. She is the author of four books of poems, including *Windfall (New and Selected Poems), A Space Filled with Moving,* and *Cold Comfort,* and editor of four anthologies of poetry.

Octavio Armand was born in Cuba to a family twice exiled. He has published several volumes of poetry and essays in Spanish, among them *Entre testigos, Piel menos mía, Origami, Son de ausencia* (poetry), and *Superficies, El pez volador, El aliento del dragón,* and *Horizontes de juguete* (essays). *Refractions,* a pairing of poems and essays, was published by Lumen Books in Carol Maier's English translation.

Rosemary Arrojo is professor of comparative literature at Binghamton University, where she directed the Translation Research and Instruction Program from 2003 to 2007 and helped implement the first PhD in translation studies in the United States. Before that she taught translation studies in Brazil for almost 20 years. Her work has focused on the interface between translation studies and contemporary thought (deconstruction, psychoanalysis, and postcolonial and gender studies). She has published extensively on the topic both in Portuguese and in English. Her work has been translated into German, Spanish, Turkish, and Hungarian.

Brian James Baer is professor of Russian and translation studies at Kent State. He is founding editor of the journal *Translation and Interpreting Studies (TIS)*, general editor of the Kent State scholarly monograph series Translation Studies, and has served on the editorial board of *PMLA* (2009–12) and *Slavic and East European Journal* (2013–present). He is the author of *Other Russias: Homosexuality and the Crisis of Post-Soviet Identity* (2009), which was selected as a 2011 Choice Outstanding Academic Title by the American Library Association. He has edited *Contexts, Subtexts, Pretexts: Literary Translation in Eastern Europe and Russia* (2011), *No Good without Reward: The Selected Writings of Liubov Krichevskaya* (2011), *Russian Writers on Translation: An Anthology* (2013), and *The Unpredictable Workings of Culture* (2013), a translation of Juri Lotman's final work. His latest works include the collected volume *Research Methods in Translation and Interpreting Studies* (Routledge, 2015), co-edited with Claudia V. Angelelli, and the monograph *Translation and the Making of Modern Russian Literature* (Bloomsbury, 2015).

Julie Boéri is currently working as a teacher-researcher in interpreting at the Universitat Pompeu Fabra (Barcelona). She is the coeditor with Carol Maier of the bilingual book *Compromiso social y Traducción/Interpretación—Translation/Interpreting and Social Activism,* published by ECOS in 2010 and distributed by St Jerome. Her work focuses on activism, the ethics, sociology, and politics of interpreting as a profession, a scholarly discipline, and a field of education.

Peter Bush is an award-winning literary translator who was now lives in Oxford. He was formerly professor of literary translation at Middlesex University and then at the University of East Anglia, where he also directed the British Centre for Literary Translation. He was founding editor of the literary translators' journal *In Other Words* and coedited (with Susan Basnett) the collected volume *The Translator as Writer.* He was awarded the Ramon Llull Prize in 2014 for his translation of Josep Pla's *The Gray Notebook* and in 2015 La Creu de Sant Jordi for raising the profile of Catalan literature in English. His current projects include Carmen Boullosa's *Before* and Najat El Hachmi's *The Foreign Daughter.*

Ronald Christ taught English literature and classical rhetoric at Rutgers University. He is currently the publisher of Lumen Books and translates, especially from Latin America and Spain. He was awarded the Kayden National Translation Prize for Diamela Eltit's *E. Luminata,* a Foreword Magazine Gold Book of the Year for Ignacio Manuel Altamirano's *El Zarco, The Blue-Eyed Bandit,* and is now completing Álvaro Pombo's *Contra Natura* with a grant from the Spanish Ministry of Culture.

Moira Inghilleri is assistant professor of translation and interpreting studies and director of Interpreting Studies at the University of Massachussetts, Amherst. She is the author of *Interpreting Justice: Ethics, Politics, and Language* (2012) and the forthcoming *Sociological Approaches to Translation and Interpreting.* She is coeditor of *The Translator: Studies in Intercultural Communication.* Prior to joining the journal as coeditor in 2011, she guest-edited two special issues: *Bourdieu and the Sociology of Translating* (2005) and *Translation and Violent Conflict* (2010, with Sue-Ann Harding). Her research has appeared in *Translation Studies, The Translator,* and *Target* and a number of edited collections.

Roberta Johnson is professor of Spanish, emerita, at the University of Kansas, where she served as chair of the Department of Spanish and Portuguese and director of the Hall Center for the Humanities. Her published work includes more than 80 articles on twentieth- and twenty-first-century Spanish literature and the following books: *Carmen Laforet, El ser y la palabra en Gabriel Miró, Crossfire: Philosophy and the Novel in Spain 1900–1934 (Fuego cruzado: Filosofía y novella en España), Las bibliotecas de Azorín,* and *Gender and Nation in the Spanish Modernist Novel.* She collaborated with Carol Maier on her translation of María Zambrano's *Delirio y destino;* she has coedited *Antología del pensamiento feminista español,* as well as three other volumes. She is currently completing a book, *Major Concepts in Spanish Feminist Theory.* Her academic honors include a Fulbright lectureship at the University of Valladolid, Spain; an NEH fellowship-in-residence at Duke University; a Graves Award; a fellowship from the Guggenheim Foundation; and the Order of Isabel la Católica from King Juan Carlos of Spain.

Suzanne Jill Levine is a translator and scholar of Latin American literature. She directs the Translation Studies Program at the University of California at Santa Barbara. Awards for her translations and critical work include a PEN prize and NEH, NEA and Guggenheim fellowships. She is the author of a literary biography of Manuel Puig and the highly influential work *The Subversive Scribe: Translating Latin American Fiction*. More recently she has edited five Penguin paperback classics of the poetry and essays of Jorge Luis Borges.

Françoise Massardier-Kenney is professor of French translation at Kent State University and director of the Institute for Applied Linguistics, Her research interests include the theory and practice of literary translation, and cross-cultural competency. She is the general editor of the American Translators Association (ATA) Scholarly Series. Her publications include *Gender in the Fiction of George Sand* (2000), *Translating Slavery: Gender and Race in French Women's Writing* (with Doris Kadish, Kent State University Press, 2009), *Translating Slavery: Ourika and Its Progeny* (with Doris Kadish, Kent State University Press, 2010), translations of Madame de Duras's *Ourika* (2000), George Sand's novel *Valvèdre* (2007), Antoine Berman's *Toward a Translation Criticism: John Donne* (Kent State University Press, 2009), and numerous articles on Sand, nineteenth-century women's writers, and translation. She is also the coeditor with Carol Maier of *Literature in Translation: Teaching Issues and Reading Practices* (Kent State University Press, 2010).

Christi A. Merrill is associate professor of South Asian literature and postcolonial theory at the University of Michigan, and author of *Riddles of Belonging: India in Translation and other Tales of Possession*. Her translations of the stories of Rajasthani writer Vijay Dan Detha, *Chouboli and Other Stories,* have recently been published. In her current book project, *Genres of Real Life: Mediating Stories of Violence Across Languages* she interrogates the category of the "literary" as it is applied to previously untranslated genres of nonfiction writing and investigates the translingual, transnational conversations that take place when mediating the truth claims of first-person narratives.

Maria Tymoczko is professor of comparative literature at the University of Massachusetts, Amherst. Her research focuses on translation studies, Celtic medieval literature, and Irish studies. Her monographs *The Irish "Ulysses"* (1994) and *Translation in a Postcolonial Context* (1999) have both won prizes and commendations. In addition she has edited several volumes, including *Born into a World at War* (with Nancy Blackmun, 2000), *Translation and Power* (with Edwin Gentzler, 2002), *Language and Tradition in Ireland* (with Colin Ireland, 2003), *Language and Identity in Twentieth-Century Irish Culture* (with Colin Ireland, 2003; special issue of *Éire-Ireland*), and *Translation as Resistance* (2006, special section in the *Massachusetts Review*). Her most recent books are

Enlarging Translation, Empowering Translators (2007), a major reconceptualization of translation theory, and the edited volume *Translation, Resistance, Activism* (2010).

Noël Valis teaches at Yale University. A Guggenheim and NEH fellow, she is the author of 25 books on realist novelists, women writers, the Spanish Civil War, bad taste and class in modern Spain, and religion and literature, including *The Culture of Cursilería: Bad Taste, Kitsch and Class in Modern Spain* (2003), which won the Katherine Singer Kovacs Prize; *In the Feminine Mode: Essays on Hispanic Women Writers* (coedited with Carol Maier, 1990); *Teaching Representations of the Spanish Civil War* (2007); *Sacred Realism: Religion and the Imagination in Modern Spanish Narrative* (2010); translations of works by Pedro Salinas, Sara Pujol Russell, Julia Uceda, and Noni Benegas (*Burning Cartography,* winner of the New England Council of Latin American Studies Best Book Translation Prize); and a book of poetry, *My House Remembers Me* (2003; with a prologue by Carol Maier). Most recently, with Carol Maier, she cotranslated the book *Two Confessions,* essays by María Zambrano and Rosa Chacel.

Lawrence Venuti is professor of English at Temple University. A leading translation theorist and historian as well as a translator from Italian, French, and Catalan, he is the author of *The Translator's Invisibility: A History of Translation, The Scandals of Translation: Towards an Ethics of Difference* and *Translation Changes Everything: Theory and Practice,* as well as the editor of *The Translation Studies Reader,* an anthology of theory and commentary from antiquity to the present. His translations include Antonia Pozzi's *Breath: Poems and Letters,* the anthology *Italy: A Traveler's Literary Companion,* Massimo Carlotto's crime novel *The Goodbye Kiss,* I. U. Tarchetti's *Fantastic Tales,* and Ernest Farrés's *Edward Hopper: Poems,* for which he won the Robert Fagles Translation Prize.

Kelly Washbourne is professor of Spanish translation at Kent State University, where he is a member of the Institute for Applied Linguistics. His works include *An Anthology of Spanish American Modernismo, in English Translation with Spanish Text* (editor, 2007) and *Manual of Spanish-English Translation* (2009). His research interests include literary translation and translation pedagogy. Most recently he has worked on cognitive load in task design, and reading for translation. He has completed a volume of Reinaldo Arenas's selected poetry and an English-language edition of Nobel Prize–winning writer Miguel Angel Asturias's *Leyendas de Guatemala* (*Legends of Guatemala,* 2011), for which he won NEA and NEH awards in 2010. He serves on the editorial board of the journal *The Interpreter and Translator Trainer* and on the advisory board of the book series Current Trends in Translation Teaching and Learning (Routledge).

Index